ESSENTIALS OF PRICE THEORY

Essentials of Price Theory

By

B. S. KEIRSTEAD

Professor of Economics in the
University of New Brunswick

With a Foreword by

H. A. INNIS

THE UNIVERSITY OF TORONTO PRESS
TORONTO, CANADA
1942

LONDON:
HUMPHREY MILFORD
OXFORD UNIVERSITY PRESS

FOREWORD

THE restrictions imposed on economic life in Canada since the outbreak of war have implied a rejection of economic principles developed in democratic countries over the past two centuries but fortunately have stimulated an outburst of publications reinforcing the belief in those democratic principles. Three volumes, the result of extensive experience in undergraduate teaching—namely H. A. Logan and M. K. Inman, *A Social Approach to Economics* (Toronto, 1939), V. W. Bladen, *An Introduction to Political Economy* (Toronto, 1941), and this volume by B. S. Keirstead—have been hastened in their publication by exchange restrictions. Professor Bladen's book is designed to meet the demands of large introductory courses; Professors Logan and Inman's, of more formal elementary classes; and Professor Keirstead's, of more advanced groups. The protests of the late Professor Robert McQueen in his notable review of Logan and Inman (*Canadian Journal of Economics and Political Science*, February, 1940, pp. 79-85) against the attempt to tell all about economics in one volume are being met by a range of texts and studies. The volume by Professor Keirstead comes near to meeting his plea for a rigid analysis throughout. The study of economic theory in Canada has been materially advanced by these volumes.

Professor Keirstead has had full advantage of the traditions of his subject in the University of New Brunswick as a successor to Professor John Davidson who held the chair of Philosophy and Political Economy for the decade from 1892 to 1902 and to his father Professor W. C. Keirstead. The interest in a broad philosophical background and its implications to the social sciences, the use of Canadian illustrations, and the humanitarianism shown in John Davidson's, *Bargain Theory of Wages* (New York, 1898) with its reliance on evidence presented in the *Report of the Royal Commission on the Relations of Labor and Capital in Canada* (Ottawa, 1889), and in the writings of W. C. Keirstead, are evident in this volume. Professor Keirstead has developed a precise, logical, and sustained argument with a lucid style.

Nothing is more heartening to the social scientist in Canada than such evidence of interest in economic theory in smaller institutions with heavy teaching loads and limited library facilities. It indicates an immediate awareness and an intense anxiety to keep abreast of advances in Great Britain and the United States and a determination not to be disturbed by questions raised on all hands as to the usefulness[1] of economic theory. It gives promise of resistance against what appears to be an overwhelming pressure toward authoritarianism. The obsession with the immediate, and the consequent temptation for the economist, to quote Professor Pigou, "to sell his birthright in the household of truth for a mess of political pottage," to become a stepfather to Confederation, to make "a contribution to the war effort," to direct policies of reconstruction are overpowering in a young country at this time.[2] The economist fails to realize that for the political partisan, again

[1] "Pure science has its indispensable place, but neither pure nor applied science can ever displace the customary and the gossipy in legislation, nor lift from decision the purely personal equation. Social science, like all science, is but a staggered strategy directed toward the citadel of life. And the social scientist, like every intelligent man, must learn to lean as much upon the unearned increment of his labor as upon the foreseeable results. Pure science is mostly waste from any narrow point of view, waste save for the fun the scientist gets out of it. The scientist is, for this reason, ordinarily wise in doing only what he wants to do—to have fun is the surest guaranty, here as elsewhere, against complete futility. But that small sector of scientific work which adds to the fun of the pure scientist a funded factuality for present or future utility is the capsule of ointment in the jar of amusing flies" (T. V. Smith, *The Democratic Tradition in America*, New York, 1941, p. 68).

[2] Under conditions of peace the student is persecuted by those who have found the light. Betraying the intellectual themselves, they are particularly zealous in charging the student with treason. In exploiting him, they obscure their tactics by charging him with exploitation. Under conditions of war, discussion of the economic implications of policy is completely checked. Full knowledge of allied strategy is not available and discussion of even such economic problems as are involved in the probable varying lengths of the war is speculative. Intelligent discussion in the press appears to be limited to the weeklies. Perhaps in a foot-note and with a plea that a measure of freedom still exists in Canada it may be suggested that the strains imposed by authoritarian efforts have serious effects on the economic strength, including the extremely important element of morale on the home front, of a democratic economy for war purposes. Wars are not won by democratic countries attempting suddenly to convert themselves into totalitarian states, nor are they lost, for democratic countries, as in Adam Smith's time, will stand a lot of ruin. But they are won more quickly by democratic countries with conviction in democratic beliefs and actions based on those convictions. It is ominous that statements concerning public policy made by Ministers of the Crown have taken on more and more the character of a strange hand. The Bergens of the civil service have become less artistic in the renderings of their McCarthys. It is more ominous that they have dispensed with McCarthy and appeared in person. Where democracy demanded silence in peace it has allowed them to become vocal in war. The masterly voices of our servants have become more threatening. But the spirit of Cobbett of the Napoleonic Wars will reappear with its well-aimed references to locusts and tax-eaters.

to quote Professor Pigou, "economic reasoning is . . . not a means of arriving at truth, but a kind of brickbat useful on occasions for inflicting injury on their opponents."[3] With a bureaucracy of economists he might have added that economic reasoning is also useful to belabour economists outside the bureaucracy. One is reminded of that great rule of safety: "never attack a public department or a newspaper." Limited cultural development evident in the weak position of universities facilitates the exploitation of economists by political parties, governments, and newspapers.[4] The economics of a Liberal administration become the economics of newspapers.[5] For those who adhere to the democratic tradition the concern with economic theory offers hope. They will find no answers such as are provided by authoritarian practices but they will retain intact the belief that they are still a free effective people.

[3]See A. C. Pigou, *Economics in Practice* (London, 1935), pp. 9-10; also A. C. Pigou, "Newspaper Reviewers, Economics and Mathematics" (*Economics Journal*, June-Sept., 1941, pp. 276-80); also "The Social Sciences in the Post-War World" (*Canadian Historical Review*, June, 1941, pp. 118-20).

[4]"Books are the means by which civilization registers the whole product of the human consciousness. It is only in so far as individuals assimilate as much as possible of this collective knowledge, in its social and human aspect rather than in the academic sense, that they can be 'forces' in their own age, or even 'good citizens,' as the phrase goes. It is only in proportion as they have assimilated some of this common stock of wisdom that they are in a position to profit by the more ephemeral information of journalism. In other words, education is the only possible basis of a profitable journalism—profitable, I mean, for the individual spirit and for society. Journalism depends for its effect upon the nature of the soil on which it falls. A country which needs good books will demand a good journalism, and the class which is accessible to literature is the class which also derives ideas from the information of the moment, which uses those ideas and translates them into action" (R. A. Scott-James, *The Influence of the Press*, London, p. 307).

[5]"Whether the subject be the national expenditure or the inefficiency of Ministers, the journalists protest, hand on heart, that their sole desire is to protect the people, to save the country, to restore an ordered and flourishing State in which shall reign contentment and prosperity. This is the correct journalistic pose. . . . A cold, dispassionate appeal to patriotism, to sincerity, to truth, looks well in print, and never fails to impress a certain number of readers" (Kennedy Jones, *Fleet Street and Downing Street*, London, pp. 6-7). "There is much to be said in favour of modern journalism. By giving us the opinions of the uneducated, it keeps us in touch with the ignorance of the community. By carefully chronicling the current events of contemporary life, it shows us of what very little importance such events really are. By invariably discussing the unnecessary, it makes us understand what things are requisite for culture and what are not" (Oscar Wilde, *The Critic as Artist*).

To no one can the encouragement of interest in economic theory be more welcome than to the economic historian. Economic history in Germany and elsewhere has been a fertile nursery for authoritarianism. Like bureaucracy it provides all the answers and none of the questions. Economic theory compels a fresh attack on the economic interpretation of history. Induction strengthens, and is strengthened by, deduction. No effective advance in economic history can be made without an advance in economic theory, particularly in Canada. The tangled character of economic development, evident in the impossibility of isolating political and economic factors, presents a challenge to the economic theorist. The interrelation explains the facility with which the economist is lured into political pursuits but at the same time it presents major opportunities to the student determined to face them. The study of a young country presents the same opportunities to the economist as the study of large mammals does to the biologist. The phenomena are on a vast scale and suggest the advantages and limitations of economic theory. The theorist who becomes concerned with economic history can extend indefinitely the third dimension of time and the historian who seizes the aid of economic theory can strengthen his interpretation. In both cases the social scientist will be compelled to recognize his limitations and protection will be given to a society threatened with a bureaucracy of the social sciences. Without theory economic history becomes neatly arranged piles of dry wood, without history economic theory becomes abstruse adventures into formal logic. Economics is essentially an economy of study and about economy. We are grateful for contributions in economic theory and particularly to Professor Keirstead.

H. A. INNIS

The University of Toronto.

PREFACE

THIS book is the result of an attempt to sharpen and clarify in my own mind the basic principles and concepts of price theory. My only excuse for publishing it, where so many introductory books on economic theory already exist, is that it attempts to be precise and it is entirely devoted to the problems of price theory. It may help some students of economics to concentrate on the fundamental problems of price theory and to master rigorous techniques in a way a more discursive book could not. I hope that it may prove such an aid to those students and teachers who have felt, like myself, the need to do this.

I had hoped to continue this study by extending the theoretic techniques that are here developed to the problems I have touched on in the final chapters—the problems of the cycle and the secular trend and of economic controls—and to indicate the unity of "static" and "dynamic" theory. It was, however, for several reasons impossible to continue during the war, the course of which will, in any case, profoundly modify some of our thinking about institutional problems. I have tried, however, to say enough to show that we cannot successfully conduct our economic thinking in separate compartments labelled "pure theory," "money and banking," "cycle theory," and so forth. Perhaps at some future time I shall yet have the opportunity to extend the argument as I had originally planned.

ACKNOWLEDGEMENTS

ONE cannot clarify one's own thoughts without some help and, in this case, I should never have been able to do this book without the assistance and encouragement of friends and colleagues and without the written works on which I have so largely drawn and for which some acknowledgement is made in foot-notes to the text. My father, my first teacher in Economics and, since my return to the University, a sympathetic and considerate colleague who has always been ready with encouragement and advice, has once again given me the benefit of his experience and scholarship. Dr. H. A. Innis, who has done me the great kindness and honour of writing a Foreword, has read the manuscript and has offered valuable criticisms and suggestions and he has also helped me with problems connected with publication. Professor Stewart Bates, of Dalhousie University, has read with care, not only the published material but large sections of manuscript which have been rejected and I am indebted to him not only for his advice in connection with the argument but also for his admirable judgment of what to delete. Professor B. W. Fleiger, of the University of New Brunswick, has drawn all the graphs and I have him to thank, not only for his beautiful draftsmanship, but also for his insistence on precise and accurate statement for purposes of pictorial representation. In the chapters on the curves of the firm and on wages several of the graphs are derived from Mrs. Robinson's *Economics of Imperfect Competition*, in particular Figures 12, 13, 26, 27, 39, 41. Dr. C. C. Jones, Dr. Bryan Priestman, and Professor W. G. Jones of the University of New Brunswick, Professor J. G. Adshead of Dalhousie University, Dr. D. B. Marsh of Barnard College, Columbia, Mr. Norman Wood of Noranda, Quebec, and Professors A. B. Schmidt, L. Grey, E. Boldyreff and Dean Chapman of the University of Arizona have all advised on certain sections of the book. I wish to thank all these for their assistance.

I should like, finally, to express my gratitude for the generous assistance my University and the Canadian Social Science Research Council have given me in publishing this work, and to the Editorial Department of the University of Toronto Press for their help in seeing the manuscript through the press.

B. S. K.

Fredericton, 1942.

CONTENTS

BOOK ONE

INTRODUCTORY

CHAPTER I

THE MEANING OF ECONOMY

SINCE the Garden of Eden, or, if one prefers, since the pre-glacial age[1] man has never enjoyed such an abundance of the necessities and comforts of life that he could afford not to economize. In order to obtain for himself even the meanest subsistence he has been obliged over the greater part of his history to husband his land and his capital and to contribute to the labours of production an unremitting toil and ceaseless vigilance. Even in these modern days of scientific machine production and of easier living there remains a basic scarcity. This scarcity is to be understood as assuming two forms. There is, first of all, a fundamental scarcity of the productive resources, land, labour, and capital, relative to the unlimited wants and needs of the world population. This basic fact is frequently obscured from our common view by the existence of unmarketed or "unmarketable" surpluses of goods and by the prevalence of waste, such as those famous watermelons which were thrown into the Potomac River or the five hundred and fifty million bushels of wheat, which in this war year of 1940 are being kept in storage by the Canadian government. But these instances, and many others, are examples of the failure of our economic institutions; they betray the inefficiency of our distributive machinery; they do not illustrate the essential economic situation to be one of abundance rather than scarcity. The watermelons could not be sold at a profit, but there were lots of little boys hungry for watermelon who continued to go hungry, and there are millions of unhappy people in Hitler's Europe who are in need of Canada's wheat, but to whom, for military reasons, it cannot be sent. There remain unsatisfied needs and wants, in excess of any "surpluses" to satisfy them. This scarcity can be seen more clearly in this way. If all goods were free and in abundance they would be like air, present to us for our taking without the expenditure of effort on our part. Actually there are few such free goods to meet our manifold needs. We have to exercise ingenuity, artifice, and effort to satisfy our wants and we have to select those we mean to satisfy. Such are the elements of an "economic situation." Man has learned to choose the wants he shall satisfy; he has pooled his efforts, learned specialization, and exchanged the

[1]Cf. Gerald Heard, *The Emergence of Man* (New York, 1932).

3

fruits of specialized labour. A whole complex of institutions has grown up for the most efficient organization of production and the distribution and exchange of produce. This institutional complex, "the economy," is the material of economic studies. "Here then," as Professor Robbins says,[2] "is the unity of subject of Economic Science, the forms assumed by human behaviour in disposing of scarce means. . . . Economics is the science which studies human behaviour as a relationship between ends and scarce means which have alternative uses."

In war-time the problem of scarcity is thrown into sharp relief, and the two main types of economic organization to obtain production and to determine the wants to be satisfied are brought into clear distinction.

The economic problem of war, considered apart from the larger problem of grand strategy consists in the methods to be used to allocate the productive resources so as to get the various needs satisfied according to the "order of importance" as designated by the military. The methods which may be used are of two general sorts. The government may acquire income from the public by taxation and borrowing and use it to bid up the prices of the productive agents (labour and capital) in the war goods industries, while at the same time the restriction in consumers' income forces down the prices of the agents in the peace time industries. This method is a general reliance on the mechanism of the price system. The other method is for the government to enter the economic field and use its compulsory powers, saying that so much labour, so much capital, so many raw materials are to be allowed various industries, establishing what are called "priorities," namely the right of essential war industries to satisfy their requirements before inessential industries are allowed to enter the labour or raw material markets, and even rationing the consumption by civilians of certain scarce goods.[3]

In a developed society scarcity assumes another form, which accounts for the anomalies which obscure and distort the basic facts. The creation of a complex social machine for the production and distribution of wealth has given a special institutional aspect to the nature of scarcity. In our society based on the institution of private ownership of capital we have solved the problem of what goods are to be produced and in what quantities in one special way. The result of this type of solution is to give to certain people a much greater voting power than the majority enjoy in the selection of goods to be produced; that is, since the production of goods is guided by the price system and since prices respond

[2]L. C. Robbins, *An Essay on the Nature and Significance of Economic Science* (New York, 1932), pp. 15-16.
[3]B. S. Keirstead, *Canada's Economic War Policy* (Dalhousie University Institute of Public Affairs, 1941), p. 6.

to the purchasing power of consumers, the rich man has much more influence in determining the direction of production than the poor man. Thus an "unnatural" scarcity may be created in necessities by the diversion of productive resources into luxury trades.

Thus our institutions are such that production can only properly be undertaken where there is expectation of a profit. That is the way, as we shall discover, that our productive resources are guided in their employment. If a portion of the community is too poor to buy, regardless of need, there will be no profit in providing for them. The scarcity which arises is one which has its source, not in basic physical fact, but in social institutions. This sort of problem is of peculiar interest to the economist, because it suggests a failure of the institutions, and promises the hope that the fault can, by proper analysis, be discovered and reformed. The basic physical scarcity is beyond removal, the institutional scarcities may be cured. The one is the physical fact on which "economy" is founded, that gives form and purpose to economic organization and from which all economic studies must start. The other is indigenous not in the physical but in the social universe and may give direction and social purpose to our studies. It arises from the very nature of economic institutions and is a commentary on their effectiveness and its existence is a challenge to the social and economic analyst.

For Marshall[4] the urgency of the problem of poverty constituted the pressing drive to economic studies. Similarly in our own day the economist must feel the rowel of social evils, the insecurity, fear, and oftentimes disaster which fill the lives and destroy the peace of the vast majority of mankind.

[4]"There are vast numbers of people both in town and country, who are brought up with insufficient food, clothing and house-room, whose education is broken off early in order that they may go to work for wages, who thenceforth are engaged during long hours in exhausting toil with imperfectly nourished bodies, and have therefore no chance of developing their higher mental faculties. Their life is not necessarily unhealthy or unhappy. Rejoicing in their affections towards God and man, and perhaps possessing some natural refinement of feeling, they may lead lives that are far less incomplete than those of many who have more material wealth. But, for all that, their poverty is a great and almost unmixed evil to them. Even when they are well their weariness almost amounts to pain, while their pleasures are few; and when sickness comes, the suffering caused by poverty increases tenfold. And though a contented spirit may go far towards reconciling them to these evils, there are others towards which it ought not to reconcile them. Overworked and undertaught, weary and careworn, without quiet and without leisure, they have no chance of making the best of their mental faculties" (Alfred Marshall, *Principles of Economics*, 2nd ed., p. 2), London, 1891.

CHAPTER II

THE OBJECTS OF ECONOMIC STUDY

A LL studies have as one object the satisfaction of human curiosity, that is of the desire to know and understand. The study of economics has this object in common with all the other sciences. But economics has, perhaps more than most, as a further object the improvement of human welfare. The existence of poverty, which we have already noticed, and the existence of unemployment and destitution at the same time that crops and other goods are being destroyed create in all generous minds the desire to find some cure for these evils of society. This cure is not to be found in idle dreamings of Utopia but in scientific analysis of the workings of the economic system to discover the causal laws that are operative, and to isolate, if possible, the causes of its inefficiency.

We must remember, however, that economics is primarily a science of means, not a criticism or criterion of ends, except incidentally. The economist tries to discover the determining or causal factors so that the means can be controlled to yield the socially desirable end, but, as an economist, he does not attempt to evaluate that end. If the society comes to believe that a perfectly equal distribution of income is a desirable social end, the economist may pronounce on it, not to say whether it is desirable, but whether or not it is practicable. If he is able to say it is practicable he must be able to say how it is to be achieved. If the society desires as a worthy object the abolition of poverty and unemployment, it can ask the economists if it can be done, and, if so, how to do it. It is unlikely that economists will quarrel with this as a social ideal, but, in any case, that question is not their affair.

Thus economics is limited in scope. It is not social ethics. It does not attempt to pronounce on the good or evil of the economic system. It does not say, or attempt to say, that the capitalist system is the "right" system or the "wrong" system. It can merely say that, to retain the example, capitalism is the right system to attain certain social ends, if these are what society wants, and the wrong system to attain certain other social ends. It must deal objectively with quantities and quantitative determination. Its methods become distinct from those of social ethics and its task is a different one. That the two must go hand in hand to

6

achieve a better society is a paramount truth we should never deny; but that, in that operation each has a distinct task, peculiar to itself, is a first principle for their mutual success.

We must, however, avoid the fallacy of supposing that, because we can distinguish means and ends, we can separate them. Means and end are two parts of, two aspects of, the complete act. The means which we choose will determine in part the end we achieve. We may wish, for example, to score a victory in a game. But if we choose dishonourable means which involve an infraction of the rules, the sort of victory we achieve is a dishonourable one, and, because we choose to cheat, unsatisfactory. Our means have, as the philosophers say, determined our ends. The entire act, of which playing, cheating, and winning are all partial aspects, is completely coloured or fashioned by the means we chose. This determination of ends by means is not peculiar to the playing field, it is characteristic of every ethical situation. Thus in the field of social policy the economic means will help determine the social end. Economics may be able to show that certain social ends are impracticable of realization in the sense that any economic means undertaken to achieve them would be self-contradictory, nugatory, or incompatible with other accepted social ends. Thus the society might desire complete and absolute equality of income as among its different members. Yet the economist might discover that this would result in such a reduction of all income that each would have less than before, and thus the reform would defeat its own purpose.

A further consequence of this intimate relation of means and end is that the economist when he comes to talk of economic reform or economic control, as many economists do, is certain to have in the back of his mind the nature and form of the social ends his reforms or controls are to serve. This means that a certain bias may be introduced to his thinking. He cannot achieve the perfect objectivity of the physical scientist. This is natural when you consider the emotional, explosive stuff with which he is dealing. Moreover the very objects which he selects for analysis will be, perhaps unconsciously, determined by his social philosophy.

Thus economics, while limited in scope to the objective analysis of the economic system, must be regarded as intimately related to social ethics. We cannot admit any sharp separation of the two fields, nor can we claim the complete objectivity and lack of bias that the natural scientist claims. We can only try not to deceive ourselves or others as to the nature of our social bias and to prevent its influencing us in any conscious way in our recognition and treatment of economic facts.

CHAPTER III

ECONOMIC METHODS

THE attempt is frequently made to draw an analogy between the methods of economics and the physical sciences. This analogy may be useful as serving to illustrate some of the procedures of economic analysis. But it is apt to be misleading, because, much as some would like to believe it, economics is unable, in many important particulars, to imitate the methods of the physical sciences.

Both the physical sciences and economics are similarly based on the fundamental logical processes of induction and deduction. Induction is the process of leading up to a generalization from the observation of a series of particular facts or events. The generalization usually takes the form of an assertion of the causal relationship. Thus, to take a simple case, the child may observe that every time the adult presses the electric light switch the light comes on. He is then able to say that the pressing of the switch causes light to appear and to predict from this generalization. The adult probes further into the matter. He knows there is an electric current travelling on the cables to which his house is wired. He knows that when he presses a switch he connects the light wires with the current, thus causing the incandescent wires to glow in the vacuum bulb. He knows that every time that connection is made there will be light. He knows that making the connection is the cause of the appearance of light. He knows, further, that if he made the connection by directly joining the wires he would obtain light. This again is a generalization from induction. The physicist goes further. He is not content with such surface generalizations. He studies the nature of electricity, makes a series of generalizations about it, of some of which he may be so sure that he calls them laws. A law is simply a generalization based on experience that has been tried and tried again until the scientist has no doubts about it. On the basis of these laws the electrical engineer is able to control electricity, to predict its behaviour, and to make use of it for light, heat, and motive power. Thus induction is generalization from experience of individual events, a moving from the particular to the general.

Deduction is the process of moving from the general to the

particular. It starts with certain simple, universal propositions which are regarded as self-evident or axiomatic.[1] Then by logical process, based on the principle of non-contradiction, particular propositions may be deduced. Thus if we begin by saying that all men are mortal, and if we postulate that Socrates is a man, we deduce that Socrates is mortal, because if Socrates is not mortal it cannot be true without contradiction both that Socrates is a man and that all men are mortal. By postulating for Socrates any other man, we can similarly deduce the mortality of any individual. This process, which seems very simple in the example we have given, is that of the Euclidean geometry, and of a great deal of philosophic and scientific thinking.

The physical sciences make use of both these methods, as, indeed, must any system of thought, but the first achieved results by breaking away from purely deductive, *a priori*, theorizing and by using inductive and experimental methods. Thus "scientific method" is usually thought of as the opposite of deductive. Actually the "scientific method" consists of the following steps. There is first the restriction and definition of the field of study. There is then observation, description, and classification of the particular facts. This is followed by the formulation of a generalization, known as an hypothesis. This is a sort of intelligent guess that is advanced as a possible explanation of the behaviour or relationships of the data, a probable generalization from which future behaviour could be predicted. Perhaps "guess" is a misleading word in this context. The formulation of a hypothesis is a genuinely creative act, highly imaginative, almost intuitive, it sometimes seems, in nature. "The physicist is bound, by the very nature of the task in hand, to use his imaginative faculties at the very first step he takes. For the first stage of his work must be to take the results furnished by a series of experimental measurements and try to organize these under one law. That is to say, he must select according to a plan which will in the first instance be hypothetical and therefore a construction of the imagination."[2] But this constructive, imaginative thought is based on the sum of his past experience and is a deduction from it. This is not to say that it does not arise from the data or is not suggested by observation of them. When the hypothesis is formed it must be subjected to a series of tests, or experiments, under controlled

[1]A deductive process may begin with a generalization which has been reached from induction. In all scientific thinking the two processes are thus used together.

[2]Max Planck, *Where Is Science Going* (London, 1933), p. 86.

conditions, to determine whether or not it is a valid generalization, viz. to determine whether cause and effect relationships obtain as predicted on the basis of the observations and the deductions from past experience. So even in science the deductive and inductive processes serve each other and are both essential to successful thinking.

Thus when his car stalls on the road, the motorist, from his experience, sets up the hypothesis that his car is out of gas and that lack of fuel is the most likely cause of the stoppage. This hypothesis is a tentative explanation and the motorist proceeds to test it by seeing if it is consonant with the facts, that is he experiments. Is the gas tank empty? If it is he has verified his hypothesis and knows what to do to get his car going again. If the tank is not empty his hypothesis is destroyed, and he must set up another. He may suppose the cause of the trouble to lie either in his electrical system or in the supply of fuel to the engine. Perhaps he has recently had his electrical system checked and found in good order. The more likely cause of trouble, then, will be in the fuel supply. So he establishes as his second hypothesis the more likely explanation that his carburettor is clogged or his gas lead plugged. In this case he opens the carburettor cock to see if he has a freely running supply of gas into the the carburettor. If he finds this to be so he examines the carburettor itself to see if the gas is flowing properly through it. He may at the same time test his spark plugs to rule out the alternative explanation that there is no electric spark to fire the mixture. He may conduct a series of these tests until he is finally sure that there is no other defect which might be the cause and that the carburettor is not working properly. He has then a theory explaining the behaviour of his motor in this instance, and if he acts on the theory he can remedy the defect and get his car started again.

Physical science is, therefore, primarily an attempt to interpret and explain the physical world in terms of cause and effect. A causal relation may be asserted when there is invariable sequence, inevitable elimination and concomitant variation; i.e., when event A is always followed by event B, when, if A is removed, B disappears, and when any quantitative changes in A are accompanied by quantitative changes in B.[3] Careful experimentation establishes hypotheses in the form of theories, and on the basis of these science

[3]Though not necessarily in the same direction. An increase in pressure leads to a decrease in volume of a gas.

is able to predict future behaviour and to control the physical environment.

The subject-matter with which physical science deals is usually material and inert, or at least unconscious and capable of exact control. It can be exactly measured, and causal relationships can be reduced to precise mathematical formulation. A similarly exact precision can be attained in the results. Given the exact change in temperature, and a constant pressure, the exact change in the volume of the gas can be predicted. This exactitude, the scientific basis of so much that is common in modern life, is the reason the physical sciences are often spoken of as "the exact sciences." Such exactitude in economics is precluded by the subject-matter and this same difficulty makes economics more abstract, more dependent on deduction from certain broad principles, and less able, except in certain of its branches, to adopt inductive and experimental methods than the physical sciences. The basic thought processes are the same but the emphasis and the special techniques of analysis differ. Instead of the experimental hypothesis the economist may sometimes use the somewhat similar device, the deductive hypothesis or assumption, a device which is also frequently used by the scientist. For example one may say, "Let us assume that the world is flat. We know that, in fact, it is not. But for certain purposes the degree of error is so small that our conclusions for all practical purposes will be correct, and the use of the assumption may enable us more readily than otherwise to achieve useful results." It is exactly on this assumption—and for these reasons—that the science of level, as opposed to geodetic, surveying is based. Similarly the science of mechanics is based on the assumption of perpetual motion. The use of this deductive hypothesis or assumption, less usual in science than the experimental, is characteristic of the existing body of economic analysis. The accepted and tried method of the economist is to set up a model economic system based on certain simplifying assumptions and limiting restrictions[4] and to infer from these the laws governing the relationships of the system.

[4]A limiting restriction is a further assumption limiting the field of study. Thus the assumption of perpetual motion is a deductive hypothesis underlying the study of mechanics. The assumption of constant pressure is a limiting restriction used in studying the behaviour of gases under varying temperatures. It defines the field of study and restricts attention to the variables whose behaviour the scientist wishes to observe. In economics the axiom that all men try to maximize their net advantage is a deductive hypothesis. The limitation of a portion of the study to a market in which perfect competition obtains is a limiting restriction.

The assumptions which are basic to established economic theory are of the nature of axioms derived from simple observation and direct experience.   They are: (1) that there are scarce means to satisfy a system of wants, (2) that each man is aware of his wants and has them arranged in an order of importance, and (3) that in the satisfaction of the wants each man tends to try to maximize the net balance of satisfactions over efforts or costs.

In this study our method will be to begin with the very simplest case of the balancing of satisfactions and costs, to construct a model economy in which certain fundamental laws will be clearly exemplified and to express in a very formal way the nature of those laws.   We shall then attempt under various restrictions to analyse the modern exchange economy and to make such modifications in our formal laws as may be necessary.   We shall hope at the same time to find historical or other observational data that will serve both to exemplify and confirm our theoretic principles.

Section 2: A Digression on Criticisms of the Abstract Method

The method we have been describing has frequently been called the "abstract method," or, to use the phrase of the late Professor J. B. Clark, the "isolating method."   It consists in the isolation in the mind of the student of certain fundamental forces whose behaviour it is desired to study free from the confusion of all the incidental forces that appear on the actual market.   Professor Clark speaks of it as the study that "creates in imagination a static society."

Abstraction consists logically in separating in the mind the common qualities or attributes—or in some cases the determinants of these common attributes—of all the members of a class from the mass of other qualities and characteristics which they possess as individual objects.   The abstracted common quality of all members of the class is the universal characteristic of the class. The qualities the objects have as individual members are the differentiating attributes which distinguish them as individuals.[5]

---

[5]"Abstraction is the detection of a common quality in the characteristics of a number of diverse observations: it is the method supremely exemplified in the work of Newton and Einstein. Newton, for example, gave us the 'laws of motion.'   Now motion is not an experience; what we observe are moving bodies. Motion is an abstraction, a quality conceived to be possessed by all moving bodies, however much they may differ in size, shape, colour, beauty, virtue or anything else.   The laws of motion express the characteristics of this common

Thus in Economics we abstract the common quality of all economic situations, the allocation of scarce means to satisfy a system of wants. We abstract the common behaviour of men in such a situation—the maximization of net advantages—and we abstract the common phenomenon of diminishing returns to scarce factors in use. Without these abstractions economic science in its accepted form would be impossible.

This method has given rise to much misunderstanding and to criticisms which are based on misunderstanding. It is frequently said that the economic theorist abstracts from reality, that the picture he presents is purely imaginative, interesting, no doubt, "but as far removed from economic fact as is the game of chess from the armed clash of war."[6] Economists, these critics maintain, establish in their minds a model of the economic system which is not the least like the real thing. Its laws, they say, are purely imaginary, and when conclusions drawn from these laws are applied to real life they are illusory and apt to prove misleading. As a result, it is alleged, the economist is never able to offer a clear-cut solution to a practical problem, or, if he does attempt to do so, the policy he advocates is apt to be unwise. Generally speaking, so the critics say, the economist tends to see in his model not a logical erection but a moral ideal, and he advocates in policy measures designed to achieve not material welfare in the conflicting, dynamic world of people, but the static equilibrium of a logician's dream.

These criticisms ought not to be too lightly dismissed by the student of economics. Though they can be shown to rest on misunderstandings they may serve to put us on guard against the danger of claiming too much for our science and they may warn us to make very sure of all the facts of any particular situation before we attempt to apply to it the conclusions of our general theory. The criticisms are valuable admonitions to the student of abstract economic theory to be careful how he uses his method and cautious

---

quality, and they are therefore a rational means of correlating a vast body of human experience . . ." (H. Dingle, *Science and Human Experience*, pp. 22-3; quoted by A. C. Benjamin in *An Introduction to the Philosophy of Science*, New York, 1937, p. 183). Cf. also E. Cassirer, *Substance and Function* (Chicago, 1923), pp. 192-4.

[6]E. H. Phelps-Brown, *The Framework of the Pricing System* (London, 1936), p. 27. Mr. Phelps-Brown, we must hasten to add, does not accept this point of view but continues with cogent argument to dispose of it. For a carefully stated presentation of the case against the abstract method in economics, see Barbara Wootton, *Lament for Economics* (London, 1938).

in its application to particular questions of policy, but as criticisms of the method itself they are irrelevant and trivial.

Economists themselves have been the first to recognize the dangers of misuse of the abstract method. Professor Pigou points out[7] that it would be perfectly possible to set up a scheme of *a priori* propositions, which bear no relation at all to reality, and to proceed by a perfectly valid logical process on a high level of abstraction to deduce an entire Wizard of Oz economic system. Alice wanders into just such a logical Wonderland where everything is upside down yet follows directly from a fanciful set of postulates. But the fundamental abstractions of economics are not fanciful. They derive directly from our experience of human and physical behaviour in the real world. The behaviour of different men in satisfying their wants will exhibit all the thousands of peculiarities of thousands of individuals. Some will want lean, like Jack Spratt, others, like his celebrated spouse, prefer the fat. Some men want beauty in their lives, others want the latest model motor car. But all do dispose of their income so as to gain for themselves the satisfaction of what are to them the most important wants in the order of their importance. This common characteristic is the distinguishing attribute of human behaviour in an economic situation. It is thus properly abstracted by the economist.

The misunderstanding which lies at the root of the criticisms can be made abundantly clear by a reference to the Law of Diminishing Returns. This law states that the increased use of variable factors with a scarce factor of production in any employment yields less than proportionate increases in physical returns. As stated it is obviously true. If it were not true, all the food in the world could be grown on an acre or so of land by the application of sufficient labour and machinery. It constitutes a proper abstraction, a fair and important underlying assumption of economic method. But it is a purely static law. It does not say that over a period of time if improvements and inventions are made physical returns per unit of effort will diminish. Yet that is exactly how the law is interpreted by the critics of economic method when they argue that the Law of Diminishing Returns is obviously false because it can be demonstrated that returns per unit of land, or of labour, or of capital have increased in a certain industry over the past fifty years.

We have to be careful to make the right abstractions. We have to be careful to understand exactly the nature of the abstrac-

[7]A. C. Pigou, *Economics of Welfare* (London, 1932), p. 6.

tions we do make and the limitations they put upon the applicability of our conclusions. But we cannot admit the strictures on the general method. Indeed no serious student of any science could ever admit these criticisms. All science works on a certain level of abstraction. The physicist assumes a perfect vacuum in defining the laws of motion of a falling body. Nature abhors a vacuum. The assumption is "unreal," as the unsophisticated[8] say. Yet no one has tried to argue that modern physics is worthless and impracticable because it works on an "unreal" level of abstraction. Perhaps, as this suggests, the final test for the validity of the basic assumptions of any science is pragmatic, and, if this is so, the achievements of theoretic economics, if not sensational, are sufficiently solid to defy the trivialities of its critics.

SECTION 3: A DIGRESSION ON THE PSYCHOLOGICAL ASSUMPTIONS

The most important of the assumptions of economics, viz. that men will always try to maximize their gains and minimize their losses, is psychological. It is a generalization about human behaviour. Since it has recently been subjected to criticism we make this brief digression to examine it.

Our problem here is similar to the general problem of psychology. As Professor Woodworth says,[9] "The individual, our object of study, is decidedly a variable quantity. The same individual varies from time to time, or one individual varies from another. How, then, it will be asked, can we hope to reach any general laws in psychology?"

The psychologist's problem involves the whole of human behaviour. He has to find general laws which apply to a manifold range of human activities. He does so by discovering that all human responses to the same stimulus concentrate about a "mode." Without discussing the technical questions involved in the definition of the "mode," we may say that it amounts roughly to the typical

---

[8]"The vulgar notion that the safe methods on political subjects are those of Baconian induction—that the true guide is not general reasoning but specific experience—will one day be quoted as among the most unequivocal marks of a low state of the speculative faculties of any age in which it is accredited. . . . Whoever makes use of an argument of this kind . . . should be sent back to learn the elements of some of the more easy physical sciences. Such reasoners ignore the fact of the Plurality of Causes in the very case which affords the most signal example of it" (J. S. Mill, *System of Logic*, London, 1884, chap. x, par. 8; quoted by L. C. Robbins in *An Essay on the Nature and Significance of Economic Science*, New York, 1932).

[9]R. S. Woodworth, *Psychology* (3rd ed., New York, 1934), p. 31.

group. We discover, also, that there are deviations from this normal or typical response. The extent of the deviations can be measured and the "standard" deviation established. It is then possible to speak of human behaviour in response to any given test or stimulus in terms of "typical response" and "standard deviation response." Moreover it is also possible to give multiple tests for the same situation and to correlate the results so as to reduce the margin of error.

The results of these tests may not tell us what any particular individual will do under the given circumstances of the test. Unlike the generalizations of the physical sciences, they do not permit us to forecast from the universal the exact behaviour of the particular. In Professor Woodworth's example of testing the hand grip of soldiers the mode of 43 kilos pressure does not enable us to say of any one soldier that 43 kilos would exactly measure his grip. But it does permit us to say of the group as a whole that the typical individual grip will be 43 kilos. If the standard deviation is a narrow one we know that all individual behaviour will approximate the mode. If the standard deviation is a wide one our generalization has validity only as applied to the group.

Now in economics it is group behaviour in which we are interested, and we have the simplified case of being interested only in one very narrow field of behaviour, that is, man's response to the price system. It may be interjected that it is fundamentally his response to the condition of having to get a living from the scarce means of subsistence; but that amounts to saying his response to price because his living is measured by the price his labour commands divided by the prices of the goods he buys.

Thus every market situation is a case study in individual responses, and when the cases are correlated we find a typical response, with, one would judge, a very small standard deviation. Certainly one may speak with confidence of the group response, which is that men tend always to sell in the dearest market, buy in the cheapest, and so to distribute their income as to get the greatest possible sum of satisfactions. So general is this response that the earlier economists used to symbolize it with their imaginary figure, "the economic man."

There have been many objections taken to this concept of the "economic man," and we might pause a moment to consider them, because to do so will prevent us from falling into common error, and will help to sharpen and clarify our understanding of the psychological generalizations on which economics rests. It must be remembered throughout that economics never claims that there are no individual variations in behaviour. To dispute the concept of the modal behaviour of the "economic man" must mean to show the average group response is different from that postulated for the "economic man."

In the first place it is frequently objected that economics assumes the validity of the crude hedonistic psychology, a theory which asserts that all our actions have as motive the attainment of maximum pleasure. It is not necessary here to outline the objections to this theory. In its crude form it is rejected by all modern psychologists. But it is not necessary to set up a defence for hedonism in order to defend the psychology of economic theory. Economics does not assert that all human action is directed by desire for pleasure. It does not say, even, that all economic action is directed by desire for pleasure. Rather it insists that actions are directed towards particular satisfactions; that is, it makes the very point that critics of hedonism make when they point out that desires are for certain satisfactions directly connected with the desires, and not for the "pleasure" that attends the satisfaction of desire.[10]

Nor does the position of the economist exclude the so-called "nobler impulses." He admits his economic field to be a narrow one and does not suppose that in limiting his field he is to be accused of denying the existence of the wide range of non-economic activities. He sees, also, that, in the field of economic activity, many men prefer aesthetic or moral satisfactions to material ones. He never attempts to argue that all satisfactions desired by men are material. This common idea involves a fundamental misunderstanding of economics. All the economist says is that men, whether their satisfactions be material or non-material, tend to achieve them so as to get the greatest possible sum of satisfaction. That does not preclude the unselfish behaviour of most men who desire the welfare of their family and their friends. What Bishop Butler calls "benevolence" is a perfectly reasonable motive of economic action. Parents may go without comforts in order to send children to the university. This is a source of greater satisfaction to the parents than any other that could be had. Thus the economists'

---

[10]". . . all that is assumed in the idea of the scales of valuation is that different goods have different uses and that these different uses have different significances for action, such that in a given situation one use will be preferred before another and one good before another. Why the human animal attaches particular values in this sense to particular things, is a question we do not discuss. That is quite properly a question for psychologists or perhaps even physiologists" (Robbins, *The Nature and Significance of Economic Science*, pp. 85-6).

psychological assumptions do not, as Ruskin said, take a "dreary" view of human nature, but are fair and valid generalizations.

The question of the pecuniary motive as an incentive to productive activity is rather more difficult. Economists have long recognized the existence of powerful non-pecuniary motives. The artist or writer is often productive, quite apart from the pecuniary reward offered. He works because of his interest in what he is doing, because of the necessity, that some feel, for self-expression. Many scientists and professional men work hard, regardless of pay, because they enjoy their work, or because they are ambitious for ecognition in their profession. Many statesmen and men of affairs are said to find in public honour and acclaim, or in service of their country and their ideals, rewards sufficient for their labours. We everywhere see evidence that men are willing to undergo hardship or labour without any adequate pecuniary compensation. To say that the pecuniary motive is the chief or only spur is simply untrue of many fields of activity.

The economist has to admit all this. He is able to say, however, that in most cases of business and industry the primary response is to the pecuniary motive. After a certain level of remuneration has been reached there may be little direct connection between pecuniary rewards and efforts. There is no reliable evidence, for example, for the often quoted statement that private profit is necessary to encourage initiative. What the economist calls "psychic income"—the enjoyment in the work, the degree of leisure permitted—comes to be an important consideration.

Perhaps this much is beyond controversy, that, other things being equal, even the artist takes his wares to the best market. This is not to say that he paints for money—though if he is a good artist that is usually a prime consideration—, it is not to say that the private profit system is necessary to get him to paint, or any such nonsense: it is merely that, though his activity has motives other than the pecuniary, when these others are satisfied or in balance, the pecuniary motive then is operative.

This all suggests a certain rationality in economic decisions, and so much it must be admitted the economist does assume. But this rationality is a rationality in the arrangement of satisfactions and the choice of means to satisfy them, it does not imply an *ethical* rationality in the evaluation of the ends themselves. Thus the objection based on the fact that the wealthy or snobbish often buy in expensive shops what could be obtained for half the money elsewhere, or that typists go without lunch to buy silk stockings misses the point. The economist passes no judgment on the wisdom with which people select their values or on the ethical, hygienic, or aesthetic implications of their choices. The rich man buys in the expensive shop because part of the satisfaction for which he is paying is made up of the service, atmosphere, and convenience of a smart shop, and part again of the knowledge that he is known to buy there. He is getting value for his money, though all the value is not contained in the article he buys. Again the stenographer who goes without food to buy silk underwear may be foolish—that is not a subject on which the economist requires to be a competent judge. But she wants the silk underwear more than hearty food. That is why she buys it. And that is all the economist says. The man who is tricked by modern advertising has a want which he satisfies. That it is an artificial want, or a want for something which is useless or even harmful, is not a relevant criticism of the economist's position. We may have to admit a paradox here, because the economist does call such advertising "uneconomic," meaning that it is wasteful to society as a whole. But this admission does not change the fact that the main psychological generalizations of economics, symbolized by the economic man, form a valid working hypothesis of the economic behaviour of men in general.

Section 4: Summary and Evaluation

The method of economic theory is, then, both inductive and deductive, but, in its abstractions forced to rely more heavily than the physical sciences on the deductive processes. We start with certain simple generalizations about human behaviour and we assume or postulate the condition of stable equilibrium. We make a series of simplifying restrictions and work on the level of abstraction so established. Our theory is a drawing out of the full implications of equilibrium and our conclusions enable us to say how, under the conditions we have assumed, prices and output are determined. Such theory claims to be rigorous and, within its limitations, exact. "Rigid demonstrability and certainty of an almost geometric kind are claimed for [it]."[11]

There is, as Mr. Harrod shows, a paradox here. The laws of economic theory concern phenomena, and are supposedly empirical. The phenomena they concern are "notoriously highly complex and unamenable to scientific handling."[12] The economist may appeal to history for verification, but he can obtain little help here, for the appeal to history is unlike the experimental check of the

[11]R. F. Harrod, "The Scope and Method of Economics" (*Economic Journal*, Sept., 1938, p. 386). [12]*Ibid.*

physical sciences.　History does not repeat itself.　Every situation, however similar, is new and different by reason of the very fact, to name one ever-present difference, that past experience must always enter into it.　Isolation and controlled conditions are impossible. Something may, indeed, be learned, but it must lack the certainty that comes from the true experimental method.

Again it is frequently noticed that economists, when asked for advice about questions of public policy, are apt to disagree.　There is the story, attributed to Earl Baldwin, of the English Prime Minister who called five economists together to obtain advice on policy and who received six different opinions, "two of them from Mr. K." How then can economists claim on the one hand absolute validity for their general theory and on the other hand approach matters of public policy with controversy which betokens lack of certainty and precision?

The answer, as Mr. Harrod points out in the article from which we have quoted, is that in matters of public policy the economist is frequently dealing with the variables that are excluded from his abstract theory and to the study of which he has to bring a different apparatus of analysis.　His general theory is certain because it is so general.　"The laws in question are deducible from a single simple principle, itself based on experience, but on an experience far wider than that vouchsafed by the study of markets and prices and extending back to the earliest phases of man's self-conscious existence. . . . The experience is so broad that the principle may be taken as an axiom of the highest possible degree of empirical probability."[13]

Every science, as Professor Schumpeter says in his *Theory of Economic Development*, tries to push its explanations of cause and effect to its own borders and there turn the causal chain over to the neighbouring science.　Thus economics traces back the causal chain to the border of psychology.　It takes certain simple psychological principles of great generality and certainty.　Of that which flows directly from these, economics speaks with certainty.　The psychological principles themselves it leaves to psychology to explain.

But the very generality of these principles and the generality and degree of abstraction imposed on all that is deduced from them constitutes the weakness of abstract economic theory in the face of questions of practical policy.　There are excluded too many variables that, in the short run, are important.　There are, undoubtedly some questions, such as that of Free Trade, on which

[13]*Ibid.*, p. 387.

theoretical economists are agreed, and on which they have offered advice based on the laws of abstract theory. And most of their efforts to deal with other questions of the day take their departure from the conclusions of abstract theory. Thus abstract or "pure" theory remains of fundamental importance, and students of economics must begin their studies with the theory. But after this departure has been taken, when the economist is fully launched on the analysis of a specific issue, such as, for example, monetary policy, he has so many variables, so few landmarks, so little control over his conditions, such limited possibilities of experimentation or verification, that it is small wonder his work is tentative and sometimes contradictory. In this field or division of economic studies he must rely on an inductive method, similar to that of the physical sciences.[14] His general theory provides him with a "map" and a point of departure. He must then depend on the analysis of his particular problem, causal hypotheses, probably suggested by historical analysis, and attempted verification by statistical methods. It is probably true to say that some of the most significant work in economics today has been done, and will continue to be done, in this field. It is further true that as this method is perfected it will find statistical and historical evidence to lend empirical support to, or to impose modifications on, the conclusions of abstract theory.

A further chapter of this introductory book will discuss more fully the assistance the theoretical student can get from historical analysis. But we must be careful not to expect too great a degree of certainty or exactitude from the inductive methods in applied economics. In this field the subject-matter is too difficult for the precision, exactitude, and certainty attained by the physical sciences. Five hundred years from now the scientists may be taking week-end excursions to Mars, but the economists will be in disagreement as to the wisest policy for controlling the interplanetary exchanges.

[14]We are in danger here, in trying to make clear the distinction between pure theory and institutional or other "applied" studies, of overstating the case. The abstract theory is primarily rigorously deductive, but it makes use of ordinary induction, and it always stands to have its conclusions and laws modified or verified or rejected by the experimental, statistical and historical work of the applied economics. Again in the applied field continual back references will be made to the laws of pure theory. The two must go hand in hand, they are complementary methods of gaining knowledge of the economic world. Our emphasis on the methods and the importance of pure theory is not to be taken as any deprecation of the importance of other methods of economic study. The student must, however, first master the rigorous discipline of theory to put himself into a position for the proper prosecution of other economic studies.

CHAPTER IV

THE HISTORICAL METHOD

Section 1: Historical Facts

THE use of the historical method in economics has already been briefly indicated. In the first place we may appeal to historical experience for some of the generalizations of theory. Or again we may try to find in history verification for our theoretical conclusions, try to see, that is, if our hypotheses can account for actual events as they have happened. Thus Adam Smith[1] appeals to the statistics of corn prices from the thirteenth century to support his thesis of the relation of rents to agricultural prices. Thus, also, the quantity theory of money gains support from historical and statistical analysis of prices during periods of debasement of the coinage and from a study of the "Assignats" issued by the Convention during the French Revolution and of other paper money inflations.[2] Again Mr. J. M. Keynes undertakes a lengthy historical analysis as a "scientific experiment" to test the hypothesis which he advances in the first volume of his *Treatise on Money*.[3] He also attempts to find statistical verification and completes a study in the truly scientific manner by applying the theories so tested and verified to the solution of problems of monetary policy.

In the second place history provides a critique of theory. By this we mean that one sometimes finds in history not the expected verification but, instead, facts and events that stubbornly refuse to fit the hypothesis, so that theories have to be discarded or modified to explain these events. Thus Tooke's *History of Prices* showed that the whole classical theory of money and bank rate was, in its accepted form, incompatible with the facts. The theory had supposed that high prices coincided with low bank rate and *vice versa*, whereas in fact, Tooke showed, the correspondence was

---

[1]Smith's language makes very clear the nature of historical verification and, at the same time, the caution which the economist must use in the employment of this method. "I do not pretend," he says, "that any very certain conclusions can be drawn from them [i.e., the corn prices]. So far, however, as they prove anything at all, they confirm the account which I have been endeavouring to give" (*Wealth of Nations*, Everyman ed., London, 1933, vol. I, p. 169).

[2]Cf. J. N. Keynes, *The Scope and Method of Political Economy* (London, 1891), p. 271.

[3]J. M. Keynes, *Treatise on Money* (London, 1930), vol. II, chap. xxx.

very inexact and the tendency on the whole seemed to be a coincidence of high rates and high prices or of low rates and low prices. This led to a reconsideration of money and bank rate theory.

In the third place historical technique may be itself a method of formulating, as distinct from testing, theory. There has been in Germany, and there is now in the United States, a whole school of economists who have argued that this is, indeed, the only valid way to reach theories of any practical significance. They point to what they have done in various institutional studies, studies in the working of tax systems, banking systems, economic legislation, trust control, etc., and they say that this method of generalization from accumulated historical evidence is justified by its results.

Again theories of economic growth and progress, dynamic theories of economic society and sociology, are largely historical in method. The advantage of this method for this type of theory we have already shown, but the idea that "economic theories established by history" should entirely supplant the deductive method is a false one.[4] Both methods have their place and are, as we have said, complementary.[5] The idea, growing in popularity, that deductive economic theory is a mere academic pastime, entirely misses the point. It still remains true that these atomistic and discrete studies do not give any general body of theory or any explanation of the price system as a whole. Yet the price system is fundamental in our economy. The abstract theory in the classical tradition is the central core of all economic thought and an understanding of it is essential to success in any economic study. It is, so to speak, the co-ordinating principle. Without it historical facts have little significance. Those who think otherwise seem to do so from a misunderstanding of the nature of historical fact. They think of history as being chronology without interpretation.

History and economics are both interpretations of life. Indeed they have been associated in the Marxist philosophy as near identities.[6] The interpretation of economic history and the

[4]Keynes, *Scope and Method of Political Economy*, p. 279.

[5]For purposes of exposition we have perhaps drawn too sharp a distinction between the historical and the abstract method. Ideally they should be used together, the one testing the other against concrete fact and the other serving the one by providing explanation and interpretation of recorded fact.

[6]It is perhaps not surprising that the philosophies of fascism and communism should have a common source in the dialectic logic of Hegel, the one seeing in history the unfolding of the idea of the Absolute under the dominance of a Totalitarian Will, and the other, "turning the dialectic right side up" (Karl

interpretation of an aspect of life which we call economic theory
are similar, interdependent studies. History is no mere set of
data in a chronological or temporal rather than a spatial setting.
Like the universe of physical objects it wears a pattern, is subject
to causal laws, and can be interpreted by the intelligent, diligent,
and imaginative mind. It is, indeed, more difficult than physics,
or astronomy, or mechanical engineering, because it embraces the
whole range of human activities, and is often so confused in its
pattern that, as in the case of economics, exactitude and certainty
of knowledge are not possible. The historian, like the economist,
and like the philosopher, must often rest content with guesses and
part truths and he must know that the very stuff of his science is
apt to change in a generation and render false much of what has
been accepted as true.

Indeed history and philosophy can scarcely be contrasted
without the realization that they are, in one sense, the same,
differing in methods of study, but alike in the range of their subject-
matter and in the singleness of their approach to the whole of life.
They form together an effort *to explain* the development of human
life and thought and human institutions. Any effort to treat
history, economic or otherwise, as a mere sequence of facts without
any co-ordinating principle, without any effort at interpretation
or without any understanding of the constant interplay of fact and
theory, "material" and "non-material" facts is bound to failure.

For some time there has been much talk rightly, that history must be
established in facts, that it is essential it recount them. Nothing can be
more true, but there are many more facts to recount, and they are more
various than at the first blush one might have believed. There are the
material facts, like battles, wars and the official acts of governments; there
are moral facts, hidden, but none the less real for that. There are individual
facts, distinct and specific; there are general facts, indistinct, to which it is
impossible to assign a precise date, that cannot be contained within narrow
limits, yet no less facts than the others and not to be excluded, without
mutilation, from historical treatment.[7]

Marx, *Capital*, Preface to 2nd ed., London, 1873, p. xxx) and discovering through
the same logic the inevitability of economic determinism, the moulding and
conditioning of thoughts and institutional forms by intransigent, inescapable,
and omnipotent economic fact.

[7]"Depuis quelque temps on parle beaucoup, et avec raison, de la nécéssité
de renfermer l'histoire dans les faits, de la nécéssité de raconter: rien de plus vrais;
mais il y a bien plus de faits à raconter, et les faits bien plus divers, qu'on n'est
peutêtre tenté de le croire au premier moment; il y a des faits matériels, visibles,
comme les batailles, les guerres, les actes officiels des gouvernements; il y a des
faits moraux, cachés, qui n'en sont pas moins réels; il y a des faits individuels qui

We must attempt, in our economic thinking, a fusion of the two procedures. The abstract theory is an integration and interpretation. It can be tested and modified by historical research, and it, in turn, will modify and serve as a principle to interpret historical facts. Statistical and institutional studies will add to our knowledge, and will extend economic studies to fields that abstract theory cannot reach. At the same time these studies must take their departure from the abstract theory, they must be informed and directed by it, and they will finally constitute, after adequate testing, an extension of it.

SECTION 2: RELATIVITY OF "THEORY" AND "PRACTICE"

The economist is always striving to do two things. He attempts to describe how any given economic system works, and at the same time he is pointing out its inefficiencies and looking forward to a new or modified system which will incorporate reforms. Thus the body of economic doctrine grows and develops with changes in the economic system. The ideal of one generation of economists becomes the accomplished fact of the next. Adam Smith describes a commercial, domestic system economy and idealizes laissez-faire. Ricardo describes a young industrial economy, feeling its way towards laissez-faire, but in need of fiscal and monetary reform. Mill announces the achievements of these earlier ideals, and simultaneously Marx denounces the system for its inequalities and brutality and prophesies that its inherent defects and contradictions will lead to its violent destruction. Later the Austrians forsake the point of view of the man of business and attempt a scientific analysis of consumers' demand at a time when a series of technical revolutions had solved the most pressing of production problems and had brought producers face to face with the various and fluctuating demand of the new *bourgeoisie* and industrial proletariat who had arisen in the place of the old corn-consuming and largely self-sustaining peasantry.

Marshall makes a fusion of the Austrian analysis and the old classical line of thought and points the way to the economics of monopoly and decreasing costs. Contemporary economists are preoccupied with the growing menace of the business cycle and with the study of monopolistic competition.

ont un nom propre; il y a des faits généraux, sans nom, auxquels il est impossible d'assigner une date précise, qu'il est impossible de renfermer dans les limites rigoureuses, et qui n'en sont pas moins des faits comme d'autres, des faits historiques, qu'on ne peut exclure de l'histoire sans la mutiler" (F. P. G. Guizot, *Histoire de la civilisation en Europe*, Paris, 1846, p. 5).

We here observe the mutual dependence of economic doctrine and economic development. A new economics is required by a revolutionized industrial system, and a new economics points the way to further changes in the world of economic affairs.[8]

Economists sometimes have failed to remember this and have treated their laws as being permanent and immutable in spite of the mutability of the data with which they are concerned. It is true, of course, that there is a permanence in the psychological postulates in which economic theory is rooted. But the final conclusions to which the economic theorist comes must be determined by the nature of the institutions through which the psychological laws work themselves out. Changes in these institutions will affect the general body of economic thought. Thus the laws of economic growth are relevant to the principles of static theory. Only in the very highest degree of abstraction where the particular form of the institutions cannot affect the problem and where the conclusions follow directly from the psychological postulates can the conclusions be held to be valid in any permanent or absolute sense. And such conclusions can only be held to have any value if they can be used as hypotheses to apply to more realistic studies, in the course of which the whole study will be determined by the nature of the particular institutions selected for analysis.

[8]"In the industrial sphere, as in other departments of human action, facts and ideas act and react upon one another, so that there results a complex bond of connexion between the historical succession of phenomena and the historical succession of ideas. Economic theories may accordingly be considered not merely in relation to their absolute truth or falsity, but also in relation to the economic facts that helped produce them, and those that they themselves helped to produce" (Keynes, *Scope and Method of Political Economy*, p. 89).

APPENDIX TO BOOK ONE

ON THE USE OF MATHEMATICS IN ECONOMIC STUDIES

M OST students of economics are not mathematicians. In consequence the occasional use of mathematics in books on economics bewilders and frightens them. They make no effort to read the passages which include mathematical notations, or, if they do read them, they do so with the idea that they will not understand, and this idea has a way of making itself come true. Now most mathematics used in economics is simple and can be followed easily if the student has in mind one or two elementary principles. The object of this appendix is to present the non-mathematical reader with such simple mathematical techniques as will enable him readily to comprehend what little mathematics is used in this book. Mathematicians are not advised to read this chapter. It adds nothing to the general argument and covers only certain elementary principles with which all students of mathematics are familiar. Also there is apt to be a degree of over-simplification with which the mathematician would find it hard to be patient.

Mathematics is a language. It is a method of expressing by means of symbols instead of words a set of relations which must necessarily follow from the nature of certain very simple ideas with which it starts. Thus mathematics is also a logic, a formal study. It tells us nothing by way of description of our world or our universe, or of any particular world or universe.

When we say mathematics is formal we mean that it asserts nothing about any particular. When we say two and two make four, we think not of apples, apes, or apartment houses. The generalization is true for application to any of these particular subjects, but it is true quite apart from them or any other particular contents. In logic we say formal argument is concerned with the form as opposed to the matter of reasoning, that is with the agreement or disagreement of ideas with one another, not with their agreement or disagreement with phenomena. Thus when we say "if all trees are coniferous, the maple does not lose its leaves in autumn," our argument is formally correct. The conclusion is wrong not because of a mistake in proceeding from the major premiss, but because the major premiss itself is not in accord with the facts. Now mathematics may deal in a world completely remote from reality. It could deal with a purely imaginative world. But once you granted its premises all its conclusions would necessarily follow. It is not concerned with the agreement or disagreement of its conclusions with the facts of the material world. When a mathematician says, "what can be inferred from next to next can be inferred from first to last,"[1] his statement refers to all series of finite numbers, and is true of all such series without reference to any particular series of objects in the world of appearance. Mathematics is thus inferential and deductive. It says if the Euclidean axioms are all true, then the Euclidean theorems necessarily follow.

Mathematical reasoning is not dependent on the existence of specific numerical data. The important thing is that the data be, not numerical, but quantitative. If we can speak of greater or less, if we can say that a quantity increases or decreases, if we can speak of a rate of increase or decrease, if we can treat of quantities as negative or positive, as approaching a maximum or minimum limit, if we know the rate of change of one quantity to depend on the change in another quantity, mathematical reasoning is both possible and useful. To take a simple example: "if A is greater than B, and B is greater than C, therefore A is greater than C."[2] Yet these quantities, A, B, C, may not be susceptible of exact numerical measurement. Nevertheless relative values for the bulk of A and C may be an essential point in the establishment of an argument.[3]

We have already observed the nature of deductive argument. It rests, we will remember, on the principle of non-contradiction. Two contradictory propositions cannot both be true at the same time. If, therefore, two statements are given as true, a third proposition defining the conditions which make their simultaneous truth possible emerges as being also true. If a straight line is the shortest distance between two points, and if the line xy is the shortest line between two points x and y, then xy must be a straight line; for if xy is not straight then one of the other two propositions must be false.

Again, to take an example more abstract, if we say $y = kx$, when $k = 3$ and $y = 9$, we can solve for x. That is we can deduce the value which x must have if it is true that y is 9, k, 3, and that $y = kx$. The only value for x that will satisfy these conditions, that is to say the only value that x can have if the other equations

[1]Bertrand Russell, *Introduction to Mathematical Philosophy* (London, 1919), p. 27.

[2]F. Y. Edgeworth, *Mathematical Psychics* (London, 1887), p. 2.

[3]Consider the following example given in Edgeworth, *Mathematical Psychics*, to illustrate the importance of unnumerical mathematical reasoning: "It is required to distribute a given quantity of fuel, so as to obtain the greatest possible quantity of available energy, among a given set of engines, which differ in efficiency—*efficiency* being thus defined: one engine is more efficient than another if, whenever the total quantity of fuel consumed by the former is equal to that consumed by the latter, the total quantity of energy yielded by the former is greater than that yielded by the latter.

"In the distribution, shall a larger portion of fuel be given to the more efficient engines? always, or only in some cases? and, if so, in what sort of cases? Here is a very simple problem, involving no numerical data, yet requiring, it may be safely said, mathematics for its complete investigation."

are true, is that $x = 3$. This process of deduction in mathematics is called determining the value of x which will make the equation a true one under the given conditions. Similarly the solution of the familiar simultaneous equations is an exercise in deduction. If $y = x + 7$ and $3y = 4x - 2y + 43$, then y must equal 15, and x must equal 8. The process of deduction is hidden here by the steps that are taken, but it is the same process. If $y = x + 7$, then $2y = 2x + 14$, and $3y = 3x + 21$. This follows from the first condition that $y = x + 7$, and from the deductive principle that in mathematics is called multiplication. Then because things that are equal to the same thing are equal to one another $3x + 21 = 4x - (2x + 14) + 43$. Then by addition and subtraction, further deductive or inferential principles, $x = 43 - 14 - 21, = 8$.

By substituting the value for x in the first equation, that is by adding to our knowns the first conclusion of our deduction, we easily discover the value of y, and we say that our two equations are true when x equals 8, and y equals 15.

Mathematics is thus a formal, deductive science. It is a method of finding the unknown from the known. It is a symbolic language in the sense that it enables us to dispose of the cumbersome use of words and take short cuts in a deductive process. Its value in economics lies in this fact that it is a short cut. It is possible to carry through long processes of deduction by means of mathematics when the process would otherwise be almost interminable. Again it is valuable because the laws of mathematical deduction are clear cut and errors of reasoning which might easily escape notice buried in a mass of verbiage are readily seen and detected. A very important case, particularly in the theory of price, is when the given conditions are not such as to make the problem determinate, that is when the given conditions are not sufficient to enable one to solve definitely for the unknowns. Purely verbal argument is apt to cover up this deficiency and lead to solutions of problems that, under mathematical analysis are shown not to be true and complete solutions at all. Further, it is possible in mathematics to show the exact nature of interdependent variables and to achieve an exactitude and clarity in the expression of functional variations which would otherwise be impossible.

Finally, graphic mathematics is a visual aid in understanding. The presentation of dependent functions by means of curves gives a picture which illustrates economic principles in a clear and precise fashion, and enables the student more easily to comprehend them and more readily to take in a whole series of related ideas.

We must remember that mathematics is dangerous in inexperienced hands. If the propositions on which a process of deduction rests are incorrect the conclusions will be false, however valid the process. In applying a formal technique to an empirical science we must realize that the most perfect deductive process will yield us nothing of value in the way of knowledge about the real world if the premisses on which the process rests are faulty, or at too great a remove from reality.

With these thoughts about the general nature of mathematics in mind, let us now consider briefly some of the simple mathematics the student of economics uses.

In the first place we make a considerable use of curves. A curve is a device to picture or illustrate the dependence of one variable upon another.

We have first what we call the independent variable or argument. The independent variable is a varying quantity whose variations are taken as given in the problem. The independent variable is then defined as affecting through every variation the dependent variable or consequent, but as itself being free of any reciprocal influence.

In all curve drawing the independent variable is plotted along the x-axis. By this sentence we mean that we draw a horizontal line—our x-axis—and mark off or plot on it in units all the variations of our independent variable which we shall call x. If x varies from 0 through 10, our x-axis will be marked like this:

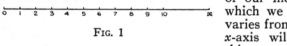

FIG. 1

The dependent variable is a quantity that varies in a certain, not necessarily uniform, way with x. It is very often known as a function of x and may be written $(f)x$. We may consider the dependent variable as the unknown, and most economic problems of a mathematical nature consist in solving for the value of y, i.e. $(f)x$, given x. But to solve for y in this fashion it is necessary to know the principle of dependence, that is the principle governing the way y varies with x. This principle we shall be able to express mathematically, but we shall discover it in our economic data. Thus if x is the number of units of goods put on the market and y the cost per unit of producing these goods, we shall need to know if the unit costs rise or fall as the total number of goods produced is increased. Let us suppose that they rise at a uniform rate, and that for every increase of one unit in x, there is an increase of 2 units in y.

Then we may write that $y = 2x$, and for any value of x we can solve for the corresponding value of y. We can say that y is determined from x. We picture this process by erecting a perpendicular on the x-axis, which we call the y-axis, and both axes come from the same origin which is given the value 0. Just as we increased our quantities away from the origin on the x-axis, so do we on the y-axis. Then our two axes look like this:

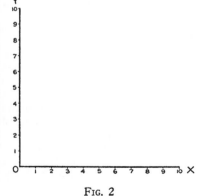

FIG. 2

To illustrate the dependence of y on x, we indicate by a series of points in the area lying between the axes the corresponding value of y for each value of x. In our example, when $x=0$, $y=0$; when $x=1$, $y=2$; when $x=2$, $y=4$; when $x=3$, $y=6$, and so on. This is shown graphically in the following manner:

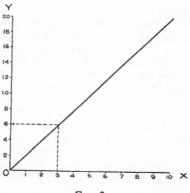

FIG. 3

The faint vertical and horizontal lines are merely guiding lines and may be disregarded. The points show the value of y for each value of x. Given any value of x we can rapidly see— that is the illustrative value of the graph—the corresponding value of y, by glancing up from the x-axis at that value to the point indicating the corresponding y value. A reference to the y-axis shows us what this value of y is. The distance along the x-axis from the origin to any value is known as the abscissa of the value and the corresponding distance along the y-axis is known as the ordinate. The co-ordinates of a point are the abscissa and ordinate for that point and the values of the co-ordinates can be read along the axes.

We may connect all the points by a line, as in Fig. 3 we have done. This curve rests on the supposition that if the variation is continuous, and if the dependent variable varies in a uniform fashion with the independent variable, as in our example it does, any point on the curve will yield the corresponding value of y for that value of x. This curve is defined by the equation we have given, $y=2x$, and at any point on it we have the true value of y for the value of x.

Our equation $y=2x$ is a peculiar and limiting example of a group of curves called parabolas which in this positive quadrant of the axes all curve upward from the origin. In our particular case the curve is a straight line. The general equation which describes all these curves is $y=ax^n$, when a is any constant and n any power of x. In our case $a=2$, and $n=1$.[4]

Curves drawn from empirical data of variations in x and y are suppositions in the interstices between the empirically known points, but if the line of the curve is at all regular the curve will be approximately true at all points.

Few curves are as simple as the one we have drawn. The simplest demand curve will have the equation $y=\dfrac{k}{x^n}$, and many

[4] Throughout this chapter we use the equation $y=ax^n$ as our general equation when we are illustrating cost curves. In this way we are able to keep our examples relatively simple. Realistic cost curves are not frequently parabolas and are much more apt to have equations of the general type $y=ax+b+\dfrac{c}{x}$ 2.

hyperbolic curves will have diabolic equations. That need not worry us, however, as long as we understand the general principles involved in graph drawing. The equation shows us the dependence of y on x. The constants are derived from our economic data. Given that y will vary in a certain fashion with x we can always solve for y. y may not vary in a uniform fashion; it may vary at first directly, then inversely. However that may be, the curve tells the story in pictorial fashion and as long as we have sufficient data to construct an equation we can solve for y for any value of x.

Moreover we can solve simultaneous equations for x and y given two curves with a point or points in common. The solution of the equations gives us the point or points which will be common to both curves. It is thus that we can determine the point in common of supply and demand curves. For reasons that we shall take up later on, price is stable at this common point. Hence if we can show how this point is determined we can show how equilibrium price is determined. If we can establish equations for the supply and demand curves the determination of equilibrium price can be determined in the form of simultaneous equations. It is often convenient and beneficial to do this. It is convenient because of the greater ease with which argument can be conducted in symbols, and beneficial because it enforces clarity and precision of thought. There is no symbol in mathematics for a vague idea.

Thus to take our two examples, if the supply curve equation is $y = ax^n$, and the demand curve equation is $y = \dfrac{b}{x^n}$ (substituting b, a specific constant, for k, any constant), we can solve the two equations for the price of the good. (We assume here the truth of our statement that price is stable at the point of intersection of the supply and demand curves.)

In both equations y equals money cost or money price, and x equals the quantities of the commodity put on the market.

$$y = ax^n \qquad \dotfill \text{(i)}$$

$$y = \frac{b}{x^n} \qquad \dotfill \text{(ii)}$$

$$\text{then } a.x^n = \frac{b}{x^n} \qquad \text{by substitution}$$

$$a.x^{2n} = b$$

$$x^{2n} = \frac{b}{a}$$

$$x^n = \sqrt{\frac{b}{a}} \qquad \dotfill \text{(iii)}$$

$$y = a.\sqrt{\frac{b}{a}} \qquad \text{substituting (iii) in (i)}$$

$$= \frac{a.\sqrt{b}}{\sqrt{a}}$$

$$= \sqrt{ab} \qquad \dotfill \text{(iv)}$$

Let us now give arithmetic values to a and b, plot our curves and observe in an actual case how the graphic results coincide with the algebraic.

Let $a = 4$, $b = 16$, and $n = 1$.

Substituting these values in (iii) and (iv) above we have

$$x = \sqrt{\frac{16}{4}} = 2,$$

and $y = \sqrt{16 \times 4} = 8$.

Thus the point, the co-ordinates of which are x equals 2 and y equals 8, is the common point which must lie on both the curves. These are the only values of x and y which will satisfy both equations.

Let us now plot the curves and observe this graphically.

Demand Curve

$y = \dfrac{b}{x^n}$, $b = 16$, $n = 1$

When

$x = 1$, $y = 16$
$x = 2$, $y = 8$
$x = 4$, $y = 4$
$x = 8$, $y = 2$
$x = 16$, $y = 1$

Supply Curve

$y = a.x^n$, $a = 4$, $n = 1$

When

$x = 1$, $y = 4$
$x = 2$, $y = 8$
$x = 3$, $y = 12$
$x = 4$, $y = 16$
$x = 5$, $y = 20$
$x = 6$, $y = 24$

We see that our equations can be solved to yield the same result as can be obtained by plotting the curves. The equation method is more suitable for complicated cases. It enables us to see with perfect precision the exact nature of price determination given the conditions of equilibrium.

We must observe that our equations are proper equations, that is that they can be solved.

A mathematical equation states a proposition; it is what is called a "propositional function." So long as it is undetermined it is neither true

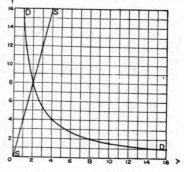

FIG. 4

nor false. It is true when it is solved for a value of the unknown which satisfies the conditions of the equation. Thus the statement "x is a human" is a propositional function;[5] as long as x is undetermined it is neither true nor false, but when a value is assigned to x it becomes either true or false. If the value assigned to x is "Mr. Brown," then the equation is a true one. If the value assigned is "our dog Fido," then it is false. The equation which can be solved for a value of the unknown must be carefully dis-

[5]See Bertrand Russell, *Introduction to Mathematical Philosophy*, p. 156 ff.

3

tinguished from the sort of an equation known as an identity. An identity is true in all cases. $x=x$ is true for any value of x. It has no unknown to be solved for, because if one side of the equation is given so is the other and by the same data. Hence from an identity we can deduce no new knowledge, whereas from a determinate equation we may. In an identity if there are any given or known quantities all are given or known and no deduction as to the value of an unknown is possible, because the equation is true for all cases and gives no special conditions that must be satisfied to find a determinate value of the unknown.

The dangers of failing to distinguish an equation from an identity are not uncommon in economics. Thus Mr. Keynes has criticized the famous Fisher equation as being an identity.[6] The price level in the equation is set down in the form of prices times transactions and it is set equal to the quantity of money times velocity, which, Mr. Keynes charges, is the same thing as the total of price transactions. If the criticism is fair the equation is an identity and does not enable one to solve for an unknown P (prices); hence P is not determinate and the equation tells us nothing about the monetary forces determining the price level. Whether or not Mr. Keynes's criticism is in this case applicable we do not now inquire. But it serves as an illustration of the danger of failing to distinguish the identity equation from the equation which can be solved. In economics we must try to organize our knowns and our unknowns so that we can set them down in equations which will enable us to solve for the unknowns.

Our account so far has described the nature of dependent variation, but it has omitted any consideration of *rates* of change.

We have treated variations as being variations of a unit quantity of finite and recognizable size. Now, without worrying about the nature of continuity[7] let us make the assumption that the increments are infinitesimally small.

When the increment in x is supposed to be very, very small we

[6] J. M. Keynes, *Treatise on Money* (London, 1930), vol. I, p. 234.

[7] Actually the treatment of finite increments and of infinitely small increments belong to different "discourses" of mathematics. It is only by a happy accident, we are told, that the use of continuous differential functions can be applied in the world of finite quantities with valuable practical results.

We might also notice that we deal throughout this chapter with continuous curves. That is, we suppose that for every change in x, even if the change is by the smallest quantity that may be thought of, there will be a corresponding change in y. For this reason the functional variations, conceived as a series of points, are so narrowly spaced as to appear as a continuous line. This method is convenient as it enables us to apply valuable mathematical aids to economic analysis. Sometimes, however, it is misleading, and we must remember that economic quantities do not actually permit of such minute division. In actual fact the points will be widely spaced, and from purely empirical data we cannot be sure that a curve joining them either exists at all or, if it does exist, that it joins them in a continuous curve. It is necessary, therefore, in applying this method to economic analysis, to allow for a margin of error.

call it dx. The corresponding change in y is called dy. The ratio $\dfrac{dy}{dx}$, expressing the rate of change of y with respect to x, is called the derivative, or differential coefficient of y with respect to x.

The derivative measures the rate of change of y as compared with ("with respect to") x. The increment, dy, in y is dependent on the increment, dx, in x. The *rate* of change of the dependent variable, is simply the ratio of change in the dependent to the change in the independent variable.

A rate of speed, to choose for example a rate of which we commonly speak in every day life, is a change in space in a change in time. If we cover 80 miles in two hours, our average speed, or rate of change of place in time, is $\dfrac{80}{2}$ or 40 miles per hour. If, on a journey from New York to Chicago, we discover that we have added 80 miles to our progress and that it has taken us two hours to do this, we can regard the 80 miles as the increment to our dependent variable and that the increment to our independent variable, time, has been two. We might write this $\dfrac{\Delta y}{\Delta x}$[8], though of course we should never bother to do so for such rough and obvious calculations as this. In this case we should divide 80 by two and say our speed or rate of change of place in time is 40 miles per hour.

But these increments are too great to give us any accurate idea of our speed at any time during those two hours. We might be accelerating and decelerating all along the road. For exact calculations we want some way of discovering our speed at any point on our journey. The process of "differentiation" enables us to do this. By differentiating the equation of a curve, i.e. the equation of functional variation, we can find the rate at which y is changing with x for any value of x.

The rules for differentiation are difficult and beyond the scope of this chapter, and we shall not need to use them. But to make clear the exact nature of the process we shall take an example, showing what we do when we differentiate, but neglecting the explanation of the technical rules governing the process.

The process of differentiation, we repeat, is that of finding the rate of change of y with respect to x. If we refer to our graphs we discover that the steepness of the *slope* of the curve pictures the rate of change. When the change in y is large with respect to the change in x the curve rises or falls sharply. When the rate of change is small the curve has a gentler slope.

Now the curve may have the same slope throughout or its slope may change. We shall deal with these two conditions separately.

Let us first take the case of a straight line, a case where the slope is constant. To discover the value for $\dfrac{dy}{dx}$ for this curve we

[8] $\dfrac{\Delta y}{\Delta x}$ is the symbol used in place of $\dfrac{dy}{dx}$ when the increments are finite and commensurable.

need only discover its slope. In mathematics the slope of the curve is dependent on the angle it makes with the x-axis or with any line parallel to the x-axis. The equation $y=ax$ is the equation of a straight line. In our example where a was 2 we plotted the curve as follows: (See Fig. 5).

The tangent of an angle, A, in a right-angled triangle (abbreviated Tan A) is defined as being the $\dfrac{\text{perpendicular}}{\text{base}}$, and this is the expression for the slope of the curve which makes the angle, A, with the x-axis or any parallel to the x-axis. We may further define Sin A as the $\dfrac{\text{perpendicular}}{\text{hypotenuse}}$ and Cos A as the $\dfrac{\text{base}}{\text{hypotenuse}}$. Thus, when we plot our curve, the expression $\dfrac{dy}{dx}$ used in the calculus

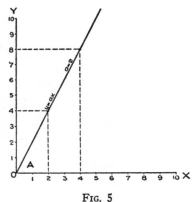

FIG. 5

corresponds to the trigonometric function, tan A. Now from the known factors in our example we see that tan A is always

equal to 2, because tan $A = \dfrac{y}{x}$

$$= \frac{2x}{x}$$

$$= 2.$$

But 2 is simply the arithmetic constant substituted for "a" in our example. For any curve of the equation $y=ax$, tan $A=a$, because

$$\tan A \;=\; \frac{y}{x}\;\frac{(\text{perpendicular})}{(\text{base})}$$

$$= \frac{ax}{x}$$

$$= a.$$

Thus $\dfrac{dy}{dx}$, for the curve $y=ax$, equals a.

This method can be of great practical use, because it enables us to calculate the value of y for any value of x, when our only known is $\dfrac{dy}{dx}$, the rate of change or slope.

When the curve is not a straight line the trigonometric problem is more difficult. It will be easier here to follow the rules for differentiation. The rule is to reduce the power to which x is raised by one and multiply by the index.

Thus when $y = ax^n$, $\dfrac{dy}{dx} = n.ax^{n-1}$

Or, if $y = \dfrac{b}{x^n}$, $\tan A = \dfrac{y}{x}$

$$= \dfrac{\dfrac{b}{x^n}}{x}$$

$$= \dfrac{b}{x^{n+1}}.$$

But for this type of curve the slope is not constant; for $\tan A$ differs with every value of x. In geometry there would be difficulties in measuring the slope at any given point, but by means of differentiation it is possible to calculate it. Thus in our curve $y = \dfrac{b}{x^n}$, when n equals 1 and b, 16, we can calculate the slope of the curve for any value of x. If we choose the point where x equals 4, $\dfrac{dy}{dx}$ equals $\dfrac{b}{x^{n+1}}$, equals $\dfrac{16}{4^2}$, equals 1. Similarly, where x equals 2, $\dfrac{dy}{dx}$ equals 4, and so forth.[9]

It is important for us when we come to the study of demand to have some way of measuring what is called elasticity. Elasticity is the proportionate change in y to the proportionate change in x. It is thus capable of being written as a fraction

$$\dfrac{\dfrac{dy}{y}}{\dfrac{dx}{x}} = \dfrac{dy}{dx} \cdot \dfrac{x}{y}.$$

From this we see that elasticities can be calculated by multiplying the derivative by $\dfrac{x}{y}$.

It would be interesting to go on with the theory of the second derivative, but it is unlikely that the student will run across this in the course of elementary economic studies.

We might fittingly bring this appendix to a close at this point. The student of advanced economics will need to make a proper study of mathematics, getting both a fuller knowledge of what we have so sketchily covered, and carrying the study beyond these limits.

This appendix will have served its purpose if it has dispelled in some readers the fear and emotional complex which sometimes prevent the intelligent co-operation of the student in economic studies.

[9] We have purposely dropped the minus sign here. Economists speak of elasticities as positive, and thus imply that the slopes of falling curves are positive. Thus this is presented so as to be in keeping with general economic usage.

BOOK TWO

THE PRICE SYSTEM IN ABSTRACTION

This Book, while it should serve to clarify the argument and sharpen certain concepts for those who find helpful the precision of mathematical treatment, is not essential to the continuity of the study and may be omitted by those who find mathematics confusing.

CHAPTER V

EQUATIONS OF THE SIMPLIFIED ECONOMY UNDER CONDITIONS OF MONOPOLY, MONOPSONY AND SINGLE AND MULTIPLE COMMODITIES

SECTION 1: THE SIGNIFICANCE OF THE PRICE SYSTEM

THE central problem of abstract economic theory is to answer this question, "What determines the prices and quantities of goods put on the market?" "Goods" in this context refers to all commodities and services which satisfy human desires and includes both commodities and services which are immediately consumed and those which are used for the further production of such consumption goods.

The determination of price is the central problem of economic theory because all economic activity is guided by price. A man's standard of living is determined by the price he can obtain for his labour and the prices which he has to pay for goods. An entrepreneur decides what and how much he shall produce and what employment he will make of the agents of production by reference to the prices offered for his output and the prices he has to pay for the productive agents.

We have, we saw, a system of unlimited wants and scarce means for their satisfaction. The purpose of an economy is to distribute these satisfactions, to guide the productive force of nature and the productive labour and capital of man into the channels that will yield satisfactions. The mechanism of guidance and distribution is the price system. It is possible to imagine an economy in which some central direction would be exercised by a bureaucrat or dictator who would decree how much of each commodity should be produced and what share of the social output should go to each unit of each productive agent. But it is doubtful if there could be devised any means whereby the bureaucrat would have adequate knowledge to do this. It is doubtful if any dictator could ever succeed in preventing some measure of free choice to consumers. In that case he would have to set up some sort of imitation of a price system in order to obtain guidance. As things are, the central directing principle of our economic system is the price system and that is why the study of the price system is central in economic studies.

Even if we want to make restricted "institutional" or historical

inquiries, price theory, we have argued, is basic. If we are interested
in a reformed fiscal system we must know what taxes and levies will
be shifted; how taxes will affect prices; what taxes might restrict
output. To know these things it is necessary to know how prices
are determined and what alterations in costs will affect prices and
output and in what degree.

Again, if we are interested in the problem of controlling the
business cycle, so as to avoid the periods of depression, we must
know the causes of economic disequilibrium. To know these requires, first of all, knowing the forces which determine equilibrium,
the "stabilizers," as one economist has called them. And to know
these is to know the laws of equilibrium price and output, which
hold in balance the quantities of goods supplied with those
demanded.

If we are looking towards some sort of economic equality as the
ideal implicit within our democratic political and social system, we
must first discover the causes of inequality, which lie within our
present system of distribution.   The key to understanding the distributive system is the price structure of goods and services.   We
must know how wages are determined if we are to know if it is
possible to raise them.

Even if our interest is in the nature of economic change and
growth we must know how prices and output are determined if we
are to understand the effect on output and standards of living of
changes in population or of production techniques.

Thus the economic theorist is concerned primarily with the
theory of price determination and it is because of the central role of
price that we have argued that theory is basic to all economic
inquiry.

SECTION 2: DEFINING THE LEVEL OF ABSTRACTION

We begin with a completely unreal but, nevertheless, illumin-
ating case. Our plan is to discover what determines output under
the simplest conditions when every possible influence but real labour
effort and real want are excluded. We shall then carry the analysis
forward to consider this balance of cost and want in terms of money
price. We shall conclude this book by extending our conclusions so
as to embrace a complete price system.

Throughout we shall assume that the men we are considering
are completely rational and accurate in their measurements of costs
and satisfactions. We shall assume that there are no forces present
external to our pricing situation. We shall assume that there are

no changes in productive technique, or in the available quantity or fertility of land.

We shall postulate a position of equilibrium. Output is in equilibrium when producers have no incentive to increase or decrease the amounts they put on the market. A study of the equilibrium position is therefore a static study. It is an inquiry as to the nature of the forces that fix equilibrium where it is. We hold the economic system in balance, so to speak, and study it as it is at that moment of balance, static and out of time.

For this first chapter we need not introduce more than one man. It is rather out of fashion nowadays to talk about a "Crusoe economy" because it is impossible to discuss a price system when only one man is involved. But it is necessary at some point in the development of theory to introduce an examination of the psychological forces of real wants, real satisfactions, and real costs and these concepts can most clearly be studied and the proper logical sequence of the argument from the psychological postulate most clearly seen, or so we believe, by beginning with the one-man economy.

This Robinson Crusoe—for so we shall call him after an established, if slightly facetious, tradition—is an abstract economic man. Our fundamental assumption is that he carefully balances costs against satisfactions and always acts so as to minimize his costs and maximize his satisfactions. The nature of our abstraction does not, however, require that Crusoe be regarded as a primitive man, an unhappy Adam in his solitary Eden. He is, rather, very like the Crusoe of Defoe's story, a social being, who has been lost and separated from all his fellows. He is rational, he has a civilized man's standard of values. He is unique only in that he is alone and that he is the personification of economic behaviour. This does not mean that we believe in the existence of such a dehumanized creature. It simply means that our abstraction of Crusoe from society is followed by a second abstraction, that of Crusoe the economic man, from Crusoe, the whole man. We shall concentrate on observing his responses to economic stimuli and situations and neglect his other activities, feelings, and thoughts.

He brings with him to his island a whole complex of wants, and a civilized man's knowledge that some of them can only be satisfied by waiting and some of them by indirect means. He is not a savage to live in the present only. What is implicit in Crusoe, the isolated social being, is explicit in society. Thus what we learn from studying Crusoe will serve us in the study of the more complicated social

economy.   We must hope to move from one study to the other
without too sharp a transition and with valuable lessons learned
from the one to help us with the other.

Section 3: Marginal Utility

We shall first consider Crusoe alone on the island and we shall
suppose him to be producing only one commodity, presumably for
immediate consumption.   We thus rule out competition among
both purchasers and producers, and our economy consists of a single
man working on the land without capital, that is without instruments or machinery, to produce a single commodity for his sustenance.

We shall call the satisfaction which Crusoe gets from the consumption of each unit of any number of like units of his commodity
the degree of utility of that good; and we shall call the satisfaction
which he gets from the last unit of any given available quantity the
marginal utility of the commodity.   The total satisfaction he gets
from consuming all the available units of the commodity we call the
total utility of that quantity of the commodity.   Thus when we
speak of the utilities of a good, "degree" refers to the utility of any
unit, "marginal" to the utility of the last unit, and "total" to the
sum of utility of all the units.   The last unit of any given supply of
the good is spoken of as the marginal unit.   Thus the degree of
utility of the marginal unit of any number of units is the marginal
utility for that quantity of the good.

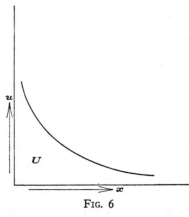

Fig. 6

Let x be any quantity of the
good; u the marginal utility; and
U the total utility of the x goods.
It is clear that for every value
of x there is a corresponding value
of u and of U, therefore we may say
that u and U are each functions of
x, though, of course, different functions.   As we know from ordinary
experience, u decreases as x increases.[1]   This is illustrated in Fig.
6.   The total utility U which is the
sum of all the marginal utilities is
given by the area under the curve.

[1] U will increase as x increases, though at a constantly decreasing rate.   The
rate at which U is increasing at any given value of x is nothing more nor less
than the marginal utility of the x goods.   That is $u \equiv \dfrac{dU}{dx}$.

Now any unit of the good is perfectly interchangeable with any other.   If Crusoe is living on turtles' eggs and possesses twelve eggs, any one of the twelve will have the same degree of utility for him. The degree of utility of any one of the twelve will be the satisfaction he would lose by possessing only eleven.   In other words the degree of utility of any egg to Crusoe is the degree of utility of the last egg he gathers, i.e. it is measured by the marginal utility.   Given any quantity of a commodity available for consumption, the degree of utility of any unit of that commodity, or the value of it to the consumer, is equal to the degree of utility of the last unit added to the quantity, that is to the marginal utility of the given quantity of goods.

A more realistic example may perhaps bring this point more vividly to the attention of the reader.

A hungry man enters a restaurant and finds the management ready to serve him with a two-ounce steak, a three-ounce steak, a four-ounce steak, or a five-ounce steak.   The price the restaurant charges works out at ten cents the ounce of cooked steak, i.e. twenty, thirty, forty, or fifty cents, according to the size of the steak ordered. Now, though our man might be prepared to pay as much as twenty cents for the first ounce of steak he consumes, if that was the only available food and all that he could have, it is not likely that he will be willing to pay that much for the second ounce, because after the first ounce has been eaten he is less hungry and his desire is less acute.   He anticipates this diminishing desire and makes some sort of rough calculation of what his desire for steak will be as it becomes progressively satisfied.   He finds that he is willing to pay twenty cents for the first ounce, if only one ounce is available, fifteen cents for the second ounce, twelve cents for the third ounce, ten cents for the fourth ounce, and nine cents for the fifth ounce.   Let us not suppose that for five ounces he is willing to pay the sum for all these amounts.   He is willing to pay for each ounce of the five ounces only the measure of the value he would lose by not consuming the fifth ounce.   If the restaurant will not sell him five ounces at nine cents the ounce, that is for forty-five cents, he will not buy five ounces.   All that he is willing to pay to retain that fifth ounce for consumption is nine cents, and if more than that is asked he will give it up.   It is the value of the marginal unit, not the value of any other unit, which determines what he will pay for any unit of the commodity offered.

For the fourth ounce of steak our man is just willing to offer ten cents to prevent its being taken away from him.   That is to say, he will pay forty cents for a four-ounce steak. He will not, let us emphasize, offer forty-seven cents for it, that is the sum of the utilities of one, two and three and four ounces. The four-ounce steak is worth to him only four times the utility of the marginal unit. Thus he is willing to pay for four ounces what the restaurant will accept for this amount, namely, forty cents, and, in our example, that determines the size steak the man will order.

Similarly for Crusoe the value of any one of his turtles' eggs will be just that of the marginal egg in consumption. Only in Crusoe's case the cost is measured in terms of labour effort, not in the money units we are accustomed to use for our measure of account. Crusoe has to labour to collect the eggs. Labour, after a certain period of activity has been passed, becomes wearying and irksome. Let us call all the dissatisfactions, such as fatigue, painfulness, etc., brought about by labour, its disutility. Let us mean by degree of disutility the dissatisfaction due to the production of any unit of a good; by marginal disutility, the dissatisfaction attributable to the production of the last unit of a good; and by total disutility, the total dissatisfaction brought about by the production of all the units of any given quantity of the good.

Let x, as before, denote any quantity of the good, l the marginal disutility, and L the total disutility for the production of x goods. It is evident that l and L are functions of x, though different functions. We know from experience that l usually increases as x increases.[2] l is frequently known as the marginal real cost of production.

[2] l increases when x increases as we know from common experience. We can demonstrate this in a manner conformable to our general treatment in this section.

An increment in output is produced during a unit increment in time. Thus output is a function of time and the rate of increase in output in time can be written $\dfrac{dx}{dt}$. The longer a man works the greater his fatigue and the less effective he will be. Statistical time studies have shown this beyond dispute. Thus he will produce less and less as time goes on. Hence $\dfrac{dx}{dt}$ is a diminishing rate. The rate of labour disutility, $\dfrac{dl}{dx}$, is an increasing rate and it increases more and more rapidly the longer a man works. It increases the more rapidly because $\dfrac{dl}{dx}$ is really $\dfrac{d^2l}{dt^2}$ and while l increases with x, x decreases with t, thus the increase of l with t is exaggerated.

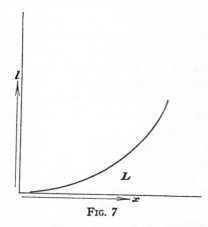

FIG. 7

The relation of x, l, and L is shown in Fig. 7. L, the total disutility, the sum of all the marginal disutilities, is given by the area under the curve.

Now we can see the answer to the question raised at the beginning of this section, what determines the price in labour cost Crusoe will pay for a unit of his single commodity, and what determines the amount he will produce?

He will produce to the amount where any further production would require a labour effort whose marginal disutility would exceed the marginal utility which he would derive from the product. That is he would produce till $l=u$, and no further.

Since marginal utility will be decreasing while marginal disutility will be increasing with increasing quantity, there will be but one value of x which will satisfy the condition that $l=u$. We can readily see this in Fig. 8, where we put our two curves together.

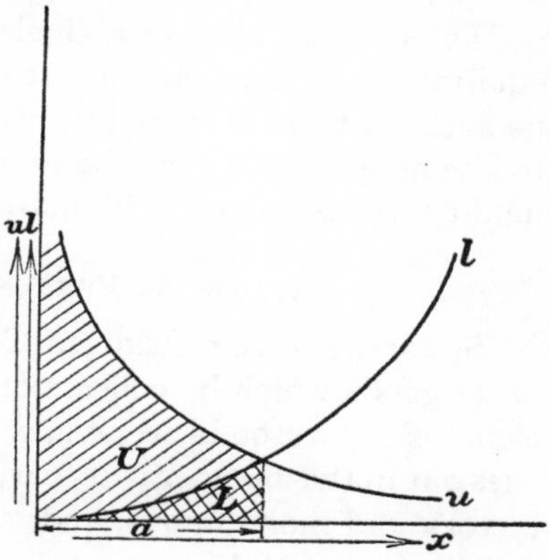

The value of x at which the two curves cross gives the quantity which would be produced.[3]

The reader will remember that we do not pretend that Crusoe's calculations will in fact be exact. We are defining in our equation the equilibrium position to which his actual output will tend to approximate.

FIG. 8

[3] The total net advantage to Crusoe in producing "a" commodities will equal the area under the utility curve bounded by the perpendicular at a and the y—axis less the corresponding area under the disutility curve, i.e. $U-L$.

a thus marks the point in output which gives Crusoe the maximum net satisfaction that can be obtained by producing and consuming this good. He obtains part of this maximum net satisfaction as the sole producer, that is as a monopolist, and part of it as the sole consumer, that is as a monopsonist. In later studies where consumer and producer are two different persons we shall have to examine the division of this gain, $U-L$, between them.

Section 4: Two Commodities

Let us now suppose that Crusoe produces two commodities. It is clear from the argument we have traced above that he will divide his labour time and effort between the two commodities in such a manner as to produce such quantities of each that their marginal utilities will in each case be just equal to the marginal disutilities of producing them, and it implies that at that point their marginal utilities will be just equal to one another.

That is, if u' denotes the marginal utility of the first commodity and u'' the marginal utility of the second commodity, he will produce those quantities of each for which u' will equal u''. But we have seen that any one commodity will be produced until $u = l$; hence if l' denotes the labour cost of producing the first commodity and l'' denotes the labour cost of producing the second commodity, Crusoe will produce the first commodity until $u' = l'$, and the second until $u'' = l''$. But $u' = u''$. Thus the condition of equilibrium output for two commodities is expressed by the equations: $u' = l' = u'' = l''$.

Thus we see that in a single person economy the condition of equilibrium is that the output of each commodity produced shall be such that the marginal utilities of all commodities will be equal to one another and that the marginal cost in the case of each commodity will be equal to its marginal utility in consumption.

Section 5: Present and Future Goods

So far we have considered Crusoe as living on turtles' eggs and other goods which he collects or produces for immediate consumption. But Crusoe is no savage. He knows that the bare living he ekes out in this manner is precarious, that, at best the diet is unsatisfactory and monotonous, and, at worst, is insecure and haphazard and likely to fail during certain seasons of the year.

He knows that if he could cultivate the rich earth of his island, if he could capture and tame goats, if he could construct a boat that would carry him safely from estuary to estuary so that he could drop fish nets across them, that then with less arduous labour he could greatly enrich his life. He also knows that he will need shelter from the tropical storms and that a season will come when turtles will be scarce and berries or other wild fruits non-existent. Unlike the savage who lives in and for the present moment only, Crusoe can and does anticipate future values or future utilities, the needs and hazards that are to come, and he is aware of the potentialities of indirect and roundabout processes of production. This does not mean that he values a possible berry in the future equally with a berry today. On the contrary; his anticipated satisfaction is less lively than a present satisfaction, and the longer the period which must elapse between anticipation and realization the less vivid seems the future satisfaction to the present mind and the greater will it be discounted when compared with present satisfaction.[4] There is the uncertainty, in Crusoe's case very great, as to the future and what it will bring him. His present appetite is great and the urge to satisfy it now is so strong that the sense of future needs and their satisfactions is dimmed. Future utilities are discounted in the sense that the marginal utility of a given quantity of berries next year is simply not as great in anticipation at this moment as the marginal utility of the same quantity of berries now. Yet it is possible for Crusoe to equate marginal utilities as between two different periods of time. If we call the present utility of his berries u, and if we suppose that he discounts this utility at the rate r for n years we can say that the marginal utility now of this quantity of berries visioned at some point in the future will be $u\left(1-\dfrac{n}{r}\right)$. Let us call this u'.

We may demonstrate this as follows.

At the end of the first year, or unit of time,

$$u' = u - \frac{u}{r}$$
$$= u\left(1-\frac{1}{r}\right).$$

At the end of the second year

$$u' = u - \frac{2u}{r}$$
$$= u\left(1-\frac{2}{r}\right).$$

At the end of the nth year

$$u' = u - \frac{nu}{r}$$
$$\text{and } u' = u\left(1-\frac{n}{r}\right).$$

---

[4]There are certain exceptions to this general rule of which we shall later take account.

With this equation we can see how Crusoe could if he wished equate his future with this present satisfactions. If we may suppose that he can work now to produce future satisfactions we may expect him to divide his work so as to produce present and future goods in such quantities that u equals u'. This point will be reached when goods for present consumption have been increased to the point where the marginal utility is reduced according to our principle of discounting to equal the marginal utility of the future goods.

Now the production of goods for future consumption is not direct. Crusoe works in the present clearing land or building a boat and a fishing net. He may not know exactly how many fish he will be able to catch or how great a crop he can expect from the land, but he will draw on his past experience as a sea-faring man and as a Brazilian planter to make an estimate. He will know that the larger the area of cleared land, or the larger the boat, the greater his crop or his catch will be. Yet the larger the boat the greater will be the labour of building and the greater the difficulty of getting it to the water and properly launched. He must balance the increased effort and marginal disutility involved in building a larger boat against the decreasing marginal utility of his future catch. Roughly he will build the boat to the size where his marginal disutility in the present will equal the discounted marginal utility of his estimated future catch. But the discounted marginal utility of his future catch must equal the marginal utility of his present consumption goods, and the marginal utility of his present consumption goods must equal the marginal disutility of gathering them. Therefore the marginal disutility of making the boat for future satisfactions must equal the marginal disutility of labour for present consumption. That is $l' = u' = u = l$, when l' equals the marginal disutility of labour on future goods, and u' the discounted marginal utility of those future goods.

We are now in position to draw certain conclusions about Crusoe's disposition of effort, and to generalize about the Crusoe economic system.

We see:

(1) that he works to produce goods for immediate consumption in such quantities that their marginal utilities are equal;

(2) that he divides his labour effort so that the marginal disutility of his labour is equal to the marginal utility of his satisfactions, and so that the marginal disutilities of labour are equal in his several occupations;

(3) that he works so as to produce goods for future consumption in

such quantities as to equate their discounted marginal utility with the marginal utility in consumption of immediate goods.

(4) that he spends such time and effort on future goods as to equate their marginal disutility with the marginal disutility involved in the production of present goods;

(5) that the value of his capital goods, or good (in our example his fishing boat and nets), is determined by the discounted marginal utility of its yield; and the size of his capital equipment is determined at the point where the marginal disutility of making it is equal to the discounted marginal utility of its yield;

(6) that the process of "saving" for the future does not take the form of accumulating hoards of consumption goods, but of distributing productive effort as between the output of goods for present and those for future consumption;

(7) that the quantities of goods brought on the market will be such that, in each case, the marginal utility of the goods in consumption will be just equal to the marginal disutility of producing them.

NOTE ON THE EQUATIONS OF THE CRUSOE ECONOMY

The equations used in this chapter are merely illustrative. They show how Crusoe makes his decisions, what factors determine his decisions, and provide a useful tool of analysis. They cannot, however, be solved by us. They are expressed in terms of purely subjective concepts. Only Crusoe knows what his utilities and satisfactions are, and only Crusoe can measure them. We have not here progressed to the field of objective measurement and objective quantities. We are not, therefore, in the field of objective science. We are rather generalizing on the basis of common subjective experience, laying the foundations for a later objective and scientific analysis.

CHAPTER VI

EQUATIONS OF THE SIMPLIFIED ECONOMY
(Continued)

SECTION 1: TWO MEN, TWO COMMODITIES

IN this chapter we welcome the advent of Man Friday to the island, and our economy becomes at once a social economy, albeit a very simple one.

Friday will have to produce a share of the social output. He may do so as an independent producer, working on his own and trading with Crusoe, or he may be employed as Crusoe's servant. In this section we shall suppose that Friday is an independent trader.

Both Crusoe and Friday realize, or soon will realize, that they will both gain by specializing in the tasks for which by nature each is best fitted, and by trading a portion of their output. For each man to attempt to produce all his wants, to be self-sufficient, would be to sacrifice the advantages to be gained from concentration of effort, the training and development of special skills, and the employment of special, individual abilities.

Friday will, perhaps, specialize in the collection of turtles' eggs. His native knowledge of the habits of these creatures enables him to gather in the course of a day a much larger crop than Crusoe. Crusoe, on the other hand, has the European's knowledge of land, and knows where it is most fertile and where he can cultivate the largest crop of berries.

Crusoe has now at the end of each day a supply of berries, Friday a supply of turtles' eggs. In what quantity will they exchange?

Crusoe will be willing to give berries for eggs, as long as the acquired stock of eggs has a greater marginal utility for him than his depleted stock of berries. Friday, likewise, will be willing to trade eggs for berries as long as berries have a greater marginal utility for him than eggs.

Let us call the total supply of berries A, and the total supply of eggs B. Let x equal the berries that Crusoe sells, and let y equal the eggs he buys.

The degree of utility of berries to Crusoe we know to be a function of the quantity of berries he has. We shall therefore call it $f(A - x)$. Similarly the degree of utility of eggs will be a function of his supply of eggs for consumption so we shall call it $f'(y)$.

The condition of equilibrium for Crusoe, or the limiting point at which he will not want to exchange any more berries for eggs will then be defined by the equation:

$$f(A-x) \cdot dx = f_1(y) \cdot dy$$
$$\frac{f(A-x)}{f_1(y)} = \frac{dy}{dx} \qquad \cdots\cdots\cdots (i)$$

Similarly we shall call the degree of utility of berries to Friday a function of the berries he has, expressing it as $F(x)$. His utility function for eggs will be $F_1(B-y)$.

Friday will only be satisfied when

$$F(x) \cdot dx = F_1(B-y) \cdot dy$$
$$\frac{F(x)}{F_1(B-y)} = \frac{dy}{dx} \qquad \cdots\cdots\cdots (ii)$$

But, because of the principle of indifference that all quantities will be exchanged in the ratio of the marginal quantities,

$$\frac{dy}{dx} = \frac{y}{x}$$

Therefore,

$$\frac{f(A-x)}{f_1(y)} = \frac{y}{x} = \frac{F(x)}{F_1(B-y)} \qquad \cdots\cdots (iii), (iv).[1]$$

The equations appear to be determinate and, once the values for the functions are assigned, can be solved for x and y.

In actual practice barter prevents the attainment of exact equilibrium because it does not permit of sufficiently small divisions of the units of goods exchanged.

Suppose, for example, that Crusoe's marginal utility function is such that he is willing to trade:

> 20 berries for 1 egg
> 30 berries for 2 eggs
> 36 berries for 3 eggs
> 40 berries for 4 eggs,

and that Friday is willing to trade

> 1 egg for 15 berries
> 2 eggs for 28 berries
> 3 eggs for 39 berries
> 4 eggs for 44 berries.

Then after two eggs have been exchanged for 28-30 berries, say 29,

[1] Cf. W. S. Jevons, *Theory of Political Economy* (4th ed., London, 1911), pp. 89-101.

Crusoe will offer up to 36 berries for a third egg, but Friday will be unwilling to accept less than 39 berries for the third egg. Thus trade may stop at two eggs for 29 berries, not an exact equilibrium point because at that point Crusoe's marginal utility for eggs exceeds that for berries and Friday's marginal utility for berries exceeds that for eggs, and both would like to trade further. But if they trade three eggs for, say, 37 berries they will not reach a point of equilibrium, because at this point Crusoe's marginal utility for berries exceeds that for eggs, and Friday's marginal utility for eggs exceeds that for berries.[2]

SECTION 2: FRIDAY AS CRUSOE'S EMPLOYEE

In the last section we supposed that Friday and Crusoe were independent traders. Friday, however, was native labour, and Crusoe was too good an English merchant not to realize the advantages to be gained from a judicious exploitation of the good fortune which had been thrown his way when Friday asked for his "protection." Indeed, if we remember Defoe's story, which we are unpardonably mangling, we know that Crusoe behaved after the best traditions of his society. He put Friday to work as his servant and at the same time endeavoured to convey to him the various blessings of European civilization and the Christian religion. In this task Crusoe had the usual measure of success, though sometimes one suspects that Friday's conversion to Christianity was rather superficial and was as much for benefits received as from a consciousness of original sin, a concept of considerable difficulty to the unlettered savage.

Crusoe, when Friday arrived, had already created some capital. He had a boat, fishing equipment, a house, arms, a plantation, and other capital goods. He had also accumulated stocks of goods, raisins, barley and grain, and other stores salvaged from the wrecked ship, of which, like the good merchant he was, he kept careful inventory. We may recall the various book-keepings he made, scattered throughout Defoe's story, though we should beware of some of his entries. Goodwill is always a questionable item, and in Crusoe's entries the good favour he supposed himself to enjoy with Divine Providence would probably arouse the suspicions of a char-

---

[2]Readers may be interested to attempt to work out functional equations for exchange under a price system. Mr. Phelps-Brown, in *The Framework of the Pricing System* (London, 1936), works out some very neat price equations with arithmetic functions (pp. 80-3) which students will find interesting and helpful to consult.

tered accountant. But even that item can scarcely be regarded as out of accord with modern corporation practices, so that, in every way Crusoe may be considered at the time of Friday's arrival as the prototype of the capitalist entrepreneur.

Thus Friday, with nothing but the ability to work, confronts Crusoe with the tools and instruments of production, stocks of goods, and cultivated land. More, Crusoe constitutes, in his own person, the authority of the state. In one person Crusoe is employer; his *alter ego* is the state. He makes the laws, he owns the weapons that will make possible the enforcement of them, and he has brought to his island certain English common-law doctrines which he imposes on his subject. Most important of these is the doctrine of property.

Crusoe believes, and his belief has the overt force of law, that by cultivating and marking out the land, salvaging the ship's stores, and so forth, he has acquired property in these goods. That means that they had become his to use and to dispose as he might will, that the usufructs, or fruits of use and cultivation, should for all time be his to enjoy or to dispose. This doctrine is important because it permits of the following logical corollary; viz., that he may dispose of certain usufructs or rewards of the capital to those whom he may set to work it, but that those who work it have no title to any of its fruits and no permanent interest in the wealth or its produce other than Crusoe may dispose to them as a reward for their labour. This corollary is the legal fundamental of the practice and theory of employment.

Crusoe, like his contemporary, the philosopher John Locke, held the unequivocal view that property involved both the rights and responsibilities of employment, and Crusoe, as the state, had the power of giving this doctrine the force of law.

So Crusoe put Friday to work, made him his servant, and gave him wages. But he preserved the form of a free contract. Friday is therefore considered as being free to decide what wage he is willing to accept and how much work he is willing to do.

Our question now is, how much work will Friday do, and what will determine the remuneration for the work, or the price of his services? Crusoe will be able to estimate the increased enjoyments that Friday's assistance makes possible. If, when he was alone, he could get only 200 bushels of wheat from his plantation, and with Friday's assistance he can increase his crop to 275 bushels, he is able to attribute the extra, or marginal, 75 bushels to Friday's assistance. He is, therefore, willing to offer up to 75 bushels to get Friday's assistance, but no more.　If he offered more he himself would have less than he previously had.　One might note here, also, that Crusoe can equally attribute to his own labour the 75 bushels, because if Friday worked alone the product, presumably, would be 200 bushels. The residuary 125 bushels revert to Crusoe, not as labourer, but as owner of the land.　We are for the moment presuming that the primitive cultivation carried on could be equally well done by either of our two men and that there is no marked difference in the quality of their labour.　Some elaboration of this point will be found in a later section of this work.

Crusoe, then, will pay Friday something under 75 bushels; or, to put it another way, the marginal utility of Friday's services as a labourer is measured by his employer by the marginal utility of the added product his labour makes possible.　We shall for the time being refer to the increment in product that Friday's labour makes possible as his "share" of the output, and we shall call each increment of his share which comes from a unit increment in the amount of labour Friday contributes his "Marginal output."

If Friday were to work on a new capital good, clearing more land, say, or building another boat, his labour to Crusoe would be worth the discounted marginal utility of the anticipated increment of future goods.

Friday finds his labour irksome.　An undisciplined savage, he would rather sleep and fight and let his women work.　He will do no more work than he has to do to keep alive.　He must be offered a reward as an incentive to labour.　The more he produces the longer and harder he has to work.　Consequently the more he produces the greater the marginal disutility of his labour.　Friday will work, like Crusoe or anyone else, up to the point where the marginal utility of his wage just equals the marginal disutility of his labour. This point may be a very vague one for Friday.　He is not accustomed to making such decisions.　He has no marginal utility for future goods because he has no idea of the future.　Once he is fed he is satisfied.　So the marginal utility of goods for him decreases very rapidly.　If we were to plot a curve representing his diminishing marginal utility as the supply of goods for consumption increases we should see that that curve had a very steep slope.

He has also a poor sense of marginal disutility.　He knows he is tired, but affection for his master, fear of the hell for lazy niggers, which is part of Christian doctrine as interpreted by Crusoe, or fear of more immediate punishment are apt to drive him to greater efforts than would result from his desire for material rewards.　He is therefore willing to work long hours and to accept a small remuneration. Hence the doctrine that native labour is cheap labour. However, there is a point beyond which Friday will not work. This point will be roughly where the marginal disutility of his labour, modified by these other considerations, is equal to the marginal utility of his wage.

Let x equal the amount of Friday's labour measured in terms of output,[3] and let w equal his wage, measured in terms of wage goods.

If $f(x)$ is Crusoe's marginal utility for the output produced by Friday's labour, and $v(w)$ his marginal utility for the wage goods paid to Friday, he will, of course, employ Friday to the point where

$$f(x) \cdot dx = v(w) \cdot dw$$

or

$$\frac{v(w)}{f(x)} = \frac{dw}{dx} = \frac{w}{x} \qquad \dots\dots\dots(i)$$

And if $F(x)$ is Friday's marginal disutility for the labour necessary to produce the output for which Crusoe's marginal disutility is $f(x)$, and $V(w)$ is Friday's marginal utility for the wage goods, then Friday will want to work to the point where

$$F(x) \cdot dx = V(w) \cdot dw$$

or

$$\frac{V(w)}{F(x)} = \frac{dw}{dx} = \frac{w}{x} \qquad \dots\dots\dots(ii)$$

These two equations thus express the conditions of equilibrium on the labour market in our simplified economy. Given the functions for the marginal utilities and disutilities of Crusoe and Friday, the wages that will be paid and accepted and the amount of work that Friday will do can be determined. Verbally stated the argument amounts to this: the point where the wage Crusoe is willing to pay just balances Friday's marginal disutility for the labour necessary to that output marks the equilibrium point of employment where Friday will have no incentive either to increase or decrease his labour.

Section 3: Friday as Investor

It is just conceivable that Friday will learn after a time the pragmatic value of thrift. He will see that in this white man's

[3]Ordinarily we measure labour in units of time, but it is common to pay wages by piece work, so that this concept should present no difficulty. We are here speaking of a quantity of labour necessary to produce 5, 10, 20, or x units of output. Similarly the wage paid to Crusoe is measured not in terms of money but in terms of the commodity in which he is paid, grain in our example.

island the only way for him to "get along" is to acquire property. Property, he sees, enables Crusoe to enjoy a much fuller life, and with far less effort, than he.   Friday becomes less the savage.   Religion has made him aware of the punishments and rewards of a future life, and poverty within sight of comparative plenty may make him aware of possible future rewards in the present life, if he can learn to save and acquire property.   He comes to value future goods, to want some measure of security, to possess a boat of his own, and so forth.

This changes his marginal utility schedule for goods for present consumption.   He will work harder, utilize his spare time perhaps building a boat or a plough or some other tool or instrument of production.   He does this, rather than work at the further production of goods for present consumption because, as we saw in the case of Crusoe, his discounted marginal utility for future goods now exceeds the marginal utility of any further present goods he might obtain for the same labour cost.   This process of establishing a claim to future goods rather than an increment to goods for present consumption we have seen to be the essential nature of saving.[4]

After a time Friday has his capital ready.   He might, of course, set to work independently of Crusoe, to use it.   In that case he would be an independent competitive producer such as we examined in Section 1.   But Crusoe is the man with enterprise and experience. He will probably persuade Friday that he would get more by lending his capital to Crusoe than by using it himself.

This additional capital good will enable Crusoe to obtain a greater yield from his farm or his fishery.   He will measure this greater yield in exactly the same manner that he measured the increased production that Friday's labour made possible; viz., in terms of the increment in output resultant from the addition of the last unit of capital.   If he increases the yield from his land by using borrowed capital by 50 bushels, he will be willing to pay up to 50 bushels per season for the use of the capital.

Friday will be willing to lend capital to the point where the discounted marginal utility of the future rewards is equal to the mar-

---

[4]We here present the classical view of interest rate as an incentive to saving. We regard this as being a true account of saving in a primitive economy, and it is important, in any case, for the student to gain an understanding of this view. We therefore include it in the formal account of the price system, which rigorously follows classical lines. Some criticisms of this view of interest rate will be found in Book Four, chapter XIX, where interest rate theory is modified to meet the conditions of the modern economy.

ginal utility of the present goods he is sacrificing. And since the marginal utility of any good at equilibrium is equal to the marginal disutility of acquiring it,[5] we can say that he will lend to the point where the discounted marginal utility of the future rewards will equal the marginal disutility of saving the amount of capital.

If x is the amount of capital measured in terms of output, and i is the reward measured in income goods paid for its use, and if $V(i)$ is the discounted marginal utility of the future rewards to Friday, and if $F(x)$ is the marginal disutility of saving the quantity x of capital, then the equation which expresses Friday's position of equilibrium for lending capital is

$$F(x) \cdot dx \; = \; V(i) \cdot di$$

or

$$\frac{V(i)}{F(x)} = \frac{di}{dx} = \frac{i}{x} \qquad \ldots\ldots\ldots \text{(i)}$$

Crusoe, on the other hand, will be willing to borrow until the marginal utility of the income goods he has to pay by way of reward to Friday is equal to the marginal utility of the increment of output the new capital makes possible.

Thus if $f(x)$ equals the marginal utility to Crusoe of the increment of output from the use of x capital, and if $v(i)$ equals the marginal utility to Crusoe of the income goods paid to Friday for supplying the capital, then Crusoe will borrow to the point where

$$f(x) \cdot dx = v(i) \cdot di$$

or

$$\frac{v(i)}{f(x)} = \frac{di}{dx} = \frac{i}{x} \qquad \ldots\ldots\ldots \text{(ii)}$$

Thus equations (i) and (ii) determine the rate of saving and investment and the rate of reward to be paid, given the functions of Friday's and Crusoe's marginal utilities and disutilities for the present and future goods involved.

Section 4: Conclusions

In this chapter we have advanced from the theory of the determination of output in an individual economy to that of the determination of output in a social economy, albeit a very simplified one. We still lack the essential of a price system but we are now in a position to procede to the theory of price determination.

From the argument of this chapter we are able to conclude,

[5]See page 47.

given the conditions under which this simplified economy is set up, that:

(1) Goods will be exchanged in the quantities that equate their marginal utilities for each party to the exchange. Since, from Chapter v we know that for each man the marginal utilities of goods will be equated with the marginal disutilities of acquiring them we may tentatively conclude that goods will be exchanged in the quantities that equate the marginal disutilities or marginal costs of acquiring them for each party to the exchange. Let us beware, however, of misunderstanding this conclusion. We do not say that labour costs are equal as between man and man. That would be to make the mistake of setting up an equality between two purely subjective values. There is no possible way, without an objective price system, of comparing Crusoe's measurement of his labour effort with Friday's measurement of his. All we can say is that Crusoe and Friday will exchange goods in such quantities as equate the *ratio* of the labour cost or marginal disutility involved in procuring good number 1 to that involved in procuring good number 2 for Crusoe with the *ratio* of the marginal disutility involved in procuring good number 1 to that of good number 2 for Friday.

(2) Labour will be supplied to the point where the ratio of marginal wage to marginal output for the employer is the same as the ratio of the marginal utility to the marginal disutility of labour effort for the employee. Here again, in effect, we are equating ratios of subjective valuations. The wage also, in units of wage goods, is determined at this point, but these ratios of incommensurables are not objective prices and we must remember that they are not.

(3) Capital will be supplied in such quantities as to equate the ratio of the marginal utility of the marginal reward to the marginal utility of the marginal output for the borrower with the ratio of the marginal utility of the reward to the marginal disutility of saving for the lender.

CHAPTER VII

THE PRICE SYSTEM IN THE SIMPLIFIED ECONOMY

Section 1: Prices of Commodities

OUR problem now is to discover how the subjective decisions we have described in Chapters v and vi are given an objective expression in terms of price, and how, consequently, prices are determined under the simple conditions of our present restrictions.

We may suppose that both Crusoe and Friday find it convenient to measure the marginal utilities of different quantities of different commodities in terms of quantities of some standard commodity. This commodity, which is to be used as a standard of reference for the measurement of all marginal utilities must have certain qualities.[1]

It must be homogeneous in quality. Otherwise it would not serve its purpose because different units of it would be of diverse qualities with different utilities, not readily interchangeable, one unit for another.

It must be non-perishable so that at all times a unit of it will be of the same quality. Thus it can be accumulated and act as a store of wealth without deterioration and loss.

It must be easily divisible into small units so that it can be used for accurate measurement.

It must be easily recognized, distinct, and hard to counterfeit.

It must be scarce, so that great quantities of it are not available, and so that small quantities will have a high marginal utility, and, consequently, so that no burdensome large quantities have to be carried around to conduct exchanges.

This commodity which is to be used as a general measure of utility must also act as a medium of exchange. We must have confidence

[1] In more sophisticated communities where paper money has come to be generally accepted "commodity" money may disappear from circulation and may even cease from being paid on demand in exchange for the paper. As long as the paper money has purchasing power and is accepted and discharges the functions of money, acting as a standard of account, it is money. We are not here insisting on the notion that money, to be money, must be a commodity with a "marginal utility" in its own right apart from its purchasing power. But it is reasonable to suppose, as we are supposing, that, in a community such as ours money, in its origins, would be "commodity" money. We do not commit ourselves in this chapter to the doctrine that money must always have a marginal utility in its own right.

that it will be readily accepted in exchange for goods. Instead of direct barter of berries for eggs, an awkward, cumbersome, and unsatisfactory way of conducting business, we sell berries for this third commodity, money, and use the money, in due course of time, to make such purchases of present goods and to hold such claim on future goods as we may desire. As a medium of exchange between present and future goods, money may be said to act as a store of value.

From what we have said it follows that money will have for any one person an unique marginal utility schedule. The marginal utility of any quantity of money will be measured by the marginal utility of the most desirable unit of any good for which it can be exchanged. The ability of money to purchase goods is known as its purchasing power. The quantity of money, measured in arbitrary units such as dollars, pounds, francs, or crowns, for which a unit of a good is exchanged is known as its price. Thus the purchasing power of a unit of money over any good is the inverse of the price of the good, and the purchasing power of money over goods as a whole, or any group of goods, is measured by the inverse of the price index measuring the average price of those goods.

The question which we have raised for discussion in this chapter is, what determines the price of goods on the market in the simplified economy we have assumed? Before we can answer this question we shall have to make some further simplifying assumptions.

We shall have to assume, first, that the money incomes of Crusoe and Friday are known to us. We shall later drop this assumption and show how their money incomes are determined.

We shall assume, second, that there are only two commodities to be considered. We shall see that the prices of all goods are interdependent and simultaneously determined. When a purchaser is deciding whether or not to buy a further unit of a commodity at a certain price, he must know the marginal utility of the money he must pay for it. But that will depend on the price of other commodities. When we decide to buy one thing we decide not to buy another. A change in the price of one commodity will cause changes in prices of other commodities. Hence when we assume only two commodities on the market we greatly simplify the problem. We do not, however, distort it, for, as we shall show, the two prices are determined simultaneously, and the principle of determination can be extended to cover any number of commodities.

Third, we shall assume that the total output of each good is given. Finally, we shall assume that Crusoe and Friday spend their entire money incomes on purchases of present goods and do not hold any income in the form of savings for the purchase of titles to future wealth.

We shall restrict our inquiry to a short unit length of time, say a day, during which income is supposed to be paid and spent and the market price adjusted.

Crusoe sells the quantity x of berries and Friday sells the quantity y of eggs. Crusoe's income in money is given us, say $2.00 a day, and Friday's, say, $1.00 a day.

The total output of berries is A, measured in units of an agreed nature, say a pint. The total output of eggs is B, measured in units of an agreed nature, say a dozen.

Each man buys quantities of the other's output, and may also be regarded as buying the residue from himself. This is not as strange as it sounds. Modern business men, careful to maintain strict accounts, never take articles out of stock for their own use without treating the transaction as a sale.

According to our psychological generalization each spends his money so as to get the maximum of satisfaction, i.e. so as to equate the marginal utilities of both commodities.

Our knowns may therefore be set down as follows.

A.—The Constants

1. The supply or total output of berries, A.
2. The supply of eggs, B.
3. The income of Crusoe, $2.00.
4. The income of Friday, $1.00.

B.—The Functional Relationships

5. Crusoe's marginal utility for berries, which varies in a known way with the quantity of berries he has. We call this $f(A-x) . dx$.
6. Crusoe's marginal utility for eggs, which varies in a known way with the quantity of eggs he has. We call this $v(y) . dy$.
7. Friday's marginal utility for berries, $F(x) . dx$.
8. Friday's marginal utility for eggs, $V(B-y) . dy$.

We also know the relationship which must obtain at equilibrium between these marginal utilities. This is given by equation (i), page 53.

Our unknowns are:

(a) The price of berries per unit, which we shall call p'.
(b) The price of eggs per unit, which we shall call p''.
(c) The quantity of berries sold to Friday, x, and to Crusoe, $A-x$.
(d) The quantity of eggs sold to Crusoe, y, and to Friday, $B-y$.

Our problem is to determine the prices of the goods and the quantities exchanged at the point of equilibrium where neither trader will have any incentive either to buy or to sell more or less of either commodity.

This point is defined by the equations:

$$\frac{v(y)}{f(A-x)} = \frac{y}{x} = \frac{V(B-y)}{F(x)} \qquad \ldots\ldots\ldots\ldots \text{(i), (ii)}[2]$$

Also we know that each man as consumer spends his entire income, so that

$$p'(A-x)+p''. \, y = \$2.00 \qquad \ldots\ldots\ldots\ldots \text{(iii)}$$

and

$$p'. \, x+p''(b-y) = \$1.00 \qquad \ldots\ldots\ldots\ldots \text{(iv)}$$

We have therefore four questions and can solve for our four unknowns.[3] Consequently we say that the prices are determinate and that we have established the conditions of their determination.

It can now be seen that the introduction of more commodities or of more producers and consumers would make no difference in principle to our theoretic position. As long as the supply of each commodity, the income of each consumer, and the consumers' marginal utility functions were given, and as long as all incomes were spent, and the total supply cleared or "unreserved," our reasoning would be valid; for with the introduction of each new commodity, implying a new unknown price to be determined, there would be introduced a new functional equation. Each new unknown would bring in a new equation for its solution. Thus, theoretically, our argument could be extended to cover an entire system of prices and commodities.

The four equations are merely statements in symbolic language of the nature of price determination. They are not to be understood as mystic formulae that business men use and solve to set prices on their goods. They are a method of describing the way the psychological forces in a simplified economy, such as our model, determine prices in that economy.

They state that prices are determined for the amount that will clear the supply of each commodity from the market, and clear the supply in such a manner that each consumer, spending his whole

[2]See equations (ii) and (iii), p. 53.

[3]The functions can only be known empirically and it is possible that they will be of a degree which would make exact solution impossible. In that case the equations could be solved for what mathematicians call "approximate" results, but the approximation would be so close to an exact solution as to make no practical difference.

income, will consume the commodities in such quantities as will maximize his satisfactions. The equation system tells us this will be true for any number of commodities and any number of consumers and producers as long as there is no reserved supply, and as long as incomes are entirely spent on goods for present consumption. It is only within the field as limited by our restrictions that these conclusions will hold true.

SECTION 2: PRICES OF THE AGENTS OF PRODUCTION

In Section 1 we assumed that the income of consumers was given to us, and that the total supply of each commodity was a given amount. Neither of these assumptions is justified as more than a temporary expedient of analysis. Incomes vary with the rewards paid to the agents of production, and the quantities of goods supplied will vary with producers' decisions as to the most profitable quantities to be put on the market.

If we now drop these assumptions, our problem is to determine the prices paid for the services of the productive agents, the quantities of the productive agents that will be employed in each line of production and the quantities of each good that will be put on the market.

Of the productive agents, land, labour, and capital, land is peculiar because in its use there is no cost incurred comparable to the disutility of labour or the cost, in discounted marginal utilities, of saving.[4] Land is passive and does not need a reward to be brought into use. If the demand price justifies the greater use of land, then cultivation will be extended, or the land already in use will be cultivated more intensively. The only real costs to be met in doing this are those of the further units of labour and capital involved. It follows, therefore, that the reward paid for the use of land will differ in character from that paid for the use of labour.

[4]In the text at this point we state, rather dogmatically, the classical theory of rent. More recent economists have attacked the view that rent is in any way peculiar and have maintained that the price for the use of land is determined in a similar manner to other prices. The reader will find this view urged in G. Cassel, *Theory of the Social Economy* (New York, 1924), and a most trenchant argument to the same effect but on a somewhat more orthodox basis is contained in F. H. Knight, "The Ricardian Theory of Production and Distribution" (*Canadian Journal of Economics and Political Science*, vol. I, nos. 1 and 2). The present author attempts to bring these views together in the chapter devoted to rent in Book Four, but in this book the approach from "real costs" has committed us to the differential treatment of rent, at the risk of over-emphasizing its peculiarities.

The wage paid to labour is determined by what employers are willing to pay for an additional unit of labour effort and what labourers are willing to accept, viz. by the amount necessary to offset the marginal disutility of further labour effort. In the case of land there is no such real cost as a basis of supply price. The land is a freely supplied productive agent.

The key to the understanding of the theory of rent on land lies in the fact that increased amounts of labour and capital, applied either extensively to poorer and poorer land, or more intensively on any given area, will produce less than proportionate increments in output. This is a special instance of the Law of Diminishing Returns which states that the intensification of use of any factor of production in inelastic supply will yield less than proportionate increases in returns.[5] This means that if we increase the application of productive factors of production, using more of all the factors save one, which is scarce, the increases in output will be less than proportionate to the increases in the factors. We alter the composition of our productive factors, using one of them more intensively, and the output per unit of productive factor is smaller than before. This law is a purely static one and supposes that no changes are made in the technique of production.

The factor which is scarce we shall call the constant factor, and the factors of production which are increased we shall call the variable factors. The increase in the total product per unit of increase in the variable factors is known as marginal productivity. Thus if land of a certain quality is scarce and more and more units of capital and labour are employed on it the marginal productivity of the labour and capital units will decrease. If the rewards paid to capital and labour are determined by the marginal productivity of capital and labour, then the total product will exceed the amounts paid to capital and labour by a certain surplus, and this surplus is known as rent.

Thus if y is the output and x the amount of the productive factors, and if we imagine x to have been increased by successive unit increments from 0 to a, then $\dfrac{dy}{dx}$ is the marginal productivity.

If $\dfrac{dy}{dx}$ is a diminishing rate then the total output, y, must always exceed in amount the product of $a.dy$. This is illustrated in Fig. 9,

[5]A fuller treatment is reserved until we have developed the notion of elasticity of supply.

where the increments in product
accruing with increments of the
productive factors are shown as
a series of diminishing rectangles,
erected on the x-axis. Consequently
the sum of these rectangles the
total area under the curve, is y,
the total product of "a" units of
the productive factors. The product of the "a" units and the
marginal product is the rectangle,
$oabc$, erected on the ordinate as
base. The difference between the
total area under the curve and
this rectangle is the differential

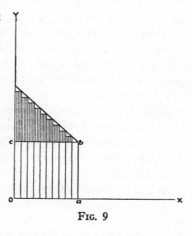

FIG. 9

surplus. If, as we shall attempt to show, the rewards of the
productive agents are equal to the rectangle, $oabc$, this differential
surplus is left to the owner of the land as a residual share in total
output of the enterprise.

This argument may be further illustrated by considering an
imaginary case of land utilization. Let us suppose the land to
be cultivated by increasing units of capital and labour with
increases in output as indicated in the following table:

Land	Labour	Capital	Total output	Marginal output
100 acres	10 units	10 units	500 bus.	....
100 "	11 "	11 "	600 "	100 bus.
100 "	12 "	12 "	675 "	75 "
100 "	13 "	13 "	725 "	50 "

Now if labour and capital get paid per unit the amount of their
joint marginal product, and we have shown in the previous argument of this chapter that is the most they could expect, their total
rewards would be 50 bus. × 13, or 650 bushels. The total output,
however, is 725 bushels. The residual 75 bushels is the differential
surplus.

We may now return to the main problem of this section. We
wish to give formal expression to the general principles we have
stated and to present them in the form of a system of determinate
equations which will illustrate the determination of the prices of
goods and of the agents of production and the determination of
output and employment.

We shall assume that there is no reserved supply, that is that all
goods in any income period are sold, that all income is spent, and

that there are no surplus profits over and above rewards for the labour of management and for investment.

We need not assume a fixed social income, because the social income will now be equal to the sum of the rewards paid to the agents (or to the sum of the total output), and will vary with variations in total rewards.

We have the following unknowns:

1. i, the rate of interest, or the price per unit paid for the use of capital, the same for all employments.
2. w, the rate of wages, or price for a unit of labour, the same for all employments.
3. C_1, the amount of capital used in the berry industry.
4. C_2, the amount of capital used in the egg industry.
5. L_1, the amount of labour used in the berry industry.
6. L_2, the amount of labour used in the egg industry.
7. S_1, the value of the differential surplus, in money units, occurring in the berry industry.
8. S_2, the value of the differential surplus in the egg industry.
   (It should be noted that, whereas i and w must be equal in both employments, there is no reason why S_1 and S_2 must be equal.)
9. p_1, the price of berries per unit.
10. p_2, the price of eggs per unit.
11. x, the output of berries in units.
12. y, the output of eggs in units.
13. R, the social income, in money units.

Because all income is spent we know that,

$$p_1 x + p_2 y = R \qquad \dots\dots\dots (i)$$

From our definition of rent we know that,

$$S_1 = p_1 . x - (w . L_1 + i . C_1) \qquad \dots\dots\dots (ii)$$
$$S_2 = p_2 . y - (w . L_2 + i . C_2) \qquad \dots\dots\dots (iii)$$

so that, by addition,

$$p_1 . x + p_2 . y = S_1 + S_2 + w(L_1 + L_2) + i(C_1 + C_2).$$

We know that p_1 will vary according to the quantity of berries put on the market, the larger the quantity of berries the smaller the price that can be charged. By experiment on the market the proper form could be assigned the function. We write this,

$$p_1 = \phi(x) \qquad \dots\dots\dots (iv)$$

Similarly,

$$p_2 = \psi(y) \qquad \dots\dots\dots (v)$$

Higher wages must be offered to attract increased quantities of labour into either employment, and the same is true of interest rate and the quantities of capital employed in the two industries.

So:

$$w = f(L_1) \qquad \dots\dots\dots\text{(vi)}$$
$$w = v(L_2) \qquad \dots\dots\dots\text{(vii)}$$
$$i = F(C_1) \qquad \dots\dots\dots\text{(viii)}$$
$$i = V(C_2) \qquad \dots\dots\dots\text{(ix)}$$

We know from our previous argument that wages and interest must equal the marginal value product of labour and capital, respectively, in the two employments.

Thus:

$$w = \frac{dx}{dL_1} \cdot p_1 \qquad \dots\dots\dots\text{(a)}$$

$$w = \frac{dy}{dL_2} \cdot p_2 \qquad \dots\dots\dots\text{(aa)}$$

$$i = \frac{dx}{dC_1} \cdot p_1 \qquad \dots\dots\dots\text{(b)}$$

$$i = \frac{dx}{dC_2} \cdot p_2 \qquad \dots\dots\dots\text{(bb)}$$

Unfortunately we are in trouble here, for the equations (a) and (aa) are based on the assumption that capital is constant and labour a variable factor of production, while the equations (b) and (bb) are based on the contradictory assumption that capital is the variable factor and that labour has been held constant. We cannot, therefore, include both the "a" and the "b" equations in the same system, because the logical assumptions of the whole system must be consistent throughout. Thus while these equations are useful expressions of the theories of marginal imputation of the rewards of the factors they are not suitable in the form in which we have formulated them for inclusion within the same equation system. We have to carry our argument a stage forward. We realize that the employer will employ labour or capital according to which is the more economic; if the cost per unit of product of an additional unit of labour exceeds the cost per unit of additional capital, he will substitute capital for labour and will continue to do so until it is immaterial to him whether he employs a further unit of labour or of capital. This equilibrium point can be defined as the point where the cost of employing an additional unit of labour divided by the value product of the additional labour unit is equal to the cost of using an additional unit of capital divided by the value products of the additional capital.

Thus:

$$\frac{w \cdot dL_1}{\dfrac{dx}{dL_1} \cdot p_1} = \frac{i \cdot dC_1}{\dfrac{dx}{dC_1} \cdot p_1} \qquad \ldots\ldots\ldots(\text{x})$$

and

$$\frac{w \cdot dL_2}{\dfrac{dy}{dL_2} \cdot p_2} = \frac{i \cdot dC_2}{\dfrac{dy}{dC_2} \cdot p_2} \qquad \ldots\ldots\ldots(\text{xi})$$

But at the equilibrium point what is true as between the two factors in one employment will also be true as between different employments. Obviously labour (and likewise capital) will flow into the different employments in such quantities as to equate the cost ratios in the two employments. If labour gave a greater return in value product per unit of labour cost in one employment than in another, on our assumption of perfect mobility, labour would flow from the less attractive to the more attractive employment. Thus at the point of equilibrium,

$$\frac{w \cdot dL_1}{\dfrac{dx}{dL_1} \cdot p_1} = \frac{w \cdot dL_2}{\dfrac{dy}{dL_2} \cdot p_2} \qquad \ldots\ldots\ldots(\text{xii})$$

$$\frac{i \cdot dC_1}{\dfrac{dx}{dC_1} \cdot p_1} = \frac{i \cdot dC_2}{\dfrac{dy}{dC_2} \cdot p_2} \qquad \ldots\ldots\ldots(\text{xiii})$$

It can be seen that our "a" and "b" equations follow from these, but that simply means that at the equilibrium point wages are equal to the marginal product of labour and interest to the marginal product of capital, but our equilibrium point is defined on a consistent set of assumptions.

We have here thirteen equations and thirteen unknowns. The equation system is determinate, and, once values are assigned to functions, can be solved for the unknowns, or solved to approximate values.[6]

[6]Certain functional values must be assigned for the solution of the equation system. Thus in equations (iv) and (v) the demand functions are empirically determined from the curves. That the system can then be solved is indicated by the following guide.

Rewrite equations (vi), (vii), (viii), (ix) as:

$$f(L_1) = \frac{dx}{db_1} \cdot p_1 \qquad \ldots \quad (\text{vi}a)$$

We can extend this system to embrace any number of commodities, because the introduction of each new commodity will at the same time add to the equation system the requisite number of equations to solve for the price and output of the commodity, and the employment of the factors in its production.   This means that our equations system is formally correct for any number of goods and for any number of producers and consumers, working under the conditions we have assumed.

But the equations are a linguistic shortcut to express the nature and relations of the forces determining prices.

Equation (i) states our limiting restriction that all income is spent on the purchase of berries and eggs.   Equations (ii) and (iii) define our concept of rent, and show the relation which must obtain between total prices and total disbursements to the agents of pro-

$$v(L_2) = \frac{dy}{db_2} \cdot p_2 \qquad \qquad \ldots \text{ (vii}a\text{)}$$

$$F(C_1) = \frac{dx}{dC_1} \cdot p_1 \qquad \qquad \ldots \text{ (viii}a\text{)}$$

$$V(C_2) = \frac{dy}{dC_2} \cdot p_2 \qquad \qquad \ldots \text{ (ix}a\text{)}$$

From equation (vi$a$), substituting therein from equation (iv),

$$\int_0^L fL_1 \cdot dL_1 = \int_0^x \phi x \cdot dx.$$

Then $L_1 = L_1(x)$.

By similar argument from (vii$a$), (viii$a$) and (ix$a$), substituting from (iv) and (v),

$$L_2 = L_2(y)$$
$$C_1 = C_1(x)$$
$$C_2 = C_2(y),$$
$$(L_1 + C_1) = \Omega(x),$$
$$(L_2 + C_2) = \psi(y).$$

so that
and

From (ii) and (iii),

$$S_1 = S_1(x)$$
$$\text{and } S_2 = S_2(y).$$

Then, in (vi), (vii), (viii) and (ix),

$$w = f(L_1) = w(x)$$
$$\text{and } w = v(L_2) = w(y).$$

Similarly i can be shown to be a function of x and y.   But wages is the same in both employments and so is interest.   Thus two simultaneous equations for x and y can be established.   From these values for x and y can be assigned and then by substitution the other unknowns can be determined.   There is throughout the assumption that the price of a unit of the money commodity is known, i.e. for example that $\$1.00 = 23.22$ grs. of fine gold.

duction. Equations (iv) and (v) simply state our generalization about the dependence of prices on the quantities of goods put on the market. Equations (vi) and (vii) give the supply functions of labour and state that wages vary (rise) to attract additional quantities of labour into employment. Equations (x) and (xii) give the demand functions for labour as determined by margin of substitution. Equations (viii) and (ix) and equations (xi) and (xiii) are the supply and demand functions for capital in the two industries. Our equations state that labour will be employed to the point where the marginal value productivity of the labour in each employment will be equal to the supply price of labour and wages will be determined for that amount where the marginal supply price and the marginal value productivity of labour are equal. Similarly capital will be employed to the point where its marginal value productivity in each employment is equal to its marginal supply price and interest will be fixed for that equilibrium amount. If we add equations (a) and (b) (or (aa) and (bb)) we discover that the price per unit must just cover the marginal cost of labour and capital.[7] Equations (iv) and (v) tell us that the price per unit is a function of the quantity put on the market. They are, as we have said, the demand functions. Thus from these equations we conclude that prices are determined for the amount where the marginal costs of production (labour and capital) are equal to the demand price. The quantities of goods produced and sold will be similarly determined for the amount where marginal demand price and marginal costs of production are equal.

Rent will be determined as the differential surpluses between total revenues and total costs of labour and capital.

These conclusions constitute the main "principles" of economics. We have set up a simple model where we might establish these laws with great generality and some exactitude. But our model is only

[7] If we take equations (a) and (b) we get the following results:

$$w = \frac{dx}{dL_1} \cdot p_1$$

$$i = \frac{dx}{dC_1} \cdot p_1$$

By addition $p_1 = \dfrac{w+i}{\left(\dfrac{dx}{dL_1} + \dfrac{dx}{dC_1}\right)}$

which is the labour and capital cost of the marginal increment in output, or the marginal cost of producing berries. The same result in the case of eggs could be obtained from equations (aa) and (bb).

a model.   It would be a mistake to say without further examination or argument that these laws apply exactly in the real world.   That we must procede to inquire.   Our model, we emphasize, has told us nothing as yet directly about the actual economy.

We may regard the argument of Book II as, first, an exercise in economic technique and method.   It provides, second, a precise formulation of the basic generalizations, and, third, rigorous deductions of conclusions "of great generality," to use Mr. Harrod's phrase, which we might treat as guides, or perhaps working hypotheses to carry forward into our future work.   The student may also observe that there has been here presented a very brief, but fairly definite statement of what is known as "classical economic theory" with whose doctrines it is important that he be familiar.

We have, thus, our model.   Let us now turn to the real world.

BOOK THREE

THEORY OF PRICE IN AN INDUSTRIAL ECONOMY

CHAPTER VIII

INTRODUCTION TO BOOK THREE

SECTION 1: FULL AND PARTIAL EQUILIBRIA

THE formal price system which we have constructed does not necessarily conform to any existing reality. It has all the artificiality of a highly controlled laboratory experiment, which may yield valuable hypotheses, but does not, in itself, pretend to the reproduction of actual situations.

We wish to take this purely formal system and apply it in an analysis of situations which we shall make more and more real. We may find out that our formal system will turn out to be not a description at all, scarcely even a partial description, but rather a technique or instrument of analysis. By this we mean that we cannot expect conditions in the real world in any way to approximate those we have set up in our simplified economy. But we may expect, with certain modifications, the same human or psychological forces to be operative, and we may expect the same methods of analysing these forces to be useful. Moreover, we may expect to find in a complex society the same balancing of forces at the equilibrium position. Fundamentally, if we can break down the complex of modern economic society so as to impose our techniques of analysis, we shall expect to find all prices simultaneously determined, and determined in such a way as to balance marginal cost against marginal demand. This balancing is basic and an understanding of the psychological forces on which it rests is basic to an understanding of any economic system.

But in breaking down this complex we shall be forced to study individual firms and industries in the equilibrium position. Thus our study will be a study of "partial equilibrium," whereas we have previously been studying the full equilibrium of the economy as a whole. Nevertheless, as we develop our theory of distribution, we shall see that the partial equilibrium of firms is only attained in a system which is itself in full equilibrium. The equilibria of all firms are only stable when the positions are regarded as simultaneously attained in a system in equilibrium. Thus partial equilibrium analysis is only a further example of the device of isolating phenomena in order to render a complex system susceptible of analysis.

This study of partial equilibrium is carried out in this and the following Book. The first chapter of this Book is something of a digression, constituting an effort to identify those institutions of modern economic society which play the part of the bargaining units.

SECTION 2: THE BARGAINING UNITS

In the economy which we described in Book Two the balancing of costs against satisfactions was done first by Crusoe alone, then by Crusoe and Friday. Consumer and producer were so closely identified that there was really direct production for consumption. There was no specialization and little exchange. Crusoe decided directly when his labour had reached the point where the disutility of further labour effort was greater than the increment to utility from consumption. Crusoe and Friday met directly together as man to man, both single individuals with equal bargaining power, and settled on the wage contract in terms of real utility and disutility. All this is very different from what we find in the actual world. Here we find large firms deciding what and how much to produce, how much to employ of each factor of production, what they must charge for the finished product and what they may pay to the factors they employ. We find workmen bargaining for wages, not as single individuals but as groups or unions. We find a tremendous specialization in industry, so that each man performs a small task in an industry which may be producing anything from machine tools to lip-sticks. The consuming public is made up of these producers, who, naturally, take nothing in kind, but rather money, as a reward for their productive services, and this they exchange for the great variety of consumers' goods which are thrown on the market. In such an economy the price system occupies a central and key position. It directs the productive agents into their various employments, it restricts consumers' demand, stimulates supply. It is itself the resultant of a million decisions made by millions of people without direct reference one to another. The units which engage in the bargaining of which the price system is the resultant are: the firm or a group of firms acting as a unit (e.g., employers' associations),the trades union or the individual workman, the individual saver, the corporate saver, and the individual consumer, and associations of consumers.

A. The Firm

A firm is an individual enterprise, organized for production and controlled by a single interest. It may be individually or collectively owned. Prior to the Industrial Revolution the characteristic firm was small.[1] The capital ordinarily could be found by a single man; a journeyman could save enough to begin in a small way on his own account and become a master. There were important exceptions. In the great export staples, in the Elizabethan "monopolies," in banking, and in developmental foreign ventures, the joint stock company was developed. The joint stock company or corporation is a device to reconcile private ownership with capital accumulation so vast as to run beyond the scope of any private fortune.

A group of men pooled their money for a joint undertaking and retained, by electing the board of management, partial control over the enterprise. They entrusted to selected individuals the management and supervision of the work. The manager, like a civil servant in the employ of the state, acted in an executive capacity and was, as long as he gave satisfaction, a permanent salaried official. He was responsible to the Board of Directors. They, in turn, like the Cabinet in our political analogy, were responsible at annual or semi-annual meetings to the "electorate," the stockholders as a whole.

A corporation, so established, had the status of a person in law. It could sue and be sued, it could be taxed, held liable in contract; it could go bankrupt. But in all instances its position was that of a person and its stockholders, as individuals, could not be held responsible. The most important effect of this corporate respon-

[1]The West Counties clothiers who employed three to four hundred men under one roof required as much as £100,000-£300,000 capital. On the other hand, the average working capital of the mass of small clothiers, ironmongers, etc., does not seem to have exceeded £5,000-£10,000. See D. Defoe, *The Compleat English Tradesman* (*Collected Works*, London, 1910); E. Lipson, *An Economic History of England* (London, 1931), vol. II, p. 9; and Adam Smith, *Wealth of Nations* (Everyman ed., London, 1933), vol. I, p. 244. Defoe says there were many enterprises of less than £5,000 capitalization, and advises against too heavy capitalization. Obviously the chief investment was in working capital and stocks. The investment in fixed capital was small. Adam Smith significantly always speaks of capital as "stocks." At the beginning of the century the trades-man usually put up his own working capital. Banks were used by the export merchants, but the domestic merchant was advised to find his own capital. See Defoe, *The Compleat English Tradesman*, p. 574. That this practice changed during the course of the century is evident from Smith's acceptance of the bank as the source of short-term loans. See Adam Smith, *Wealth of Nations*, p. 264, vol. I. Of great importance is the fact that the merchants of the domestic system did not require large fixed capital investments. Any industrious, skilled, provident journeyman could become a master workman. Heavy fixed investment, the corporation, and the fixed and established position of the workman are characteristics which came with the introduction of heavy machinery requiring large fixed capital investment.

sibility has to do with the position of stockholders in the case of bankruptcy, because they could lose no more than their original investment.

Because of this limited liability the invention of the corporation made possible investments which otherwise would not have been made. If every investment made the investor individually liable to the full extent of his personal fortune in the event of bankruptcy, there would be very few who would risk funds in enterprises beyond the scope of their own supervision and control. Few individuals, for example, would have risked their entire fortune in an undertaking as speculative as the construction of railways in the Argentine or Canada. The corporation, moreover, made possible the reinvestment of the great surpluses of profit flowing into the hands of British industrialists during the nineteenth century, and, since much of this reinvestment was in foreign countries to develop there markets and raw material supplies, it was this that enabled the new countries of the world to be opened up.

The ability to control a corporation rests in the hands of those who control a majority of the stock. The tendency towards monopoly, which we shall shortly discuss, the ability of money to breed money, and the fact that many small stockholders do not vote, mean that a small number of large financiers are able to control blocs of stock in all the more important industries, and these blocs are usually large enough to give them control of the industry. Thus corporation finance has tended to concentrate the control of industry and to give to the financial interests a disproportionate power in the economy and in the state.

Hostility to the corporation is by no means new. In very early days the private tradesmen or small manufacturers were bitterly opposed to them. So great was the hostility towards the Wool-Staplers, who marketed and exported the produce of England's primary industry, that prohibitive legislation was obtained against them[2] in the seventeenth century. In spite of this the Staplers continued to flourish. They dealt apparently on "terms," that is their operations were financed by short-term credits, which they were better able to obtain than the small-scale, unknown, independent manufacturer. They were organized to conduct large-scale export marketing and that is why they survived in spite of resistance and prohibitive legislation.

The large corporation grew as its need became felt in an ever wider range of economic activity. At first confined to foreign mer-

[2]Lipson, *Economic History of England*, vol. II, p. 23.

chandising and banking it later became necessary in manufacturing. The Industrial Revolution, which saw the introduction of power machinery, put an end to the small-scale manufacturing tradesman and the domestic system of production. The new machines required large accumulations of capital for their purchase; they required to be housed in large buildings; they required power and the generation of power on a large scale; they required great numbers of workers gathered together under one roof to tend them; they ate through raw materials in quantities. Only a large-scale organization sufficed to provide adequate capital for their inception and maintenance.

The new corporation manufacture rapidly drove the small-scale producer out of business. It was able to produce in much larger quantities at lower costs. For example, British imports of raw cotton, which had increased between 1700 and 1770 only from one to two million pounds, increased from 1770 to 1800 (after the Industrial Revolution) to 60,000,000 pounds. Needless to say a 3,000 per cent increase in raw material consumption measures the increase in the productive capacity of the industry. The fall in unit costs can be obtained by comparing the increase in the figures of volume of export and the increase in the value of export goods. Thus British exports from 1815 to 1844 increased in volume by 300 per cent, but in value by only 60 per cent, that is to say that unit costs decreased as from 100 to 40.[3]

The economies of large-scale production are not, however, to be attributed entirely to the large-scale firm, some of them are to be attributed to the large-scale plant. We defined a firm to be a productive enterprise under single ownership and direction. A plant is a productive unit, the unity of which consists in its unity in place, that is an assembly of factory buildings and equipment, usually but not necessarily,[4] with one source of power, located in one place. There are two types of economies from large-scale organization, those which can be attributed to large-scale plant, "internal economies," and those which can be attributed to large-scale management embracing a number of plants, "external economies." The economies of the early days of the

[3]If we let the index number 100 equal the value of export goods in 1815, and 100(v) equal the volume of export goods in 1815, then the unit costs will be measured by the price divided by volume, that is the index number 100. In 1844 the index number of value is 160, while the index of volume is 400. Dividing again, volume into value, we find the unit costs equal 40. Thus unit costs have fallen from 100 to 40.

[4]Many of the pulp and paper mills, for example, have both hydro-electric power and a steam-generated "standby" plant.

Industrial Revolution which resulted from the increase in the size of plant, more efficient machinery, and power production were "internal economies." They arose both from improved technical efficiency and from the high ratio of fixed costs which means, as we shall later show, decreasing costs per unit of output as output is increased. But the corporation also meant amalgamations and mergers, the formation of large firms controlling several plants. Sometimes, as in the case of the tobacco trusts, the mergers were "horizontal," that is an amalgamation of plants engaged in the production of the same type of product; sometimes, as in the case of Dominion Steel in Canada and of the "Big Steel" trust in the United States, they were "vertical," that is amalgamations of plants engaged in a series of productive operations all the way from the mining of the ore and the coal, through the production of pig iron and steel ingots to the final production of steel commodities as various in nature as guns, ships, and fencing wire. The "Dosco" group in Eastern Canada own the Wabana iron ore fields in Newfoundland, they maintain their own fleet of cargo vessels, through their subsidiaries they control the coal fields of Cape Breton, Pictou, and Cumberland counties in Nova Scotia, they own and operate their own railway from the Glace Bay coal pits to the Sydney steel mill, they manufacture pig iron and steel ingots and bars, they control subsidiary companies in Nova Scotia engaged in steel shipbuilding and in munitions, steel car and steel rail manufacture, and in Quebec they own plants engaged in the manufacture of steel wire and fencing materials.

These amalgamations, made possible by corporate methods of finance, and made profitable by technical improvements and decreasing costs on large-scale fixed investments, have the added attraction that they involve further economies of their own. The large-scale firm can take advantages of economies in management, economies in mass purchase of materials, and it can gain extra profits by reason of its dominance of the market. The process, initiated by the power revolution of the eighteenth century, helped on its way by the technique of corporate financing, has fed on itself. It has by no means been restricted to manufacturing. Mining has also definitely developed from a small-scale, individualist enterprise to a large-scale corporate undertaking. The romantic prospector, bearded individualist of the anarchical West, no longer roams the dusty streets of Tucson or Carson City. In his place, in offices of polished stone, are the giant corporations of Anaconda Copper Inc., their subsidiaries and their competitors.

Again, in agriculture, the same process is discernible, though in this instance the small producer is able to hold his own in certain areas and in the production of certain crops. Small-scale, owner-operator farming has more than held its own in dairy farming, poultry farming, hog-raising, breeding of registered stock, truck-gardening, and in certain types of fruit-growing. This has been especially true when the small operators have made use of the co-operative principle in marketing and in the purchase of machinery, seed, or stock. Again in parts of Europe and Eastern Canada and the United States small-scale mixed farming has maintained itself. In Europe the peasant owner has been able to continue raising a mixed crop for his own sustenance and in France, Switzerland, and parts of Germany he is still characteristic. In the United States and Canada he has fought a losing battle.

But in the culture of specialized cash crops, wheat, wool, wines, beef cattle, potatoes, etc., the typical firm has become a large enterprise, owned by a large landowner or corporation, and worked by wage labour.

The movement towards large-scale agriculture, known to economic historians as "the disappearance of the small proprietor," began in England in Tudor times, when the growth of the woollen industry made possible a market for a cash crop, namely, raw wool. It was accomplished by the enclosure of the common lands and the forced surrender of small holdings. The woollen enclosures of the sixteenth century were followed by a constant stream of "Enclosure Bills" throughout the seventeenth century and then a vastly increased movement towards enclosure in the eighteenth. These Acts of Enclosure were private bills, introduced in Parliament by interested members, providing for the enclosure of common and tenant's land. The peasant proprietor was dispossessed, though not necessarily without compensation, the tenant had his land enclosed and lost his right to Commons. He might remain a tenant on a cash basis or he might be driven from the land in favour of large-scale cultivation by machinery and wage labour. Thus the essential nature of the enclosures was to put an end to small-scale subsistence farming, to destroy the manorial system, and to introduce the "cash nexus"[5] as between tenant and labourer and the large landowner.[6]

[5]This convenient term to describe the new wage relationship between land-owner and worker or between master and employee, as distinct from the old feudal, paternal relationship, is used by Mr. Lipson (*Economic History of England*, vol. II, p. 43).

[6]A further important result which we may note in passing was that fewer

A very interesting point, that confirms our thesis that the large firm unit is a natural growth in an expanding industrial economy, is the correlation of the movement towards large-scale agriculture with the commercial expansion of England in the eighteenth century. Prior to the Industrial Revolution the bulk of British exports were agricultural produce and woollens. The expansion of British commerce is indicated in the following table:[7]

TABLE I

DEVELOPMENT OF BRITISH OVERSEAS COMMERCE, 1705-1800

Year	Exports £	Imports £	Total Foreign Trade £
1705.............	6,000,000	4,000,000	10,000,000
1710.............	7,000,000	4,000,000	11,000,000
1720.............	8,000,000	6,000,000	14,000,000
1730.............	12,000,000	8,000,000	20,000,000
1740.............	9,000,000	7,000,000	16,000,000
1750.............	15,000,000	8,000,000	23,000,000
1760.............	15,500,000	10,000,000	25,500,000
1770.............	14,500,000	12,000,000	26,500,000
1775.............	17,500,000	14,500,000	32,000,000
1785.............	18,000,000	17,000,000	35,000,000

Introduction of Power Machines

1800.............	41,500,000	31,000,000	72,500,000

During the early eighteenth century the discovery of more scientific methods of crop rotation, artificial fertilizers and deep ploughing, and the growth of commerce and the commercial towns, made cereals, roots, and meats good cash crops. The enclosures, which continued at an accelerating pace during the eighteenth century, were not therefore, at this time, so much for the production of wool as for the commercial production of foodstuffs for the growing urban population. Later enclosures, after 1780, do not seem to be correlated

---

men were needed for cultivation of the land and large numbers were driven to the towns where they created a supply of cheap unskilled labour, available for industry in the new factories of the industrial revolution. Cf. A. H. Johnson, *The Disappearance of the Small Landowner* (Oxford, 1909), *passim*.

[7]This table is prepared from figures given in P. Mantoux, *The Industrial Revolution in England in the 18th Century* (London, 1928). M. Mantoux's figures are taken from official sources.

with any change in the size of the average unit of cultivation. They were probably enclosures by small holders, enclosing their own land.[8]

In the New World the cultivation of the premier cash crop of the South, cotton, has from the earliest times been carried on on a large scale. Slave labour, later a form of wage labour, has been employed by big landowners and commercial entrepreneurs. In the West the development has been unique. The farms were large, but, under the Homesteading Acts no great accumulations of capital were required to gain them. At the same time great tracts were granted the railways for developmental purposes. Of recent years the land of the West has been increasingly coming under the control or ownership of financial corporations and the great capitalist corporation makes its appearance as the firm unit in agriculture.

Thus in all types of production the growth of the large-scale productive unit, the large-scale plant, and the large-scale firm, has been a characteristic of the development of the post-Industrial Revolution economy. When we ask what are the limits to the size to which plant and firm can profitably grow, it is hard to give *a priori* answers. There are physical limits to the size of plant, dependent on power resources, availability of raw materials, and so

[8]It is possible from the Land Tax Assessments to discover whether the taxpayer was owner, occupier or tenant, and to deduce the size of the holding. Thus these records enable us to determine the extent to which the change from small-scale to large-scale agriculture was complete by 1780, the date which marks roughly the beginning of machine production in industry. The Land Tax Assessments were first studied by Johnson, *The Disappearance of the Small Landowner*. Mr. E. Davies later made a more complete study, investigating a sample of over two thousand parishes in several counties. Mr. Davies's conclusions are summarized in the *Economic History Review*, vol. I, no. 1, pp. 87 ff.

Briefly, he found:

(1) By 1780 the disappearance of the small landowner was very nearly complete. Only about 10 per cent of the tax was paid by, and only about 10 per cent of the land was held by, small occupying owners in 1780. The large landowners held 64 per cent of the land, and about 25 per cent was held by non-occupying owners.

(2) There was a slight increase in the number of small landowners after 1780.

(3) There seems little necessary connection between enclosure and the disappearance of the small landowner. There was no increase in large holdings after 1780 although enclosures continued until well into the nineteenth century. There was no perceptible difference between the ratio of large to small holdings in the enclosed counties as compared with the unenclosed counties.

(4) The disappearance of the small landowner cannot be attributed to the industrial revolution. On the contrary, the movement was nearly complete when the industrial revolution began.

forth, but there is no reason to believe that new technical improvements will not continually expand these limits.[9] Other limitations on the size of plant are of an economic rather than physical nature. A large plant means high overhead costs and standardized production. It is only profitable if a large output can be marketed so as to get advantage of the decreasing unit costs that a high ratio of fixed costs makes possible. The plant cannot be profitably expanded beyond the point which the potential market indicates as profitable. Idle plant and excess capacity with high fixed costs are not profitable. If the commodity being manufactured is of such a nature that a standardized product cannot be sold, then mass production is not possible. There is, finally, a limit to the size of plant that can be efficiently managed by a single management.

The limits to the size of firms are even more tenuous. Public opinion and government interference may limit the size of a great trust and there may be some limitations in the size that can be efficiently directed by one Board of Directors, but this limit can be circumvented by subsidiary companies under individual direction but merged in joint ownership. A study of the actual facts gives us, perhaps, a better guide to the intangible factors determining the most profitable size of plant. If we make the not unwarrantable assumption that the ideal size of plant is that which tends to survive in any particular industry, we can then discover the typical firm which has emerged in different countries in various industries. The same may be done, though with less confidence in the underlying assumption, with the size of firm. We discover, for example, that everywhere the large plant is typical of the pulp and paper industry, the small plant, of sawmills. Textiles, automobiles, iron and steel, railway works, chemical industries are in Canada, the United States, England, and Germany characterized by the large plant. Boots and shoes, woollen goods, furniture are characterized by medium-sized plants. Women's clothing, particularly the more expensive gar-

[9]Since the above paragraphs were written the author has been engaged in some statistical studies of the size of plant and though the results are indefinite as yet they are sufficiently established to indicate a qualification to the argument of the text. It would appear that in most industries the advantages of large-scale plant increase to a certain point, which might be called the point of optimum size. Plants of this size appear to be large enough to obtain all the present advantages of large-scale organization and their larger competitors do not appear to enjoy any technical superiority. On the contrary, the statistical evidence would suggest that there is a falling off of efficiency in establishments of more than optimum size, an indication which supports the notion that there is a rising marginal cost of management with extensions in the size of plant.

ments, bakeries, breweries, hosiery, and knit goods have smallish or medium-sized typical plants, and luxury articles, jewels, bespoke tailoring, brick and cement manufacture have a small typical plant.

The large-scale firm is, of course, typical in industry with the large-scale plants, and also in mining, chemical industries, cement, tobacco manufacture, meat packing and distributing, and some types (cheaper standardized lines) of retail distribution.

The clear suggestion of these facts is that the big plant and the big firm are most profitable when personal contact with the consumer and individual attention to consumer demands and peculiarities are not important. For the rest, even where, as in brick, cement, and tobacco manufacture the large-scale plant is not necessarily an advantage, the large-scale firm seems to be emerging as the dominant productive unit of our economy.

B. *The Trades Union*

The Industrial Revolution divorced the worker from his tools. He could no longer work with his own loom in his own cottage. He had to come with hundreds or thousands of his fellows into a great factory where he worked with the tools and machinery provided for him by his employer. He could no longer hope by industry and providence to work up through the hierarchy of apprentice-journeyman-master to become an independent craftsman. He became dependent on his wage and fixed in his position. Born a wage-earner, he died a wage-earner.

His standard of living depended on the money wage which the employer was willing to offer. Individually he was in a weak position to bargain for a good wage. He now lived in a crowded town. He had no bit of sustaining land to fall back on. He had no tools, no ability to work independently. He had to take whatever job he could get and accept what wages were offered. If he was not offered a living wage, and most frequently he was not, he could put his children to work, or he could starve.

But if labour individually was in a weak bargaining position, labour collectively was in a strong one. The great amounts of capital tied up in any one enterprise made the employer very anxious to continue production without any loss of time. Labour, by collectively refusing to work, could drive a very shrewd bargain. Almost at once labour learned this. Trades unions of a sort had existed before the Industrial Revolution where large numbers of workers were gathered together under one roof; particularly at Spittalfields and in some of the West Country woollen towns. As the workers were brought together in factories, as the isolated country worker was urbanized and made to feel his solidarity with his fellows, and as the advantages of organization became apparent trades unions were formed. The reaction of the employers was likewise immediate. The Combination Acts, passed by a notoriously reactionary government in 1799, made all organizations of workers illegal. Working class radicalism was thus given a stimulus for underground revolutionary activity and the Tory government replied by persecution, the destruction of all civil liberties, and even massacre. Eventually the Combination Acts were repealed, just before the Reform Bill was passed. But the struggle for unionism was far from won. The unions were not permitted to picket, they were not recognized as corporations in law and could not sue for damages or for recovery of funds if a treasurer absconded. The organization was weak and the leadership divided; the public was hostile and the employers could, and did, make use of the police power of the state to break up strikes, arrest union leaders, and have them transported and disperse the union. After some unsuccessful strikes in the thirties, labour turned its attention to political reform. The Chartist movement was the result, but it was unsuccessful, and its failure brought labour back to the way of trades unionism.

In the fifties and sixties the unions acquired some strength and set up a national organization. Legislation of the Gladstone Liberals improved the legal position of the unions and the country came to accept them. Collective bargaining is established now in England, and the unions are accepted as the bargaining agency of labour. They are recognized as a definite institution, contributing to the welfare of labour, the stability of the national economy, and the formation of national policy. Since the reversal of the decision in The Taff Vale Case no effort has been made to destroy their power, though Conservative governments since the General Strike of 1926 have passed legislation which the unions regard as hostile to their interest.

In the United States the history of Trades Unionism has shown a similar struggle on the part of the unions for recognition. The craft unions of the American Federation of Labour, existing largely for the protection of skilled workers in specialized tasks, have gained recognition and public acceptance, but industrial unions similar to those of England have been bitterly opposed. Until the Roosevelt administration government has been either hostile or an unfriendly neutral, and employers have frequently been able to use the police power of the state to destroy the unions, and even to use extra-legal or illegal force to break up strikes with complete impunity. Thus in America collective bargaining is merely in process of becoming what it has become in England, a recognized and accepted institution of the modern economy. But the American unions, late in developing, are experiencing a sort of "telescoping" in their institutional history. Unions everywhere are suffering from some of the internal strains of large-scale organization which we saw imposed certain rather indefinite limits on the size of large-scale firms. These strains manifest themselves through union rivalry, personal friction between leaders, and the growth of "vested interests" within the union. Thus the struggle between the A.F. of L. and the C.I.O. in the United States was partly a matter of personal rivalry between the leaders, partly because the growth of trades unions had run beyond the organizational machinery of the A. F. of L. and very largely because the skilled crafts of the A. F. of L. had established a sort of vested interest which they did not want to share with the unskilled or semi-skilled industrial workers. That the A. F. of L. showed a shrewd perception of its own interests, at least in the short run, our theoretic analysis will demonstrate.

Again, it is true, noticeably in Great Britain, that the administrative officers of trades unions come to have a vested interest in the social *status quo*. They exist to conduct collective bargaining and to protect the union members within the framework of capitalist society. Certain important changes in that society would change their function and even the administrative form of the unions. It is not, therefore, unnatural to find the trades union executives of the Labour party more at ease with their Conservative political opponents than with the Socialist wing of the Labour party.

While these considerations suggest limits to the effective growth of a unified trades union movement and, to some minds, limits to their social usefulness, they do not affect the general economic function of the union. This is to confront the corporate employer who is purchasing labour with the corporate supplier of labour and thus to give some equality of bargaining strength in wage negotiations. By making possible a reservation of labour supply trades unions give reality to the concept of a supply price of labour.

C. The Individual as Saver

At first sight it may seem as though in the capital market the available supplies of new capital are provided by individuals making decisions which approximate those made by Crusoe when he decided to save in order to have a canoe to increase his catch of fish. Actually a good deal of saving in the modern world is of such a nature, abstinence on the part of individual income earners. But these savings are marshalled by banks, insurance companies, and investment corporations, and on the capital market the corporation strikes its bargain with other corporations which have established control over the mobilized capital resources. More will be said on this subject in the chapter in Book Four on "Interest." For the moment we note that once again the corporation rather than the individual appears on the market as the bargaining unit.

D. The Consumer

The finished products of industry which appear on the market are bought by individual consumers. Ultimately the demand for consumable goods is made up of the choices of individuals as expressed through the price system. We shall argue in a later chapter that the demand for any specific product cannot be deduced from any knowledge of individual behaviour, but can only be known empirically from actual experience in marketing the commodity. Mass demand is made up of individuals' demand and will thus depend on the psychological forces determining individual behaviour on the market, but, because the schedule of a consumer's choices is known directly only to himself, objective market demand can only be described in terms of actualized responses to a series of prices.

The tendency towards the corporate unit which we have elsewhere noticed can be discerned in consumers' organizations. There are consumers' co-operatives though these are less wide-spread than the producers' co-operatives. There are also the various consumers' organizations in the United States. These organizations attempt to give expert advice to consumers on the value and quality of different goods on the market. The sensitiveness which producers have shown towards these organizations suggests that the consumers' potential power over industry is greater than has yet been realized. In an age when the consumer is not generally able to ascertain exactly for himself the qualities of various commodities and brands, and when advertising has been developed to a skilled science of suggestion, it is obvious that consumers' organizations have a distinct function. Though manufacturers and advertising concerns have palpable reasons for not welcoming them, it is probable that the consumers' organization is an institution that will grow and develop and play an increasingly important part in economic life.

CHAPTER IX

THE CURVES

SECTION 1: ASSUMPTIONS AND DEFINITIONS—THE FIRM'S COST CURVES

OUR hypothesis, carried forward from Book Two, is that price is fixed at that point where marginal demand price is equal to marginal cost. We shall attempt to apply and to test that hypothesis in the modern industrial economy.

We shall be working on a level of abstraction which will involve the following assumptions:

(1) We shall assume that equilibrium requires that no producer shall have any incentive to increase or to decrease his output.

(2) We shall assume that no consumer will leave unsatisfied a more important desire in favour of a less important desire.

(3) We shall assume that there is an immediate adjustment of the economy to any changes so that each unit of each factor of production is always employed in its most remunerative employment.

(4) We shall assume that no motives other than economic prevail.

(5) We shall assume that no irrational considerations of optimism or pessimism with regard to the future will influence the behaviour of entrepreneurs.

(6) We shall assume that each man is to behave as though present rates of output, employment, consumption, and price are to remain constant.

(7) We shall assume that the money system is neutral; that is that no independent changes in price will result from the behaviour of the banking and financial system.

We do not assume either perfect competition or full employment of the agents of production for these assumptions are unnecessary. Equilibrium may exist without either or both; they are only special cases of equilibrium. At times we shall *restrict* our study to perfect competition and at times to imperfect competition. Such restrictions are a necessary device of analysis, but they involve no unreal assumptions about the nature of the real world.

In the formal statement of Book Two we distinguished two costs, working and waiting. These are fundamental human costs of production; they underlie all the costs which the business man must meet in his business, and all of what we popularly call costs may be resolved into these components. They are the *"real costs"* of economic enterprise.

For the present, however, we are going to accept the business man's point of view and suppose that the rates of remuneration which must be paid to the agents of production, i.e. wages, interest, rent, and other costs are all fixed at a market rate which the business man has to pay. By his own individual action he cannot appreciably affect the rates which must be paid for the agents of production. In other words we are supposing that the costs of the factors are given quantities in our problem. We must first analyse, classify, and define these costs as they appear to the entrepreneur. There is no common or objective measure of costs other than money so that all our definitions must be in pecuniary terms.

The sum of all pecuniary costs incurred in the production of any number of goods is known as the *total cost* of production. But total cost is made up of two types of cost, *prime, operating* or *variable costs*, and *supplementary* or *fixed costs*.

Prime costs or operating costs are those which vary in total amount directly with output. Thus wages, fuel or power, raw materials, interest on short-term loans, processing taxes, etc., are all operating costs. Because of this variation it will be convenient to call these *variable costs*.

Supplementary or fixed costs are those whose total amount remains unchanged regardless of changes in output. Rent, payment for plant, maintenance and depreciation on fixed machinery, long-term debt service, real property taxes, etc., are all fixed costs.[1]

Total unit cost is the total cost divided by the number of units of output, or the average total cost per unit.

Variable unit cost is the total of variable cost divided by the number of units of output, or the average variable cost per unit.

Fixed unit cost is the total of fixed cost divided by the number of units of output, or the average fixed cost per unit.

Fixed costs per unit of output will decrease approaching a limit of zero, as output increases. This follows from the arithmetic principle that if you increase the divisor, keeping the sum constant, the quotient must decrease.

Let us illustrate this with a very simple arithmetic example.

Let us suppose that our fixed costs are 3 cost units. (These units

---

[1]We postpone for later discussion the possibility of output expanding to plant capacity. Beyond that point further expansion can only take place with an addition to plant, which necessitates an addition to fixed costs. This results in an entirely new structure of cost curves which we shall consider in due course.

are quite arbitrary. They may be units of a hundred dollars each, or a thousand dollars each, or a hundred thousand dollars each: it will make no difference in principle.)

When our output is one unit of produce—again the unit of measurement is arbitrary, it may be so many pairs, boxes, tons, gallons, or kilowatts—our fixed cost per unit is 3. As we increase output fixed costs per unit must decrease according to the following table:

TABLE II

Total Fixed Costs	Output in Units	Fixed Unit Cost
3	1	3
3	2	$1\frac{1}{2}$
3	3	1
3	4	$\frac{3}{4}$
3	5	$\frac{3}{5}$
3	6	$\frac{1}{2}$
3	7	$\frac{3}{7}$
3	8	$\frac{3}{8}$
3	9	$\frac{1}{3}$
3	10	$\frac{3}{10}$

It is important to notice that though the rate of decrease remains unchanged, the *decrease in absolute amounts* is progressively less.

Variable unit costs behave in a different way. The variation in total variable costs, as output increases, makes the variation in variable unit cost more complicated. As output increases total variable costs increase, but they increase at a varying rate. If the increase in variable cost is less than proportionate to the increase in output, average variable cost must fall. This follows from the arithmetic relationship. If the sum, total variable costs, is increased less than in proportion to the increase in output (units of output being the divisor), the quotient, variable unit cost, must decrease. The opposite argument holds true when total variable costs are increasing more than in proportion to the increase in output. When variable unit costs are falling with increases of output, we shall call the condition that of *decreasing variable unit costs*; when they are increasing with increases in output, we shall speak of *increasing variable unit costs*.

At first the returns which may be imputed to the variable factors using a given fixed establishment may increase. This is because the variable factors have not been in sufficient number to make proper utilization of the plant. As the variable factors increase, however, the fixed plant remaining unchanged, and there being no change in the technique of production, returns per unit of variable factor begin to diminish. When that happens it follows that variable costs per unit of output must increase. Consequently we accept the fact that in the utilization of any fixed establishment after a period of decreasing variable unit costs, increasing variable unit costs will set in.

We may illustrate this process in the following table.

TABLE III

Units of Output	Total Variable Costs	Variable Unit Costs
1	7	7
2	13	$6\frac{1}{2}$
3	18	6
4	25	$6\frac{1}{4}$
5	37	$7\frac{2}{5}$
6	51	$8\frac{1}{3}$
7	67	$9\frac{4}{7}$
8	85	$10\frac{5}{8}$
9	105	$11\frac{2}{3}$
10	127	$12\frac{7}{10}$

We observe here that the absolute decreases in fixed unit cost are sufficiently large to offset the increase in variable unit cost when the latter first begin to increase. But as the output continues to increase, the decreases in fixed unit cost are so small in absolute amounts as to fail to offset the increases in variable unit cost. But in our example the fixed costs are a comparatively small proportion of the total cost. In an industry where fixed costs represented by

TABLE IV

Units of Output	Fixed Unit Costs	Variable Unit Costs	Total Unit Costs
1	3	7	10
2	$1\frac{1}{2}$	$6\frac{1}{2}$	8
*3	1	6	7
†4	$\frac{3}{4}$	$6\frac{1}{4}$	7
5	$\frac{3}{5}$	$7\frac{2}{5}$	8
6	$\frac{1}{2}$	$8\frac{1}{2}$	9
7	$\frac{3}{7}$	$9\frac{4}{7}$	10
8	$\frac{3}{8}$	$10\frac{5}{8}$	11
9	$\frac{1}{3}$	$11\frac{2}{3}$	12
10	$\frac{3}{10}$	$12\frac{7}{10}$	13

*Marks point where increasing variable costs set in.
†The point where increasing total unit costs begin.

In Table IV, column 2 comes from Table II; column 3 comes from Table III, column 3; and column 4 is the sum of columns 2 and 3.

far the largest proportion of total costs, decreasing fixed unit cost would continue to offset increasing variable unit cost, thus giving rise to a situation of decreasing total unit cost. Thus industries with high fixed costs relative to variable costs tend to be industries with decreasing unit costs, whereas industries with a high proportion of variable costs tend to be industries operating under conditions of increasing total unit costs.

In Table IV, where we combine Tables II and III, we may observe an illustration of this. At three units of output increasing variable costs set in, but increasing total unit costs do not begin until more than four units of output are being produced.

In industry the entrepreneur is interested not only in his average unit costs as analysed in the foregoing paragraphs, but also in *the rate* at which he adds to his total costs. We have seen that the increase in total utility expressed as a ratio of the increase of goods for consumption is called marginal utility, and that the increase in total product to the increase in employment is called marginal productivity. Similarly the rate at which total cost increases with an increase in output is known as *marginal cost*. Thus if O is output and C is total cost, marginal cost is defined as being $\dfrac{dC}{dO}$.

As long as increments in output are finite quantities measurable in units, we may calculate marginal cost for any quantity of output. Marginal cost can be calculated as the increment in total cost divided by the increment in output.

From Table IV we may now calculate the marginal cost for any output from 2 units to 10.

TABLE V

Units of Output	Total Unit Cost	Total Cost 2×1	Marginal Cost
1	10	10	..
2	8	16	6
3	7	21	5
4	7	28	7
5	8	40	12
6	9	54	14
7	10	70	16
8	11	88	18
9	12	108	20
10	13	130	22

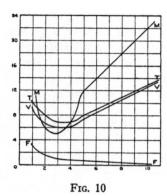

FIG. 10

We may now present the data given in these four tables on a graph. We notice that variable unit cost, fixed unit cost, total unit cost, and marginal cost are all dependent variables of output. If units of output are plotted on the x-axis and cost units on the y-axis we shall have four curves illustrating the dependent variation of fixed unit costs, variable unit costs, total unit costs, and marginal cost. This is done in Fig. 10, where F is the fixed unit cost curve, V the variable unit cost curve, T the total unit cost curve, and M the marginal cost curve.

SECTION 2: THE RELATIONS OF THE CURVES

In this section we shall be concerned to show the relationships between the marginal and total unit cost curves. For purposes of brevity we shall refer to the total unit cost curve as the average cost—more generally the "AC"—curve.[2]

1. The marginal curve always cuts the AC curve at the latter's lowest point.[3]

When marginal cost is less than average cost that means that one is adding to the sum of total costs less than in proportion to the increment in output. Thus as long as marginal cost is less than average cost average costs, must be falling. On the other hand, when marginal cost exceeds average cost, average costs must be rising. If average costs are falling as long as marginal cost is less than average cost, and if, as soon as marginal cost exceeds average cost, average costs must be rising, it follows that average costs fall to the point of intersection of the AC and MC curves, and beyond that point rise. Thus that point must be the lowest point on the AC curve.

[2]It has been deemed wise in this section simply to state the relationships which will be of importance in later studies. In an Appendix to this chapter some of the argument is demonstrated in mathematical terms. For a full geometric treatment the reader should consult Joan Robinson, *The Economics of Imperfect Competition* (London, 1936), chap. II.

[3]This assumes that the curves are at first falling, then rising. If the curves rise at first and then fall, the marginal curve cuts the average curve at the latter's highest point. If the curves rise or fall continuously there will be no intersection. The case which we examine in the main text is in practice the most important one.

2. When the average curve is rising, the marginal values must be positive. This is obvious. For if average costs are rising, total costs must be rising faster than output. Thus marginal cost must be positive.

3. If the average cost curve is falling and has an elasticity greater than unity, the marginal values must be positive.

4. If the average curve is falling but has an elasticity of unity, the marginal value will be zero.

5. If the average curve is falling and has an elasticity of less than unity, the marginal values will be negative.[4]

We must digress briefly here to explain what we mean by elasticity. By *elasticity* we mean the proportionate change in output (quantity) with respect to the proportionate change in cost (or price).[5] Thus if unit cost is four when output is eight, and unit cost falls by one when output increases by one, the proportionate change in unit cost has been 1/4, while that in output has been 1/8. The elasticity of the AC curve at that point would be $\dfrac{1/8}{1/4}$, or $\dfrac{1}{2}$.

Thus an entrepreneur who finds that a slight decrease in price enables him to sell a much larger output is able to speak of an elastic demand for his product. Most comforts and some luxuries have an elastic demand. On the other hand, changes in price may have little effect on the sales of some commodities. These are said to have an inelastic demand. Such are most necessities, and habit-forming comforts such as coffee and tobacco.

We may now illustrate propositions 3, 4, and 5.

The following table gives an output varying from 10 units to 20, with average unit costs falling from 12 to 7. In the third column the elasticity is calculated, and in the fourth column the marginal cost. It will be seen that while elasticity is greater than unity, marginal cost values are positive; when elasticity is less than unity, marginal cost values are theoretically negative. The elasticity for that part of the curve lying between output 16 and 18 is 9/8, but at the point 18 it would be unity. For that elasticity the marginal cost is zero.

A graph illustrating these relations will be found in the geometrical appendix to this chapter, Fig. 12.

[4]These propositions are all demonstrated in the Appendix. The non-mathematical reader must be content to accept them.

[5]See Appendix for a full treatment of elasticity.

TABLE VI

Output	Average Unit Cost	Elasticity	Marginal Cost
10	12	..	..
12	11	$\frac{12}{5}$	12
14	10	$\frac{11}{6}$	8
16	9	$\frac{10}{7}$	4
18	8	$\frac{9}{8}$	0
20	7	$\frac{8}{9}$	−4

The various relations we have observed in this section will all be of importance in our later studies and will take on significance in their proper context.

Information as to the point of intersection of marginal curves corresponding to two intersecting average curves—information which will be of value in considering certain problems of monopoly output—is summarized in Table VII and the following paragraphs in the geometric appendix to this chapter.

APPENDIX TO CHAPTER IX

ELASTICITY AND SOME RELATED CONCEPTS

ELASTICITY we defined as the proportionate change in output divided by the proportionate change in cost (or price). This can be expressed by saying that

$$e = \frac{dx/x}{dy/y} \quad \ldots\ldots\ldots\ldots\ldots\ldots\ldots\ldots \text{(i)}$$

$$\text{or } e = \frac{dx}{dy} \cdot \frac{y}{x} \quad \ldots\ldots\ldots\ldots\ldots\ldots\ldots\ldots \text{(ii)},$$

which means that

$$e = \frac{\text{slope of line joining } P \text{ with } O}{\text{slope of tangent at } P}$$

where O is the origin and P is any point on the curve.

It can be shown by similar triangles[1] that $e = \frac{PT}{Pt}$, when T is the point the tangent cuts the x-axis, and t is the point the tangent cuts the y-axis.

$$e = \frac{PT}{Pt} \; ; \text{ we shall number this equation} \quad \text{(iii)}.$$

If we consider a falling curve of an elasticity of unity throughout we can derive the equation of the curve by setting $e = -1$, and integrating from equation (i), which gives us $xy = k$, when k is any constant.

The curve which satisfies this equation will be a rectangular hyperbola, with the co-ordinate axes the asymptotes, such as we have drawn in the Appendix to Book One in Fig. 4. We have now a general curve and a general equation to define the falling curve with an elasticity of unity[2] throughout.

We have defined elasticity at a point, and this may be known as "point elasticity." In the rectangular hyperbola the elasticity of every point on the curve is unity, and we say it has an elasticity of one throughout its length. But most curves will not have this uniform point elasticity. When we refer to the general elasticity of a curve, or of a section of a curve, we must mean some average of the point elasticities. When we calculate the average propor-

[1]A. Marshall, *Principles of Economics* (2nd ed., London, 1891), Mathematical Appendix, note iii.

[2]Actually $e = -1$. This is because the curve is falling and changes in y are always negative to changes in x. But in economics we commonly drop the minus sign and speak positively of an elasticity of unity or of more or less than unity. This is because elasticity is of most consequence in connection with demand curves, which are falling curves, and it avoids the nuisance of constantly referring to negative values.

tionate change in "x" to the average proportionate change in "y" over any length of the curve we have what is known as the average elasticity for that section of the curve.

We can compare the slope of any part of any given curve with our standard rectangular hyperbola, and see at once if it has an average elasticity of more or less than unity. If the curve we are testing has a steeper slope than the standard curve (i.e., if the proportionate changes in x are less than equal to the proportionate changes in y) the curve has an elasticity of less than unity; if, on the contrary, the curve has a more gentle slope than the standard curve, the elasticity is said to be greater than unity.

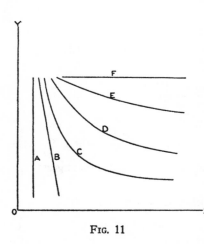

FIG. 11

Thus in Fig. 11, Curve A has a point elasticity of zero, throughout its length; B an average elasticity of less than unity, and curve C has an elasticity of unity throughout. Curves D and E have an average elasticity of more than unity, and Curve F has an elasticity of infinity.

We may now establish three propositions describing the relationship between the elasticity of the average curve and the marginal values. These are:

Proposition 1.

If the average curve is falling but has an elasticity (at all points) greater than unity, the marginal values must be positive.

Proposition 2.

If the average curve is falling with an elasticity of unity, the marginal value will be zero.

Proposition 3.

If the average curve is falling and has an elasticity of less than unity the marginal values must be negative.

These three propositions are illustrated in Fig. 12.

We may now proceed to the demonstration of these three propositions.

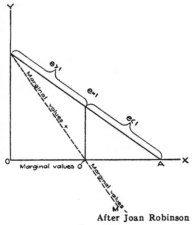

After Joan Robinson

FIG. 12

In Fig. 13, draw any average curve A, and from any point P on the curve drop a perpendicular to cut the x-axis at M.   Draw TP the tangent to A at P, and extend it to cut the x-axis at E.   Draw PP_1, the perpendicular to the y-axis from P.   Let CM be the corresponding marginal value to the average value PM.

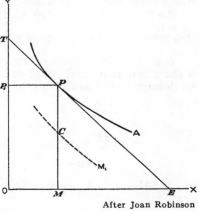

Then the elasticity of the average curve at P is $\dfrac{PE}{TP}$, equation (iii) page 99.

Now the triangles TP_1P and PME are similar triangles, i.e. their corresponding angles are equal.

Therefore $\dfrac{PE}{TP} = \dfrac{PM}{TP_1}$.

But $TP_1 = PC$ (an easy geometric demonstration of this is given in Joan Robinson, *op. cit.*, page 30),

Therefore $\dfrac{PE}{TP} = \dfrac{PM}{PC}$.

After Joan Robinson
Fig. 13

But elasticity at P equals $\dfrac{PE}{TP}$.

Therefore elasticity at P equals $\dfrac{PM}{PC}$.

This means that the elasticity of an average curve at any point is equal to the average value at that point divided by the difference between the average and marginal values.

If we call elasticity e, average value A, and marginal value M, we may write this,

$$e = \frac{A}{A-M},$$
$$\text{or } A = e(A-M)$$
$$= eA - eM.$$
$$eM = eA - A,$$
$$M = \frac{A(e-1)}{e}.$$

Now, if $e=1$, $\dfrac{A(e-1)}{e} = 0$.

Therefore, $M=0$ when $e=1$, which establishes proposition 7.

If e is greater than 1, then $\dfrac{A(e-1)}{e}$ is positive, and M is positive, which establishes proposition 6.

If e is less than 1, then $\dfrac{A(e-1)}{e}$ is negative, and M is negative, which establishes proposition 8.

An interesting corollary which we may draw as a by-product of this proof is that the average value, A, is always equal to $M.\dfrac{e}{e-1}$.

A much neater demonstration of these propositions is possible if the calculus is used. For example, the seventh proposition may be demonstrated as follows:

$$e = \frac{dx/x}{dy/y} = -1$$

$$\therefore \quad \frac{dx}{x} = -\frac{dy}{y} \ .$$

$$\therefore \quad y \cdot dx = -x \cdot dy$$

$$\text{Marginal Revenue} = \frac{d(xy)}{dx}$$

$$= \frac{y \cdot dx + x \cdot dy}{dx}$$

By substitution:

$$\text{Marginal Revenue} = \frac{-x \cdot dy + x \cdot dy}{dx}$$

$$= 0.$$

$$\text{Q.E.D.}$$

CHAPTER X

THE INDUSTRIAL SUPPLY CURVE

THE industrial supply curve represents the functional dependence of costs per unit of output for a series of outputs all considered as potential in a unit of time. Thus the concept of a supply curve, or a supply schedule, does not involve the idea of a passage of time. If we wish to construct a schedule for a period of time, we must prepare a series of supply schedules for various moments during that period, plotting the variations in cost and output against time changes shown along a third axis. Such a supply schedule over a period of time is illustrated in Fig. 33. But before we can deal with these rather complicated relationships we must understand the static equilibrium position of the firm and the industry. When the industry is constituted by a single firm, the notion of a supply curve for the industry presents no difficulty. We are assuming throughout this discussion that the firm (or industry) is producing one (and one only) product. The industrial supply curve, in such a case, coincides with the firm's curve, because the firm supplies the entire output of the industry.

When, however, several firms in competitive production of like products constitute an industry, the concept of an industrial supply curve is more complicated. It would be a false assumption to suppose that all firms in the industry would have similar cost curves, and that, consequently, any firm's curve could be regarded as representative of the industry as a whole. We are forced, therefore, in constructing the supply curve of a competitive industry, to take account of the differences between firms. Granted that there will be differences in firms, in their relative efficiencies, and, consequently, in their schedules of unit costs, what will determine what share of the industrial output will be contributed by each firm? What will govern the relations between the cost schedules of the different firms? And, for our whole analysis of the industrial supply curve is directed towards a theory of price determination, what costs will be relevant to the determination of selling price?

It is clear that we can start with two self-evident propositions.

1. Each firm in the industry will sell at the point where the price just covers its marginal cost.[1] This point, where the marginal cost

---

[1]This is assuming competition. A full examination of this point, including the case of monopolistic competition, is reserved for chapter XII.

equals price, is the point where profits are at the maximum. When marginal costs are less than price every increment in sales brings in more than it adds to total costs, and thus increases total net profits. When marginal cost exceeds price each increment of sales brings in less than it adds to total costs and thus results in a diminution of total net profits. Hence the equality of marginal cost to price fixes the point of maximum net profits.

2. The least efficient firm in the industry cannot sell for less than its average unit cost. When price per unit does not cover average unit costs including normal entrepreneur's profits,[2] the firm is taking a net loss on each unit of output and cannot for long stay in business.

To these we shall add one further proposition which we shall demonstrate later in our chapter on demand, Chapter IV. It is that the demand curve, or price curve, for the output of any firm in a competitive industry is a straight line parallel with the x-axis. This means that in a competitive industry no single firm, by altering its output, can effect changes in the price for which it can sell.

We shall call the least efficient firm which can continue in competition the marginal firm, and by this we shall mean the firm which at the ruling price can just produce, covering all costs including interest on capital and entrepreneur's salary, but nothing over and above cost.

The intra-marginal firm is the name we shall give to any firm more efficient than the marginal firm.

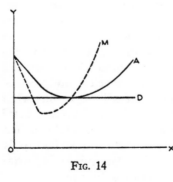

FIG. 14

The marginal firm, by definition, just covers its average unit costs. But the marginal firm, like all others, sells at the point where marginal cost equals selling price. Consequently the marginal firm sells at the point where marginal cost equals average cost, that is at the point of lowest average unit cost. This is illustrated in Fig. 14, where D is the straight line demand curve, A the average unit cost curve, and M the marginal cost curve.

The intra-marginal firm sells at the point where its marginal cost cuts the price curve, that is, in Fig. 15, at the point P, when D is the price curve, A the average unit cost curve, and M the marginal cost curve.

[2] "Normal entrepreneur's profit" equals entrepreneurial salary plus normal return on any investment of capital by the entrepreneur.

It is probable, however, that some or all of the intra-marginal firm's superior efficiency is owing to the superiority of some one of its agents, an abler manager, a better situation with respect to raw materials or markets, more fertile land, superior capital equipment, etc. To the owner of this agent the firm must pay a surplus reward which we shall call a rent.[3] Thus the surplus, above the costs of the marginal firm will be paid out to the landlord, the manager, the entrepreneur, or whomever it may be who disposes of the factor that has made possible the superior efficiency. Thus, from the accountant's point of view this rent constitutes a cost to the firm, and must be included as such, though the economist accords it special treatment in his concept of costs.[4]

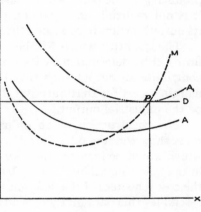

Fig. 15

In Fig. 15, the curve A_1 represents average costs inclusive of all rents, and it will be seen that the selling point is where this curve is at its lowest point. It is apparent that the selling price must cover the total average costs including rents. Also the firm must sell at the point where marginal cost equals selling price. Thus it sells at the A_1 curve's lowest point.

The supply schedule for a competitive industry will be a complex of the cost schedules of the constituent firms. For a series of different cost points there will be a corresponding series of industrial output points, the total output in each case consisting of the contributions of the various firms, each contribution being determined by the individual firm's ability to produce. The total industrial output will be such that the price which the demand will pay for that output will just cover the average unit cost of the least efficient firm in the industry and the least efficient firm will be producing to the point of its lowest average unit cost. If the least efficient firm in the industry is not producing to this point, it means that it is not

[3]This statement will be shown to be consistent with our general treatment of rent in Book Four, chap. XVIII.

[4]He must do so for reasons which will be fully explained in Book Four, chap. XVIII.

producing to the point where marginal cost is equal to price, that is, it is not realizing its maximum profits. It will therefore increase its output until it has reached the point of lowest average unit costs.

The quantity which will be contributed by each intramarginal firm will be determined by its marginal cost curve. Each firm will contribute an output such that the price will just be equal to the marginal cost for that output. The sum of the firms' outputs will be the industrial output.

The construction of an industrial supply schedule, therefore, must show the sum of the firms' outputs, and the average unit costs which would be incurred for a series of outputs. This is illustrated in the following tables. Table VII provides the relevant data as to the cost schedules of the different firms, A, B, C, and D. Table VIII assembles this data and yields an industrial supply schedule, showing how these firms will produce through a series of prices from $7.00 to $13.00.

TABLE VII

	Firm A			Firm B			Firm C			Firm D	
Output	AUC.	MUC.	Output	AUC.	MUC.	Output	AUC.	MUC.	Output	AUC.	MUC.
1	10	..	1	12	..	1	14	..	1	16	..
2	8	6	2	10	8	2	12	10	2	14	12
3	7	5	3	9	7	3	11	9	3	13	11
4	7	7	4	9	9	4	11	11	4	13	13
5	8	12	5	10	14	5	12	16	5	14	18
6	9	14	6	11	16	6	13	18			
7	10	16	7	12	18						
8	11	18									

TABLE VIII

Price	Output					AUC.				MUC.			
$	A	B	C	D	Total	A	B	C	D	A	B	C	D
7	4	..	..	..	4	7	..	..	..	7	..	..	..
9	4+	4	..	..	8+	7+	9	..	..	9	9	..	..
11	5−	4+	4	..	13	8−	9+	11	..	11	11	11	..
13	5½	5−	4+	4	18½	8½	10−	11+	13	13	13	13	13

NOTE: + designates a fraction less than ½ over the figure given.
— designates a fraction less than ½ under the figure given.

A study of Table VII will show how each firm's cost schedules obey the laws of the cost curves as we have explained them. At the point of lowest average unit cost the marginal cost coincides with the average. Table VIII shows the variations in total industrial supply, as determined by the cost positions of the firms, with changes in the ruling price. When price is $7 only firm A can produce and cover its average unit costs. Neither B, C, nor D can manufacture at $7, for, though B has a marginal cost of only $7 for 3 units, its average unit cost for that amount is $9, and it would therefore be taking a loss. Firms C and D are in still more unfavourable situations. But at $9 firm B enters as the marginal firm and firm A hitherto the marginal firm becomes intra-marginal. Firm A is now able to sell above the point of lowest average unit cost, but, because for A marginal costs are now in excess of average, it is able to increase its total net profits by doing so. At $11 firm C becomes the marginal firm and B now enjoys the advantages of an intra-marginal firm. Firm C can sell only 4 units because the price of $11 will not cover its average costs beyond that output. At $13 firm D is able to compete. It adds four units to the total output. This production enables it to cover its average costs, but it makes no surplus profits. The other three firms, producing to the various points where their marginal costs equal $13, are all able to increase their outputs and to realize profits. (These points could not be exactly indicated without making the tables unduly complicated, but they run roughly as follows, as the reader can see for himself:

A—output 5½, Average cost $8½, rent per unit $4½.
B— " almost 5, Average cost almost $10, rent per unit just over $3.
C— " over 4, Average cost over $11, rent per unit less than $2.)

It is interesting to notice from Table VIII that the marginal cost of the marginal firm coincides with the marginal costs of the intra-marginal firms for the outputs they put on the market, but their average costs do not coincide. Thus it is possible to speak of an industrial marginal cost. The industrial marginal cost is the marginal cost of the marginal firm, which is equal to selling price. Since every other firm will produce to the point where its marginal cost is equal to selling price, the marginal costs of all firms in the industry will be the same for any given output for the industry. This marginal cost may be spoken of as the marginal supply price.

But, because of superior advantages, the marginal cost of each firm, though the same for the output put on the market, will be a marginal cost for varying outputs. The most efficient firms will put a larger share of the total output on the market than the marginal firm. Moreover their average costs will be lower. The average cost of the marginal firm will just be equal to its marginal cost, and it will be therefore earning nothing over costs of production. The average costs (excluding rents) of the intra-marginal firms will be less than their marginal costs because they will be producing beyond the point of lowest average unit costs. The price per unit will thus exceed the average cost per unit, and these firms,[5] in consequence, will be earning surpluses or rents.

The total output column in Table VIII shows the total industrial supply. It will be seen that it increases as a result both of the increases in the outputs of the intra-marginal firms and of the increase contributed by the addition of a new firm on the margin of production.

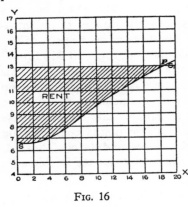

FIG. 16

This can be shown on a graph as in Fig. 16, where on the x-axis the units of industrial output are plotted and on the y-axis the selling price. Such a curve is an industrial supply curve and may be compared with the firm's cost curves, from which it is, in effect, constructed. It will be seen that the industrial supply curve by itself does not yield much information about the costs of the firms in the industry, beyond telling us, by implication, what the marginal cost for each firm must be for its particular share of the total output, and what the average unit cost of the marginal firm must be. It does, however, show us the response of industrial output to changes in price.

We might finally note that the rents per unit of output are equal to the marginal cost less the average unit cost. Thus for firm *A*, when price is $13 the rent is $4.50 per unit of output. In Fig. 16 the total amount of all rents in the industry is represented by the area lying between the SS_1 curve and the perpendicular from P to the y-axis. The shape of the SS_1 curve for the first 4 units of output corresponds to the average unit cost curve of firm *A*.

[5]The reader may plot on a graph any of these firms' curves and may see how they correspond to the generality of cost curves as we have shown them in the last chapter.

CHAPTER XI

CONSUMERS' DEMAND

SECTION 1: MARGINAL UTILITY RECONSIDERED

AT this stage we must undertake a reconsideration of our concept of marginal utility. The reader will remember that in the abstract treatment of Book Two the consumer was presumed to balance the marginal utility of one good against the marginal utility of another, or against the marginal cost of obtaining it. This marginal cost might be considered as the marginal cost of labour in obtaining the satisfaction, as it was in the first instance of Crusoe working alone to collect turtles' eggs. Or the marginal cost, from the consumer's point of view might be considered as the sacrifice of other satisfactions entailed by obtaining this one, for with limited purchasing power the consumer has to choose what desires to satisfy, and must balance the marginal utility of goods on the margin of acquisition against one another. When he decides to buy one commodity it must be that the marginal utility from that purchase will exceed the greatest marginal utility which could be obtained from the purchase of an additional unit of any other commodity. Thus the purchase of one good means the sacrifice of other satisfactions which might have been bought with the same expenditure. The marginal cost of this sacrifice may be considered as being measured by the greatest possible marginal utility of any alternative satisfaction. In this sense the consumer more usually balances marginal utility against marginal cost.

The application of the theory of marginal utility to the theory of demand presents some difficulties. In the first place we have presumed that all buyers behave so as to maximize their satisfactions by balancing marginal cost against marginal utility. When we have to explain apparent contradictions of this rule in everyday life, we say that there is no objective criterion of marginal utility but that we must suppose the subject to be behaving according to the rule. We say everyone's subjective evaluations must be different, and the apparently contradictory behaviour is to be explained by the eccentricity of our subjects. Thus if a young woman prefers to spend a dollar on silk stockings and go without her lunch, we maintain that this is no contradiction to the rule that people maximize their satisfactions. We say the young woman, foolishly perhaps, prefers silk stockings to food.

This type of argument is dangerous.   Our general rule is supposed to be based on observation of human behaviour.   It is supposed to be a generalization, valid as a description of how humans behave.   Yet how are we to know that in general they do so behave if there is no agreement as to what constitute the more important satisfactions?   How, that is, if all the utility judgments are so subjective as to fail to receive any general agreement, is any observer in the position to say that men are usually acting so as to maximize satisfactions?   Clearly we have to admit a similarity in human judgments, a generality of behaviour.   In that case exceptions have to be admitted as such, and the young woman buying silk stockings instead of lunch might be one of these exceptions. In our introductory book we argued that there was no universality in human behaviour, merely a tendency to conform to a norm.   One can generalize about human behaviour and be sure that in a large group of humans the behaviour will conform to the norm, but one admits deviations and cannot therefore predict with certainty from the generalization about the behaviour of any one individual. Thus one cannot be sure that any one individual will always behave so as to achieve an exact balance between satisfactions, but one can be sure that in any large market the demand curve for a good will be constituted by consumers whose normal behaviour will be to maximize their satisfactions according to the law of marginal utility.

In the second place, marginal utility analysis assumes the possibility of infinitely small divisions of an homogeneous commodity, and infinitely fine gradations of satisfaction.   Obviously many goods are not susceptible of this treatment. This objection does not invalidate the marginal utility argument.   That argument, for precision in statement, is worked out on the basis of the simplifying assumption of infinitely divisible goods and infinitely fine gradations of satisfactions.   This makes possible the precise argument of the differential calculus.   When the simplifying assumption is dropped, we need merely qualify our conclusion by saying that in actuality consumers' decisions will approximate the maximization of satisfactions.

Finally, the theory of marginal utility is generally held to imply the notion of "consumers' surplus," the idea, that is, that the consumer enjoys a surplus of satisfaction in the consumption of all units of the commodity other than the last unit consumed.   If a man is willing to pay $5 for one shirt, $4 for a second shirt, $3 for a third shirt, and $2 for a fourth shirt, and if the price of shirts is actually

$2, then the man may be said to enjoy a surplus satisfaction in the consumption of four shirts which is measured by $14 − $8, i.e. $6. This notion of consumers' surplus is, as Marshall says,[1] of considerable theoretic importance in welfare economics. If, for example, one is considering the hardship which a tax on income will inflict on different social groups one can conclude that an equal tax will impose much greater sacrifices of real satisfactions on the part of those groups whose "consumers' surplus" is low than on the part of those whose "consumers' surplus" is high.

But the whole notion of "consumers' surplus" has come under fire. That there can be a surplus of satisfaction to an individual over and above the marginal utility of a good to him is not denied; but that "consumers' surpluses" can be compared, that they can be added, that the "consumers' surpluses" of social groups can be spoken of as being susceptible of measurement, all this seems very difficult. The difficulty may not prove insurmountable, but whether it may or not does not appear to be important for our immediate purposes, for we are not now directly concerned with questions of welfare. We wish to obtain a conception of an objective demand curve for commodities on the market and the objective demand curve is not a sum of subjective utility evaluations. If it did, indeed, rest on some summation of subjective marginal utilities, it would be open to the criticism that such summation is impossible. It is the resultant of consumers' behaviour expressed in terms of price. In any particular case it could be obtained from the statistical data of the market. The theory of marginal utility is the explanation of why consumers behave as they do. The demand curve is the objective measure of the results of their decisions.

As long as society uses money as a purchasing medium, individuals will measure their subjective utilities in terms of price. To buy or not to buy is decided by comparing the marginal utility of the projected purchase against the marginal utility of the money which will be expended in buying it. The marginal utility of the money will depend on alternative purchases which could be made with it. A thousand consumers so behaving, all expressing their decisions by buying or not buying at a certain price, will determine the number of commodities to be sold at that price in that community of a thousand persons. The number of sales so determined at that stated price will fix a point on the demand curve for the commodity. Similarly will other points on the demand curve be

[1]A. Marshall, *Principles of Economics* (2nd ed., London, 1891), Book Three, chap. VI.

the resultants of consumers' subjective decisions. Thus the demand curve is the objective resultant of marginal utility decisions. That is all that is meant by saying that the theory of marginal utility is the theory underlying the demand curve. The resultant curve, an objective measure of consumers' behaviour *en masse*, becomes a relevant fact in the determination of price.

SECTION 2: THE DEMAND CURVE

In any community the price which will be paid on the market for any commodity will vary with the quantities of goods put on the market. Thus there will be a schedule of demand prices which may be represented as dependent functions of different quantities of goods.

Not only does the price which each purchaser is willing to pay alter with the quantity of goods, because of the change in marginal utility, but, because of different income levels, the number of purchasers willing to buy will alter. Thus from these two sources is derived the functional variation of the demand curve.

We may, for example, imagine a community of five persons, *A B, C, D*, and *E*, whose marginal utility schedules are represented in the following table.

TABLE IX

Price	*Quantity each consumer is willing to buy* (as determined by the marginal utility of the good, balanced against the marginal utility of his money):				
	A	B	C	D	E
$10..........	10	8	6	4	2
$8..........	14	10	7	5	3
$6..........	16	12	8	6	4
$4..........	18	13	9	7	5
$2..........	19	14	10	8	6

Then the total demand schedule of the community shows the variation of output and price determined by the sum of the variations of all members in the community. This is represented in the following table.

TABLE X

At	Units will be sold
$10.............................	30
$8.............................	39
$6.............................	46
$4.............................	52
$2.............................	57

This may be plotted on a graph showing the dependent variation of price on quantities brought to the market.

Demand curves of a general nature can always be deduced from our assumption as to the nature of demand. In actual business practice they can be plotted more or less accurately from empirically determined data, gained by the entrepreneur by "trial and error" on the market.

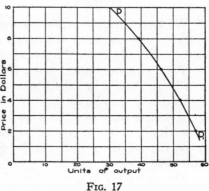

FIG. 17

The reader should notice that a demand schedule and a demand curve do not represent shifts in demand over a period of time. On the contrary they represent the possible prices for various outputs at any moment of time. Thus it is not proper to speak of there being a "change in demand" because price varies from $10 to $8 as quantity varies from 39 to 30. This dependence of price on available supply is the essence of our concept of the demand schedule or demand curve. A "change or shift in demand" properly speaking results when after the passage of time consumers' behaviour towards this commodity changes so that at any given price they buy more or less than before. This "changed demand" must then be represented by a new schedule and a new curve.

We must finally define here the term "marginal or effective demand price." By this phrase we shall mean the price for any output which will just carry the last unit from the market. Thus for 30 units the marginal demand price is $10. If any more had been charged the full 30 units could not have been sold. For 39 units the marginal or effective demand price is $8, and so forth.

The presumption of any demand analysis dependent on the assumption of buyers' competition, is that the marginal demand price will be the effective price, for if the whole quantity is to be marketed some units at least must be sold at the marginal demand price or they will not be sold at all. But if some units are sold at the marginal demand price all must be, for, though some consumers would be willing to pay a higher price if necessary and if the quantity on the market were less, they will nevertheless insist on buying as cheaply as possible. Consequently they will insist on buying at the lowest price quoted and thus the marginal demand price will prevail on the market.

SECTION 3: ELASTICITY OF DEMAND

We have already explained what we mean by the term "elasticity." The elasticity of the demand curve indicates the response of the consuming public to changes in price.

Thus when an entrepreneur finds that a change in price results in a large change in sales,[2] he is selling in a market in which the demand is said to be elastic. When on the other hand a change in price results in a small change in sales, the demand is inelastic. Elasticity is unity, of course,[3] when the change in sales is inversely proportionate to the change in price, and total outlay remains constant.

The causes of differing elasticities of demand are to be found in the varying intensities of consumers' needs for different commodities and in the possibilities of satisfying a need by different commodities. Thus, if there are no possible substitutes, the demand for necessities of life will be inelastic, because people have to have them to keep alive and if the price of such a good goes up consumers will sacrifice less essential articles of consumption. Similarly the demand for habit-forming goods such as tobacco is inelastic. In spite of the sharp increase in the price of cigarettes in Canada since the war the manufacturers announce there has been no diminution of total tobacco sales. By contrary argument comforts generally have an elastic demand, sales responding quickly to price fluctuations.

These general conclusions must be modified when we consider the effect of substitution. When two or more commodities are sufficiently similar to satisfy the same need, substitution of one for another may occur. Thus candles, oil lamps, and electric light may be regarded as substitutes. As long as electricity is the cheapest as well as the best form of illumination no substitution would occur, but if electricity were increased in price some consumers would use paraffin lamps. If habit and convenience give a strong preference

[2]The reader will notice here that we have dropped the usual practice of speaking of price as the dependent and quantity as the independent variable, and have actually reversed the process. This is because from the entrepreneur's point of view, as he studies the market, this is the way it appears to him, and for the moment we are adopting his point of view. From the point of view of the economist solving the problem of price determination, price must, of course, be treated as the dependent variable. Hence our usual custom of so regarding it. The reader will find our treatment here quite consistent with our mathematical treatment in the Appendix to chapter IX, where the elasticity of falling curves was treated as being always negative.

[3]See Geometric Appendix, Book Three, chap. IX, p. 99.

to one commodity, as in the case of electricity, the price of this commodity will have to rise sharply before there will be any great substitution.   Thus the elasticity of substitution of oil lamps for electric bulbs, that is the rate of change in quantities substituted to rate of change in price, is very low.   The elasticity of substitution of cigarette tobacco for cigarettes is, however, high, so that Canadian tobacco manufacturers have kept up their total sales since the war by increasing sales of tobacco to offset the decline in cigarette sales. When the elasticity of substitution for a necessity is low, its demand curve will be inelastic.   When, however, other goods are readily substituted for it in consumers' favour, the demand will be elastic, necessity or no.

Very expensive luxuries may have a fairly inelastic demand. They are bought by the very rich who have such large incomes that changes in price are immaterial to them.   Indeed some commodities sold to the very rich will actually have a rising demand curve.   They will become more desired as they rise in price, because as they become more expensive they become indicative, in their possession, of great wealth.   Such goods we call briefly "snob goods" and their value is "snob value."

Many goods have, naturally, varying elasticities.   At very high prices they are luxuries, enjoyed by the very rich, with inelastic demand.   As price is reduced, however, they become objects of expenditure by the middle classes and their demands become elastic. Finally, the fall in price may go so low that demand becomes relatively inelastic again.

As we shall see later, entrepreneurs may take advantage of varying elasticity to split the market and to market the same commodity under different labels at discriminating prices.   This is a frequent practice where competition is imperfect.[4]

Varying elasticities may also give rise to the interesting problem of multiple points of equilibrium, which we shall later examine.[5]

Section 4: Interdependence

In Book Two we made the observation that all prices were interdependent, and were simultaneously determined.   We represented this important fact by setting out our price equations in the form of mutually dependent, simultaneous equations.

We have just now observed this fact again.   A change in the price of a necessity will, we said, result in consumers buying less of

[4]See Price Discrimination, Book Three, chap. XIII, section 3.
[5]See Multiple Points of Equilibrium, Book Three, chap. XIII, section 2.

comforts.   Again we saw that changes in the price of certain goods will result in the purchase of substitutes.   Hence any demand schedule is dependent on other demand schedules.   When, therefore, we talk in terms of individual commodities, and make our price analysis in this discrete fashion we slightly misrepresent the problem.   The more accurate treatment is that of the simultaneous equations in the simple case discussed in Book Two.   In this book, however, we are forced to discuss price determination in terms of single commodities.   No harm will be done as long as we remember that every demand curve is a picture not only of consumers' marginal utilities for the commodity in question, but of their choices in relation to all other commodities.   Thus when we come to say: "This is the stable equilibrium price," we are always adding: "Provided that all other prices are stable."   A stable equilibrium price structure is determined where all single prices are stable and in equilibrium with regard to their own costs and marginal demand prices, but also with regard to one another in such fashion that at the stable position no price may exist which would encourage any consumer to make substitution.

SECTION 5: MARGINAL AND AVERAGE REVENUE

Our treatment of demand has so far been to analyse it from the standpoint of the buyer.   We have seen that a demand schedule is made up of the various prices consumers are willing to pay for various quantities of satisfactions.   From the point of view of the entrepreneur a demand schedule is a statement of the average revenue he can expect for various outputs.   If the demand price is $10 for 1,000 units, $12 for 800 units, and $15 for 600 units, it is clear that the average revenue to the entrepreneur for each of these various outputs will correspond to the marginal demand price for that output.   Thus the demand curve is, to the entrepreneur, the average revenue curve.

In a competitive industry, whatever may be the shape of the demand curve for the output of the industry as a whole, the average revenue curve for each firm in the industry will be a straight line parallel to the x-axis.   This is because any change in output on the part of a single firm will effect no appreciable change in industrial output.   Consequently there will be no change in price.   We can put this another way and say that if the entrepreneur tries to raise his price above the marginal demand price for the industrial output as a whole, he will lose all his sales.   He will not try to lower price except under exceptional circumstances to be considered later, because to do so would be to reduce his net profits.

In a monopolistic industry the firm's average revenue curve corresponds with the industrial demand curve. This average revenue curve has a corresponding marginal revenue curve. Marginal revenue may be defined as the ratio of the increment in total revenue to the increase in output, so that marginal revenue bears to average revenue the same relation as marginal cost to average cost. All that has been said in Chapter IX about average and marginal curves applies alike to revenue and cost curves.

Thus in our illustration of average revenue, corresponding marginal revenues would run as follows:

TABLE XI

Output	Average Revenue or Price	Total Revenue	Marginal Revenue
600..................	$15	9,000	..
800..................	$12	9,600	$3
1,000..................	$10	10,000	$2

Column IV is derived by dividing the total increment in revenue by the increment in output, thus $\frac{\$600}{200} = \$3$ and $\frac{\$400}{200} = \$2$.

When there is no change in price with changes in output, as in the case of a firm in a competitive industry, marginal revenue is obviously equal to average revenue. Consequently the marginal revenue curve for such a firm corresponds to the average revenue curve, a straight line parallel to the x-axis, the intersection on the y-axis determined by the effective demand price.

CHAPTER XII

THE DETERMINATION OF PRICE

SECTION 1: DEFINITIONS

W E shall discuss the determination of price first in the short term, then in the long term under three assumptions, (*a*) of perfect competition, (*b*) of monopoly, (*c*) of imperfect or monopolistic competition.

When we speak of short and long term in economics we have in mind periods of "functional" rather than of "clock" time.

Functional time is time measured not in minutes, hours, and days, but in terms of functional units, e.g. each unit task in the processing of leather until it becomes a pair of shoes.

The short term, so measured, is a term too short to permit of change in the quantities of a good supplied; that is to say, it is a period of time shorter than the period of production. Thus, in agriculture, the short term is a period less than the time it takes for the crop to be sown, grown, and harvested.

The long term period is one longer than the process of production.

By monopoly we shall mean the condition when there is only one firm in the industry, so that the firm's average revenue curve corresponds with the industrial demand curve, and its average cost curve with the industrial supply curve.

By perfect competition we shall mean the condition that obtains when the average revenue and marginal revenue curves of the competing firms correspond and form a straight line parallel to the *x*-axis.

By imperfect or monopolistic competition[1] we shall mean the condition that obtains when two or more large firms compete in an industry, but where the firms are so large that changes in the output

---

[1]There is not complete agreement among economists in the use of these terms. Some prefer to distinguish between imperfections in a competitive market and monopolistic competition or oligopoly. The great area between theoretically pure competition and theoretically complete monopoly is divided into two parts: (1) where the conditions are predominantly competitive but where the conditions of competition are not perfect, and (2) where there are a few large firms whose behaviour is essentially monopolistic. It is this second area which is described as monopolistic competition or oligopoly. In the sections that follow we have avoided the additional complications of this distinction and have used the terms "imperfect competition," "monopolistic competition," and "oligopoly" as synonyms, the conditions which they describe being defined as those under which the revenue curves of the firms are negatively sloped.

of a single firm affect the marginal demand price, so that the marginal and average revenue curves of the firms are not parallels to the x-axis.

The level of abstraction will remain as before. We shall be dealing with the real world, but we shall be deducing the conditions of static equilibrium and thus we presume all adjustments to take place instantaneously without friction, disturbance or time lag.

SECTION 2: SHORT-TERM PRICING

Our problem is to state what determines the price at which a commodity will be sold on the market.

In the short term the amounts put on the market cannot be varied. Once the amount appears, therefore, its price is determined by the marginal demand price for that amount.

If we take as an example a typical product for short term pricing, strawberries, we shall see that, once the crop is planted, the quantity of berries to be put on the market is determined for that growing season. Now, when the berries come on the market in quantities which for that season cannot be varied, they must be sold at the marginal demand price of that quantity. In the case of strawberries, we observe the early berries appearing in small quantities on the so-called "pre-season" market commanding, because of their paucity, a very high marginal demand price. As the domestic crop comes on the market in increasing quantities, the price falls. Its fall is not limited by cost of production or by anything which the producer can do—it is determined entirely by the marginal demand prices for the various quantities which appear on the market, the prices falling as the quantities on the market increase.

The only limit on the power of the marginal demand price to determine the actual market price in the short term is the possibility of a carry-over. Short-term pricing is not the rule with manufactured goods because they appear on the market in a regulated flow and the quantities appearing on the market can readily and quickly be changed, but in most agricultural produce there is a considerable element of short-term pricing; it takes a season for the crop to grow and, once it is planted, it is difficult to control the quantity put on the market. Now, if the agricultural product is a perishable one, like strawberries, so that it cannot be carried over to a later market or held off the market in any quantity, the conditions of pricing will, as we have said, be entirely governed by the demand. If, however, the crop is like wheat—not perishable—it can be carried over to another season; that is to say, to another market. It will be so carried over if the costs of storage, insurance, and other carry-over costs are considered to be more than compensated by the anticipated price on the future market. A guide to the anticipated price is furnished by the future exchange market and this tends to maintain a fair degree of stability and continuity in the prices of agricultural goods which permit of carry-over.

So important has this stabilization of the prices of basic agricultural products become that the natural adjustments of the market, slow to operate and working hardships on individuals as they do operate, have been supplemented by attempts of governments to stabilize prices from season to season. Government agencies in various countries have undertaken to market base products, and these agencies, frequently with the aid of subsidies from public funds, have been able to reserve large quantities of "bumper crops" when individual farmers could not have afforded the carryover costs. This policy has not infrequently been co-ordinated with a policy of subsidizing crop reductions or changes to new types of product when surpluses have accrued over a series of years. The Office du Blé under the Popular Front government of Leon Blum attempted to follow the first policy. Acreage restriction and greater variety of crops have been the principal aims of the A.A.A. in the United States. In Canada the government has undertaken to store a reserved supply of wheat. The Canadian wheat crops of 1939 and 1940 could not be marketed because of the war, and a large carryover, amounting in 1941 to an accumulated total of 585,000,000 bushels, was held in granaries and elevators at public expense. This reserved supply was maintained at an average price of 70 cents a bushel which was advanced by the Canadian government which accepted the responsibility of marketing the wheat. In this case the price of the reserved supply probably bore no particular relation to any anticipated future price because it would be impossible to entertain any notion of world wheat prices after the war: it was probably arrived at after a certain amount of political bargaining on the basis of the pre-war price and represents the minimum, or a little less than the minimum necessary to keep the western wheat farmer from destitution. But it is interesting to notice how even a war-time government responds to this situation by an imitation of the natural market response. The declared wheat policy of the government in the spring of 1941 is to subsidize acreage restriction among grain-growers, encouraging the farmers to reduce their crops of grain and to change to other agricultural products.

Section 3: Long-Term Pricing—Perfect Competition

This possibility of carrying over to offset the demand domination in the short-term market indicates to us the possibility of varying the amounts supplied. In short-term pricing we had assumed the amounts supplied to be given and the problem of determination of price was solved as soon as we knew the functional demand price of the given quantity. But in long-term pricing the quantities supplied and the costs of supplying them are not given but are themselves variable. It is to this problem of how price is determined in the long-run period to which we must now give our attention.

It is clear, as Marshall says, that if short-term pricing results in losses or additional profits to the entrepreneur, he will, in the next period, adjust the amount he supplies. If his adjustment is perfectly made, the price will be determined according to the laws of long-term price determination, and the long-period trend is to bring the market price close to this long-term equilibrium. To the extent that entrepreneurs fail in exact anticipation of the demand, short-term pricing prevails, and this accounts for short-term variations about the long-term equilibrium.

The hypothesis which we carry forward from Book Two is that price will be in equilibrium at the point where marginal cost and marginal utility are equal. We have now seen that this concept of marginal utility must be interpreted as effective demand price in the sphere of objective pricing. Thus our proposition implies that price will be stable for the amount and at the point where effective demand price and marginal cost are equal. Each firm behaves so as to maximize its profits. The total net profits of any firm will be at maximum when the firm's marginal revenue equals its marginal cost, so each firm will produce to that point.

But in a perfectly competitive industry the marginal revenue curve of the firm is the same as its average revenue curve, a straight line parallel to the x-axis. Thus each firm produces to the point where its marginal cost curve cuts the average revenue curve. For the least efficient firm in the industry this will be at the point of lowest average costs. All intra-marginal firms will be earning excess profits or rents. We have, however, to ask, what determines, not each firm's output, but the total industrial output, and what determines the height from the x-axis at which the firms' average revenue curves intersect the y-axis.

These questions can be answered more easily if we state them in another form. The average revenue or price for each firm will be the same (i.e., the height from the x-axis of the average revenue parallels will be the same for each firm), and this is because each competitive firm must sell at the same price. This price will be the marginal demand price for the total industrial output. Consequently if we know the total industrial output, we shall know what determines the average price or average revenue for each firm. If the total industrial supply amounts to OM, in Fig. 18, such that the industrial supply price is less than the marginal demand price for the industrial output, the marginal firm in the industry is making a profit above costs, i.e. is not selling at the point of lowest average costs. Consequently new capital and enterprise will be attracted to this industry.[2] The result is either that each firm will find that the marginal demand price exceeds the marginal cost of its output, and consequently will expand output, or a new firm may be attracted to the industry.

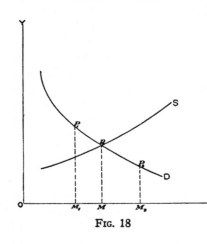

FIG. 18

If the effect of the entrance of the new firm[3] is to increase industrial output to M_2, the effective demand price of which, P_2, is less than the supply price for that amount, the marginal firm is failing to cover its average cost and is taking a loss. Or it may mean that intra-marginal firms have expanded output so that the new effective demand price (thus marginal revenue) is less than marginal cost. Consequently all firms will curtail output, the least efficient firm may have to drop out, until demand price covers marginal costs.

Equilibrium will be achieved at the output OM, the point where the effective demand price P, just covers the average and marginal costs of the marginal firm (i.e., the point of lowest average costs for

[2]This argument rests on the assumption, which must be rendered explicit, that in the economy rewards are equalized in all industries and that the society will employ its productive agents to their fullest capacity and in their most remunerative employments. Thus in any industry or firm the costs incurred equal the full rewards which the agents, including enterprise, could earn anywhere else, and if any industry is able to offer a surplus over and above those costs it attracts enterprise and capital from less remunerative industries.

[3]This new firm need not become the least efficient. It may be better organized and may well force one of the older firms to the margin.

this firm). At that point the marginal firm is content to produce, neither expanding nor curtailing output. The intra-marginal firms accept that effective demand price and produce in such quantities as to equate it with their marginal unit costs. Thus, given the determination of industrial output and effective demand price, the output of each firm is simultaneously determined for that price, and for each firm the rule is that marginal demand price must be equated with marginal cost.

In actual practice the adjustments which we have been treating as instantaneous and frictionless occur over a period of time and there are various "frictions" which militate against perfect adjustment. Firms do not readily go out of business. If they can possibly hang on during a bad period they will do so, and the least efficient firms will strive to improve their efficiency and they will consume reserves of capital to cover their losses during "bad times."[4] This may well enable a particular firm to survive for a while or even permanently, either at the expense of some other firm which is forced to the margin, and beyond, in its place, or by reason of an improvement in the demand for the product. If in the short run individual firms take losses the chances are more in favour of a general all-round restriction in output than of the decease of a firm. Adjustments to demand in what might be called the "short-long" period will be of this sort. But in the long run the inexorable pressure tells against the less-efficient (usually the smaller) firms. In Canada from 1871 to 1931 the number of firms engaged in manufacture decreased from 41,259 to 23,083, although the capital invested in manufacture increased during the same period from $77,964,000 to $3,705,702,000 and the gross value of the product from $221,618,000 to $2,555,-126,000. This indicates both the gradual disappearance of the smaller less-efficient firms and the growth of a considerable degree of imperfect competition.[5] The suggestion of these figures is that in the long run there has been a general tendency towards the larger firm unit.

[4]"Bad times" usually come not from a temporary over-investment in a particular industry, but from a general depression of a "dynamic" nature. But the principle of the firm "hanging on" is the same.

[5]This process was particularly marked in the Maritime Provinces. In 1890 the number of firms in Nova Scotia was 10,495; in 1937 it was 1,135 though capital invested had increased from $20 million to $95 million and the gross value of the product from $31 million to $84 million. The number of employees engaged in industry had, however, declined from 35,000 to 18,000.

Section 4: Monopoly

When a single firm contributes the entire industrial output its average cost curve constitutes the supply curve of the industry and its average revenue curve constitutes the demand curve to the industry.

Now in the Crusoe economy, when we said that the marginal utility of the commodity was equal to the marginal cost, our statement was true in two different ways. The marginal utility to the purchaser was equal to marginal cost; the marginal utility of the value received in exchange was, to the seller, also equal to his marginal cost. Under competitive conditions this double equality is retained. The marginal demand price is equated to marginal cost for each firm, and, because the marginal and average revenue curves correspond, the marginal revenue (for Crusoe the marginal utility of the value received in exchange) was for each firm equated to its marginal cost. The social implications of this are made clear in Chapter XIV.

Under monopoly the case is different. The monopolist, freed from the competitive behaviour of other firms, is able to consider his own best interests and maximum profit not only by varying his costs with variations in output but, because his supply is the only supply on the market, by varying prices or average revenue with variations in output. His position is such that he can control output so that his marginal revenue coincides with his marginal costs, and he can sell at the price (average revenue) which will be paid for that output. In this case the average revenue curve will always lie above the marginal revenue curve (the marginal curve is marginal to a falling average curve); consequently the price the consumers pay will always be in excess of the marginal cost. In Fig. 19 AC is the average cost curve of the firm (the supply curve of the industry) and MC is the corresponding marginal cost curve, AR is the average revenue curve of the firm (the demand curve to the industry) and MR the corresponding marginal curve.

As long as MR exceeds MC the firm is adding to its total net profits, because each

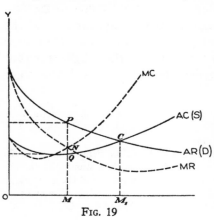

Fig. 19

increase in output results in a larger increment of revenue than the increment in cost. When MC exceeds MR the increase in output results in a larger increase in cost than in revenue. Consequently the point of maximum profit is where $MC = MR$ or where the two curves intersect. On the graph, Fig. 19, the output corresponding to this point is the amount OM.

We may notice that the firm does not sell at the highest possible price, as is sometimes carelessly assumed. Such a price would be for a minimum output and though profits per unit might be high, they would not total very much. Nor does the firm sell at the point of lowest unit costs for the same reason. Again, we should avoid the mistake of supposing the firm to take a loss beyond the output OM. As long as price exceeds average cost per unit the firm is making a profit, but its total profits will for no output be as great as for the output OM.

The price for the output OM will be determined by extending the perpendicular NM to cut the average revenue curve at P for, of course, the average revenue curve shows the price per unit consumers are willing to pay for different amounts. Since MQ is the average cost per unit of making the good, and MP is the price per unit obtained from its sale, PQ is the profit per unit, and the rectangle $ABPQ$ is the total profit. From our definition of the marginal curves it follows that this rectangle is the largest that can be formed lying between the two curves and erected on the intercepted section of a perpendicular to the x-axis.

Since we suppose that the monopolist will want to maximize his total profits we conclude that under monopoly, price will be stable for the amount determined by the intersection of the marginal cost and revenue curves and there will be no tendency to increase or decrease this amount. The price at which this amount will be sold will be the corresponding marginal demand price which will be on the average revenue curve and will always exceed marginal cost.

In Fig. 19 for the purposes of comparison we have indicated the corresponding competitive price and output for this industry. The supply and demand curves intersect at C for the amount OM_1 indicating that the amount produced under competition would exceed that produced under monopoly and the price would have been less. But the reader should draw no conclusions from this illustration because it is true only for curves of the shape shown here and depends on the unlikely assumption that the supply curve of the monopolist firm would exactly coincide with the supply curve built up from the average costs of a group of competing firms. Comparison of monopolistic and competitive output will be attempted in a later chapter.

SECTION 5: MONOPOLISTIC OR IMPERFECT COMPETITION

Both perfect competition and perfect monopoly are special cases of theoretic interest but of little more than academic and historical importance.   Some agricultural prices are determined under conditions approaching those of perfect competition, but they are subject to such slow adjustment that it is doubtful if any but a short-term analysis is of much practical importance in connection with them.

Complete monopoly is unusual outside the public utilities,[6] and these are so completely regulated today that, wherever monopoly price might be determined if the monopolist were free to set his own price, price is generally so regulated by government as to be very much lower than the unregulated monopoly price.

By far the most usual condition in the unregulated markets of private capitalist states is that which we have defined as imperfect or monopolistic competition.   Consequently the pure theory of price determination in the imperfectly competitive market will be of the most practical importance in the understanding of the everyday world.   The reader will find, however, that the study of pricing under perfect competition and under monopoly is logically necessary to an understanding of this section.

Before picking up the thread of our argument we must undertake a short digression on "decreasing costs," in order to provide ourselves with data we have not previously needed but now require. We must distinguish between short- and long-run decreasing costs.

Short-run decreasing costs exist when increases in output are accompanied by falling average unit costs, i.e. marginal cost is falling.   This condition we have pictured as occurring for a short period in all firms, but it is not usual after the firm has developed an economic output.   As the plant is used towards capacity, unit costs, as a general rule, rise.   There are, however, certain industries, notably transportation, in which unit costs continue to fall.[7]   This is true of

---

[6]Professor Reynolds, in his book, *The Control of Competition in Canada* (Cambridge, Mass., 1940), lists a number of Canadian monopolies which include aluminium, cement, lead and nickel, explosives, heavy electrical equipment, and others, but in many cases these are "near monopolies" rather than perfect monopolies.   Cf. *ibid.*, pp. 8-10.

[7]Even here they cannot continue to fall indefinitely.   Complete accuracy of statement would require us to distinguish between those industries (the majority) in which increasing costs appear well before the intersection of the marginal cost and marginal revenue curves, and those in which the equilibrium point is reached

industries in which fixed costs are high relative to variable costs. Under such conditions it is said that the firm operates under conditions of "decreasing costs."

With long-run decreasing costs we are not here interested. They apply to industries as a whole and exist as a result of technical developments, rationalization, improvements in fixed plant, etc., and they result in a new set of cost curves for each firm in the industry. Each firm's curves, at any given time, might be increasing, but over a period of time the point of lowest unit cost will be falling.

We contrast short- and long-run decreasing costs in Fig. 20, where Chart I illustrates short-run decreasing costs for a firm, and where Chart II illustrates long-run decreasing costs for a firm over a period of time, with short-run increasing costs existing at any moment during the period.

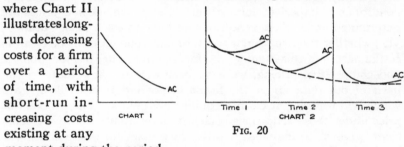

CHART I

Time 1   Time 2   Time 3
CHART 2

Fig. 20

Throughout this section we shall use the phrase "decreasing costs" to refer to short-run decreasing costs.

When decreasing costs exist in a monopolistic industry, no special problem is created. The firm will still sell at the point of maximum profit. The only complexity arises in the case of multiple points of equilibrium, which is not, however, an exception to the general rule.[8]

But when decreasing costs exist in a competitive industry, a special problem is created, for under such conditions price is indeterminate and competition unstable. As long as a firm's costs are decreasing it will try to expand its output, sell at a lower price, and take trade from its competitors. But if its competitors have decreasing costs as well, they will respond by doing the same thing. Each firm will sell below cost in order to attract trade, in the hope that its additional sales will enable it to expand output and thus decrease its costs to the point where they are reduced to the lowered level of price. But such behaviour on the part of all firms will con-

before the appearance of increasing costs. Thus in the first case all adjustments to equilibrium occur under conditions of increasing costs, and in the second case the equilibrium adjustment occurs under conditions of decreasing costs.

[8]See Multiple Equilibrium, chap. XIII, section 2.

tinually push price down faster than the firms can reduce their costs. This price war can continue until the weaker firms are bankrupt and a monopoly or partial monopoly attained, or until a price agreement is reached that enables the firms to behave monopolistically, or until increasing costs set in and stable competitive price is achieved.[9]

This cut-throat competition was characteristic of the railways in early days and resulted in amalgamations, rate agreements, and rate regulation by the governments. It has also been the cause of numerous mergers and amalgamations in other industries and tends to create monopoly and imperfect competition.

We may now return to the problem of price determination under conditions of imperfect competition. Before we ask *how* prices are determined under these conditions we have to ask a prior question, viz., whether the situation is a determinate one. Let us be clear as to the nature of this inquiry. So far, in our studies of monopolistic and competitive pricing, we have been able to show that, on the basis of our data about the firm's behaviour, forces will operate which will fix price at certain equilibrium points. The problem of price under those conditions is clearly determinate; there are sufficient "givens" to enable us to solve the problem of where prices will be fixed. But when we approach our present problem of pricing under conditions of monopolistic competition, we have to inquire very carefully if our data are sufficient to enable us to solve the problem of where price will be fixed.

We may take as our example the classic case of duopoly. Duopoly is the special oligopolist situation which exists when only two firms share the market. Each firm will try to maximize its net profits. When there is only one firm in the market this maximization is immediately possible. When there are two firms it is only possible if each firm proceeds on the assumption that any change in the quantities he offers on the market or of the price at which he will sell will have no effect on his rival. If the two firms operate on this assumption about each other's behaviour each will behave as though it were a monopoly in a section of the market. Since there can be only one price in the market, the two firms will continuously readjust their outputs until they have divided the market in the proportion determined by the proportion of their outputs at the optimum point. This case, where the situation is determinate, is that examined by

[9]Competitive instability under decreasing costs was first demonstrated by A. Cournot in his *Recherches sur les principes mathématiques de la théorie des richesses* in 1838; but his demonstration seems to have been largely neglected until recently.

Cournot in his famous *Recherches sur les principes mathématiques de la théorie des richesses.*[10]

The situation is also determinate when each firm acts on the assumption that there is a certain total output at which both firms will maximize their satisfactions and that, if firm one restricts its output to its share of that total, its rival will do likewise. In this case there is an assumption which amounts to an assumption of a tacit understanding between the firms, and, as we shall shortly show, this case is clearly determinate.

But we have to ask if, in fact, the firms will make such assumptions about each other's behaviour. Professor Pigou deals with this question in conclusive language. He says:[11]

Consider first Cournot's assumption. The settlement to which it points is the optimum settlement for each Jones [firm], only provided that, if he himself departs from it, the other will not do so. But in fact the other will do so; and everybody knows that perfectly well. We cannot suppose that either will deliberately ignore this knowledge. In other terms, since each Jones [firm] knows that the other's output is a function of the price, he cannot without inconsistency believe *both* that, by varying his output, he will cause the price to vary—which is the condition of his acting monopolistically at all—*and* that, by varying his output, he will *not* cause his opponent's output to vary. Cournot's assumption thus not only need not represent the facts: its character is such that—among rational beings—it *cannot* do so. The alternative assumption is more plausible. That it is theoretically possible for each Jones [firm] to reason and act in the way it requires, nobody would deny. The question is whether in fact they do so act. Experience in the analogous field of a few competing *firms*—not individuals—strongly suggests that they do not. Even when kartel agreements have been entered into, they frequently break down because some of the members try to steal one another's markets. When there is no formal, or at all events informal agreement, conduct of the type which this assumption postulates has probably *never* been known.

Unless these, or similar, assumptions are made, however, the situation under duopoly (and oligopoly) is indeterminate. When two or more large firms share the market, each firm will know that any change in its output will effect the price and thus cause changes in its rival's output. We may distinguish four possibilities. Price will be unstable if one firm, slightly or appreciably stronger than the other, decides to drive it out of the market and cuts prices, even to

[10]The student will find Cournot's classic statement summarized and explained in clear, non-mathematical language in Professor E. Chamberlin's excellent study, *The Theory of Monopolistic Competition* (Cambridge, Mass., 1936), chap. III, pp. 32-7.

[11]A. C. Pigou, *Economics of Stationary States* (London, 1935), p. 94.

9

the point of selling at a loss, until it is able to behave monopolistically. Price may also be unstable if the two firms jockey for position, each effecting small changes in output and price in an effort to improve its position vis-à-vis its rival. Price may be stable if there are strong forces of public opinion, custom, or law which restrain the firms. It has been frequently pointed out that even monopolists hesitate to arouse public disapproval by tinkering with accepted and customary prices. Finally, stable prices will result from agreements between the oligopolist firms.

A study of actual cases shows that agreements are rapidly reached. A period of unstable price and keen competition of the "cut-throat" variety is followed by one of stability with prices tacitly or explicitly established. The rapidity and ease with which the firms will come to an "understanding" will depend upon the degree of equality of size and efficiency between them. If they are, or believe themselves to be nearly equal in strength and size, as was the case of the American rubber companies, and if there has been an industrial tradition of bitter rivalry, the period of unstable competition will continue either until increasing costs have set in or until the weaker firms have been destroyed. But if there is great inequality the dominant firm or firms readily impose their will and "understandings" are rapidly achieved. The conditions under which agreements are reached may be distinguished as in the following paragraphs.

A—*Where a kartel or price agreement is made by the firms in the industry.* In this case one of two things may happen. If the agreement is an international one each firm may behave monopolistically in its own national market with tariff duties graduated so as to offset differences in the various domestic market prices. In this case price is determined in each national market according to the laws of monopoly price. During the inter-bella period the armaments manufacturers appear to have had an agreement of this sort. The British, American, and German chemical industries seem to have had a similar agreement.

If the market cannot conveniently be shared according to regions or countries the most important firm or firms may set the ruling price which will be a monopoly price for their output. Each of the other firms then accepts the monopoly price of the leader and regards it as a straight-line revenue curve and produces to the point of maximum profit. In such a case there might be a marginal firm just able to produce at the point of lowest unit costs. In this case pricing corresponds in part to pricing under conditions of perfect competition, except that the straight-line average revenue curve is set by agreement, not by the natural forces of competition. Thus firm A, the most powerful firm, determines its price as illustrated in Fig. 27, taking as its marginal revenue curve that which it has actually found to exist for its share of the market. This differs from the marginal revenue curve of a complete monopoly in that it is not marginal to the demand curve for the industrial output as a whole. In Fig. 21, AC and MC are the firm's costs, and AR and MR its average and marginal revenues for its output on the market. Because of competitors these curves are more elastic than those of the same firm behaving as a complete monopoly.

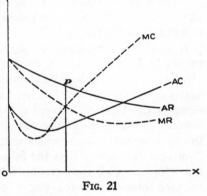

Fig. 21

The price, P, having been established, becomes the price for the entire industry. Each firm in the industry then behaves as in perfect competition producing to the point where the marginal cost curve cuts the price curve (straight line marginal revenue curve) as in Fig. 22. For the industry as a whole the situation is illustrated

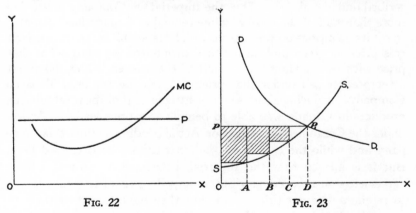

Fig. 22   Fig. 23

in Fig. 23, where the various firms, including a marginal firm, are represented as each producing a share of the total output. In Fig. 23 the line SS_1 represents the average cost of each firm for its output, the curve DD_1 the industrial demand curve, and the line PP_1 the price curve. The rectangles suspended from PP_1 and shaded represent the difference between average cost and price and thus the net profits of the firms A, B, and C. Firm D makes no profits above costs of production, which include, of course, interest on capital invested and entrepreneur's reward.

Evidence of actual price agreement is hard to obtain and the theoretic evidence of stable prices is far from conclusive as it might equally indicate the stability of agreement or the stability of competition. An agreement among the manufacturers of farm implements in Canada though denied by them, was suspected by the House of Commons Special Committee on Farm Implement Prices,[12] and a similar agreement has been suspected among the meat packing firms in the United States,[13] many of whom have Canadian subsidiaries. There is a definite steel kartel in the United States and an informal or tacit agreement among the steel companies in Canada. Professor Reynolds[14] lists the following Canadian industries as having a formal price agreement: fertilizers, leather, rubber footwear, tobacco products, most paper products except newsprint, most plumbing and heating equipment, many hardware products.

B—*Price Leadership.* Price leadership exists whenever one firm in an industry is able to dominate it, set its price, and have it accepted by the lesser competitors. In this case the conditions of price agreement are reproduced, except that the agreement is tacit rather than explicit. The theory of price determination is as described under A above. Thus the Imperial Oil Company producing more than half of the total gasoline refined in Canada has been able to set its own price on the product. The lesser oil companies accept this price as given and adjust their own output so as to sell at that price with the maximum of benefit to themselves. They have not attempted to sell under that price. Again the Imperial Tobacco Company, producing about seventy-five per cent of the total tobacco products in Canada was able to behave as a price leader. Action under the Combines Investigation Act is pending against this Company and while the case is *sub judice* it cannot be discussed here. But it is alleged that the Imperial Tobacco Company did force agreements on tobacco distributors impelling them to refuse to sell to retailers who cut prices, and that they have forced retailers to cease the distribution of the products of a rival company that at-

[12]*Report of the Special Committee on Farm Implement Prices* (House of Commons, 1937), p. 1264; quoted by L. G. Reynolds, *The Control of Competition in Canada* (Cambridge, Mass., 1940).

[13]A. R. Burns, *The Decline of Competition* (New York, 1936).

[14]Reynolds, *The Control of Competition*, p. 8.

tempted to sell at a lower price. Whether or not this is established, it serves to illustrate some of the methods which may be used by dominant firms to impose their price leadership on such of the weaker brethren as might hesitate or show reluctance in surrendering their independence.

C—*Commodity Differentiation.* Commodity differentiation is the practice of marking off the output of a particular firm as unique and different from its competitors' output. This practice is carried on by extensive advertising and expert psychological manipulation of the public mind. Thus fairly homogeneous, similar products, such as cigarettes, are broken up into distinct groups. Lucky Strikes are "toasted," Camels are made of "costlier tobaccos," Chesterfields "satisfy," and Old Gold are "double mellow," and so forth. Perfumers, tobacco manufacturers, soap-makers, and many others are at present engaged in this game of making the public believe that their product is unique, differentiated from its fellows. This advertising is not primarily directed towards increasing sales, though that is an incidental effect. It is primarily directed towards establishing a public for a firm's product as distinct from a demand for the industrial product. Thus there are "Camel smokers," "Old Gold smokers," etc., and not tobacco smokers. By creating this special demand for its product each firm becomes an industry to itself. Instead of competing in the cigarette industry the manufacturers of Camels have a monopoly of the "Camels market." Thus where commodity differentiation exists, each firm can behave monopolistically with respect to its own demand.[15]

The competition that exists is not price competition, but competition to enlarge the sphere of the firm's monopoly. The phenomenon of modern advertising is the result of this type of competition. It is most successful in markets where there is a highly gullible and suggestible public.

To the extent that commodity differentiation is not complete, there will be a residue of consumers who will buy any firm's output irrespective of the firm's brand name, and these consumers will limit the monopolistic behaviour of the firms. Theoretically these can be allowed for by admitting the firms' revenue curves to be highly elastic.

[15]The demand is a highly elastic one, however, for commodity differentiation can never rule out substitution. This high elasticity of the demand curve means that changes in output will not produce large changes in the rate of marginal revenue, and this means there will not be the same limitation of output that there would be under pure industrial monopoly.

Thus where commodity differentiation exists price tends to be monopolistically determined. Where differentiated commodities sell at the same price, a price agreement or price leadership may also be suspected.

Consequently the general trend under imperfect competition is for a monopoly or quasi-monopoly price to obtain.

It is interesting at this point to consider the position of the firm under imperfect competition which earns no surplus profits. It is at least theoretically possible that, with differentiated products, small firms can continue to exist within an imperfectly competitive industry selling at prices which depart slightly from the price of the dominant firms. This can only be when the product has been differentiated so that in the minds of the public, or a section of it, the variations in price represent differences in the quality or appearance of the commodity. These firms will have sloping demand curves, because, having differentiated their product, they find that alterations in their selling price will affect the quantity of their sales. The sloping revenue curves will be more or less elastic according to the degree of differentiation; the greater the differentiation, the less the elasticity of the revenue curve.

The limiting case for such firms is that of the firm which makes no surplus profits. This case is illustrated in Fig. 24. Here it will be seen the revenue curve is a tangent to the average cost curve. There is only one output at which this firm can sell. For any other output, greater or smaller, it would have to sell at a loss.

There is a temptation to think of this limiting case as exactly similar to that of the least efficient firm under perfect competition.

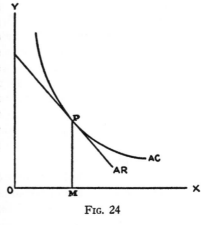

FIG. 24

But there are important differences. Under perfect competition there is complete freedom of entry to the industry. In actual fact, where there is perfect competition, there will be firms at the no-profit point. Moreover, the superior firms will also be earning no profits once their rents are regarded as costs. That is to say, if rents are added to costs, included in them, all firms under perfect competition will be producing at the no-profit point.

Under imperfect competition this is not so. The no-profit firm exists by permission of the dominant firms. There is only the one point at which it can continue in production, and only by coincidence will that point be at the ruling price of the dominant firm. If the dominant firm wishes, it could readily lower its price to the point where it would overcome what differentiation the smaller firms had established and force them from the business. It is only restrained from doing so by the consideration that the trouble and loss that would be incurred is not balanced by the gain. Yet it would and does do so, not infrequently, if the smaller firms become too numerous or attempt to expand and so cut into its privileged position. This is to say that there is not the same freedom of entry to an imperfectly competitive industry that there is to a perfectly competitive industry.

Again, as we shall argue later, there is a real distinction to be drawn between the surplus earnings which the superior firms obtain in a competitive industry from those earned by the dominant firms in an imperfectly competitive industry. In the first instance the extra earnings are rents or quasi-rents and can be claimed in entirety by the agents whose superiority has enabled the surpluses to be earned. In an imperfectly competitive industry the surpluses of the dominant firm, so far as they can be attributed to its special position in the market and the differentiation of its product, are properly monopolistic gains and are retained by the owners of the firm. Saks of Fifth Avenue undoubtedly earn surpluses over the marginal costs of their least efficient competitors, but these surpluses are paid out in the form of rent for the special site value of their land. This differs from the surpluses of Coates who control the imperfectly competitive cotton thread industry; these surpluses are monopoly gains and are retained by the owners of the firm.

From the social point of view there are differences too. In the one case, where perfect competition obtains, the greater the extension of the margin—the greater, that is, the total output—the greater will be the rents. In the other case the monopoly gains are maximized by stern restriction of output. Thus for various reasons it is important to distinguish between the position of the least efficient firm in a perfectly competitive industry and that of a no-profit firm under imperfect competition.

CHAPTER XIII

SOME FURTHER PROBLEMS IN PRICE DETERMINATION, JOINT COSTS, MULTIPLE EQUILIBRIUM, PRICE DISCRIMINATION

Section 1: Joint Costs

IN this chapter we shall be concerned with some further problems of pricing, tying up loose ends, so to speak, and with some conclusions which will be of use to us in later chapters of this study.

Some commodities are produced jointly, mutton and wool, for example, or gasoline, paraffin, and vaseline. The final commodities emerge for consumption as a result of a single productive process. Under conditions of joint production it may be impossible to allocate to each of the joint products its own, specific, average unit cost. Of course, no by-product will be produced that cannot cover the particular expense of separating it and putting it on the market. But as long as it pays its by-product expense it may be marketed whether or not it pays a proportionate share of the joint costs.

Equilibrium for the joint products will be achieved when the amounts of the joint products are in such proportion that the sum of the marginal revenues from the sale of the joint products is equal to the sum of the marginal costs of joint production.

If there should be any change in the demand for any one of the joint products, a new equilibrium would be attained by variations in the output of all the joint products, so that a change in the demand price for one of them results in a change in the equilibrium prices of all.

A brief illustration may clarify this point. Diesel oil, gasoline, heavy fuel oil, and paraffin are all joint products. Let us suppose, as is not too unreal, that a quantity of crude oil, say a barrel, produces the joint products in the proportion of 10 units of diesel oil, 15 units of gasoline, and 12 units of paraffin, and about 45 units of heavy fuel oil with 18 per cent waste. Let us also suppose that this quality of crude oil costs $1.50 and that the total processing costs are $2.30, so that the total undistributed costs of turning a barrel of crude oil into 10 parts diesel, 15 parts gasoline, 12 parts paraffin, and 45 parts heavy fuel are $3.80. Let us further suppose that the marginal revenue of the diesel oil is 84 cents, of the gasoline is 10 cents, of the paraffin is 5 cents, and of the fuel oil, 2 cents. Then the revenue obtained by working the barrel of crude is:

from gasoline...................... $1.50
from diesel........................ .80
from heavy fuel.................... .90
from paraffin...................... .60

a total of $3.80. We have here a condition of equilibrium where the marginal cost of processing an additional unit of crude oil is just covered by the sum of the marginal revenues of the joint products in the proportion in which they will be yielded.

Now if, for some reason, the demand price for diesel oil changes so that the marginal revenue from diesel oil drops to 75 cents, then the production of diesel oil must be curtailed. But the production of diesel oil can be curtailed only by a diminution in the total quantity of crude oil worked or by costly changes in the technique of refining. Thus the amounts of gasoline and paraffin will also be diminished. Perhaps they will be restricted so that the marginal revenue from gasoline will be increased to $1.55 and that of paraffin to 65 cents, the marginal cost of processing remaining at $3.80. At this point a new joint equilibrium will be attained. Thus a change in the demand price for one of the joint products has forced a change in the equilibrium prices of the other two.

The interdependence of the price of joint products is an extreme case of the mutual interdependence of all prices. Sometimes, as in the case of joint products or in the case of substitution the interdependence is clearly marked and can be specifically attributed either to the link in costs (as in the case of joint products) or to the low elasticity of substitution (as in the case of cigarettes and cigarette tobaccos). But there is a sense in which all costs are linked and a sense in which all products are possible "substitutes." A shift in the costs of production of any commodity will disturb the equilibrium in that industry and affect the supply of the factors of production. If the industry is an important one and the shift is marked, the results will be apparent in the whole economy. Ordinarily the changes in one industry are too minute for their effects to be noticeable except in the case of joint products where the link in costs is very intimate, but we sometimes have examples which sharply illuminate the nature of the interdependence of the cost structure throughout the entire economy. The Dominion of Canada in 1940 increased its expenditures on defence from $34 million (peace-time level of 1938) to almost $850 million. There was a tremendous initial shift in the munitions, steel, and construction goods industries. Of course such a spending programme by government had other direct effects on the general economy and it is impossible to sort out and measure the indirect effects on peace-time industry of the increased employment in war industry. Yet many of the changes in the peace-time industries, the restriction in available labour supply, the increased cost of raw materials, the scarcity in certain regions of power, and the consequent readjustments in the cost and output structure throughout the entire peace-time economy can be attributed to the shift in employment and costs in the basic war industries. The effects here are reflected in *shifts in cost curves* not in changed elasticities. Similarly in the case of demand we notice that war-time spending on munitions reduces our available income for motor cars, gramophones, radios, and washing machines. These are hardly "substitute commodities" in any strict sense of the term, but the decision to spend income, whether the decision be individual or social, on one type of good, is a decision not to spend on other goods. Consequently a decision to buy aeroplanes is a decision to do without radios or new books. When an important shift in demand occurs for one commodity it is reflected in shifts in demand for every commodity. Thus *potential substitution*—the possibility of substitution—affects the *elasticity* of the demand for a commodity. Important *shifts* in any single commodity demand which is of real consequence are reflected in *real shifts* in the demand for other goods. In the latter case the new demand curves may show, as well, a modified elasticity.

Every equilibrium price is a part of a wider equilibrium price system. Each price is stable, not only when it satisfies the demand-supply equation, but also when all other prices are stable. We have represented this interdependence of prices in the price equations in Book Two. In that section we were dealing with an extremely simplified economy, but our conclusions are valid for any price system in equilibrium. In equilibrium the price of each commodity must be such that marginal cost for each firm is equal to marginal revenue and such that the marginal cost to the marginal firm is equal to the marginal demand price for the commodity. For the entire economy to be in equilibrium, the price of every commodity on the market must be such that there is no incentive for any consumer to change the order and proportion of his purchases. No consumer may have any greater marginal want unsatisfied and no more remunerative employment of the marginal productive factors may be left unfilled. It is for this reason that all shifts are reflected throughout the economy, though the consequent adjustments are minor as compared with the adjustments in the case of joint products except where, as in the case of an economy at war, the initial change is of important magnitude.

SECTION 2: MULTIPLE EQUILIBRIUM

We have so far observed pairs of curves which have but one point of intersection.   One of the special problems in price theory is that of curves with varying elasticities which have more than one point of intersection.

Under competition it is usually possible to determine which of several points of intersection will be the point of stable price.

In Fig. 25 the demand curve is at first inelastic, but as price falls the curve becomes elastic. The industry is pictured as one with large fixed costs so that there is a long period of falling costs.

At points P_1 and P_2 price will not be stable because firms will still be operating under decreasing costs.   At P_3 price

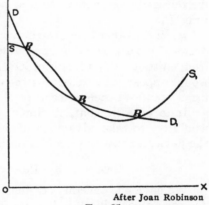

After Joan Robinson

Fig. 25

will be stable because costs are increasing.

Under monopoly or imperfect competition the case is more complicated.

In Fig. 26 we have three points where the marginal curves intersect, marking the outputs OM_1, OM_2, and OM_3. The prices which correspond to these outputs are indicated by the points P_1, P_2, and P_3 on the Average Revenue Curve.

Of these points P_2 represents a peculiarity.   Such are

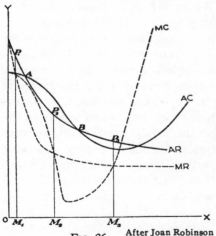

Fig. 26   After Joan Robinson

the shapes of the average curves between points A and B that the marginal curves lie throughout this distance in a relation the opposite of their usual; marginal cost exceeds marginal revenue. Consequently the point where they cross represents the point of maximum losses. Thus under no conditions would entrepreneurs sell at this point.

If a complete monopoly exists from the outset the price will probably be stable at P_1. That is a point of maximum profit and the monopolist would have no reason to go beyond it. If he did so he would find, not only that his net profits decreased, but, as soon as he reached point A, that he was sustaining losses. He would be discouraged from expansion and would return to output OM_1 and price P_1.

If, on the other hand, the industry started competitively P_1 with decreasing costs would not be stable. The price war would be fierce from output OM_1 to output OM_3 and monopolistic competition would appear. In this event the emerging duopolist or oligopolist firms would set their price at or about P_3.

It is possible that, if circumstances permitted, a monopolist would try to take advantage of the two maximum profit prices by the device known as price discrimination.

Section 3: Price Discrimination

We have had several occasions to observe the tendency towards decreasing costs in all industries from increased capitalization and mechanization. We have seen that this tends to emphasize the tendency towards monopoly. We have here to observe a further effect this has on the monopolist's power of selective behaviour.

It sometimes happens that the monopolist is able to divide his market, behaving as an independent monopolist in both the resultant divisions. This occurs when he sells across national frontiers and is able to obtain tariff protection to offset price differences in the two or more national markets. It occurs also when, by advertising or other methods, he is able to give two brand names to the same product and sell one brand in the "snob" market and the other in the general market. Thus a soap manufacturer may add some colour to a small portion of his output, wrap it in attractive wrappers, advertise it, and mark it off as a distinct commodity. He will then sell the wrapped soap at, say, 50 cents a cake, and the other soap at, say, 5 cents.

How does the monopolist determine the discriminatory prices in the different markets? His object is to maintain maximum profits. Obviously he will not bother to divide the market unless it will increase his profits to do so. It will not increase his profits to do so if the demand curves are identical in both the potential markets. In that case his maximum profit point would be the same as if he sold to the single market as a whole. And he would have to lose the advertising and other incidental costs of dividing the market.

The condition, therefore, of profitable price discrimination is two or more potential markets with differing demand curves, that is curves on different levels or of differing elasticities. In the market where the demand curve is at a lower level or where the elasticity of demand is less, and, therefore, where marginal revenue falls most sharply,[1] he will greatly restrict his sales. Otherwise the marginal revenue values will become negative. In the market where the demand is at a higher level and its elasticity is great and marginal revenue consequently high, he will increase his sales. His total sales will be so divided as to equate his aggregate marginal revenue from the two markets with his marginal cost and so as to equate the marginal revenues in each market with one another and with the marginal cost of the output as a whole.

The entrepreneur must obtain the aggregate marginal and average revenue curves for the two markets. This is done by lateral summation.

If, for example, the two markets, A and B, exhibit, after marketing experimentation, the characteristics as shown in Table XII, we can add them as in Table XIII, showing the aggregate average and marginal revenue curves for the two markets.

TABLE XII

| | A MARKET | | | B MARKET | |
Output	Average Revenue	Marginal Revenue	Output	Average Revenue	Marginal Revenue
	$	$		$	$
10,000	10	..	10,000	12	..
20,000	8	6	20,000	11	10
30,000	6	2	30,000	10	8
40,000	4	−2	50,000	8	5
			80,000	6	2

TABLE XIII

Average Revenue or Demand Price	Output A	Output B	Output Aggregate	Aggregate Marginal Revenue
$				$
12	....	10,000	10,000	..
11	....	20,000	20,000	10
10	10,000	30,000	40,000	9
8	20,000	50,000	70,000	5.33
6	30,000	80,000	110,000	2.5

[1]See Geometrical Appendix to chap. IX.

We observe here that Market A is the less attractive market with an inelastic demand and a marginal revenue curve that soon reaches negative values. The aggregate marginal revenue curve in conjunction with the marginal cost curve determines the total output. The division of the output as between the two markets is determined so as to sell in each market the amount the marginal revenue for which just covers the marginal cost. This is illustrated in Fig. 27.

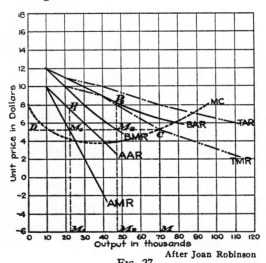

FIG. 27   After Joan Robinson

Let "A"AR and "B"AR be the average revenue curves for the markets A and B, and let "T"AR be the aggregate or total average revenue curve for the two markets. Let "T"MR be the corresponding marginal curve to "T"AR and let "A"MR and "B"MR be the marginal curves corresponding to the average curves "A"AR and "B"AR. Draw MC the marginal cost curve of the firm. Let MC cut "T"MR at C. (We have calculated our marginal cost so that this point C corresponds to the output of 70,000 units of output.) Draw perpendiculars from C to the x and to the y-axes. Call the points of intersections of these perpendiculars on the x and y-axes M and D. Then OM is the total output which it will be profitable to put on the two markets, and OD is the marginal cost of the firm's output OM.

Let CD cut "A"MR at M_1 and "B"MR at M_2. Erect perpendiculars from the x-axis to M_1 and M_2 and extend them to cut "A"AR and "B"AR at P_1 and P_2. Then OM_1 and OM_2 will be the quantities sold respectively in the A market and the B market, and P_1 will be the selling price in the A market and P_2 will be the price in the B market.

Our graph shows the revenue curves drawn to the data of Tables XII and XIII. The data from which the MC curve was drawn were not, of course, given in our tables, but the data of the firm's costs can be readily calculated from the graph. The graph enables us to say with precision the quantities to be sold and the prices prevailing in the *A* and *B* markets. Approximately 22,500 units will be sold in *A* at a price of roughly $7.75, and approximately 47,500 units will be sold in *B* at a price of about $8.10.

By equating aggregate marginal revenue with marginal cost, the entrepreneur is able after the usual fashion to determine the output which will give him the maximum profit. By equating marginal revenue in each market with marginal cost for the total output, the monopolist makes sure that any change in output or in the division of it between the two markets would result in adding less to his total revenue than he would be adding to his total costs, and thus reducing total net profits.

This device of price discrimination is often defended as being of advantage to a home industry and the home market when the monopolist sells abroad. The argument is that the firm is able to reduce its price at home because of its sales abroad. The firm may even ask for tariff protection on those somewhat specious grounds. Actually the home consumer will benefit or not according to the relative elasticities of demand in the two markets. Ordinarily price discrimination is a monopolistic device for increasing profits and is not directed by concern for social welfare.

CHAPTER XIV

DECREASING COSTS—COMPARISON OF COMPETITIVE AND MONOPOLY OUTPUT

SECTION 1: DECREASING COSTS FURTHER CONSIDERED

SO far our treatment of price has been based on assumptions that have excluded any consideration of the effect of the passage of time. We have asked what would determine price at any given moment of time. We considered output as an independent variable and cost as a dependent variable and we supposed that a cost schedule represented the various costs that would be incurred for the various outputs at any given moment of time.[1] We did not consider increases in output to take place over a period of time, but regarded various outputs as potential at any given moment. Adjustments of cost to output and of output to price were regarded as immediate. We saw that ordinarily the greater outputs would require a more intensive use of the given equipment so that, after a certain point in the utilization of the fixed factors, greater production would only be possible at increasing unit costs. We discussed decreasing costs only as an exceptional variant of this rule.

To bring our treatment a stage closer to reality we propose now to introduce another variable, time. We shall now suppose production to take place over a period of time so that output changes in time. In this event we may no longer suppose the same rigidity of fixed capital and the same tendency to increasing costs. On the contrary we must see that in the "very long run" new inventions, new fixed capital, and new techniques will be introduced. The effect of these is to create decreasing costs over a period of time, even in industries in which increasing costs are the rule at any given moment under the static assumption. This is partly because of the improvements in techniques and machinery which make for more economical production and partly because the tendency is to invest in labour-saving machinery so that fixed costs constitute a larger proportion

[1]Our distinction between short- and long-run periods may seem to controvert this statement, but it does not. Our short-run and long-run concepts were devised so that we could make certain necessary time considerations. The short-run assumption enabled us to show the nature of price determination when entrepreneurs had no opportunity to adjust output to the market. In the long run they had that opportunity. Given that as a working assumption we treated price determination as instantaneous and immediate.

of total costs.   The effect of heavy fixed costs relative to variable is always, as we have seen, to produce decreasing costs.

We have to remember that the Law of Diminishing Returns[2] is a static law.   It states that if one factor is in scarce supply and is held constant and if other factors are applied in increased quantities, the imputed increments of output will be less than proportionate to the increases in the variable factors.   This law supposes that there shall be no changes in techniques or the arts of production. As stated it is obviously a true generalization.   But it is important to see what it does *not* mean.

It does not mean that if all factors are in equally elastic supply and are increased proportionately to one another that there will be less than proportionate increments in output.   Indeed, Euler's theorem, by which it is asserted that if *all* factors are increased by proportionate quantities the increase in total output will be likewise proportionate, though challenged by Pareto,[3] is generally accepted by economists.

It does not mean that increasing costs prevail in all industries. Increasing costs are *not* the same as diminishing returns.   Increasing average unit costs arise when the total increase in costs is more than in proportion to the increase in output.   But it would be quite possible to have constant average unit costs coexistent with diminishing returns.   The *total* increase in all costs would be exactly proportionate to the increase in output that would yield constant costs per unit, but if factors in elastic supply were increased more than in proportion to the increase of the factor in inelastic supply there would be diminishing returns imputed to those agents.   The augmented surpluses imputed to the scarce factor would offset the diminishing returns imputed to the other factors and the total sum of costs would be increased in proportion to the increase in output. Thus over a period of time the fact that decreasing costs may be discovered in industry is no relevant comment on the truth of the Law of Diminishing Returns.

Moreover, industries with increasing variable costs may continue over a period of time to introduce inventions and improvements in techniques.   These will give decreased costs in time. Diminishing returns to variable factors of labour and capital applied to land and fixed capital (relatively scarce factors) are offset over a period of time by improvements in the arts of production.   This

[2]The Law of Diminishing Returns is stated in Book One, p. 13.   It is applied in Book Two, p. 66, and in Book Three, p. 94 ff.

[3]V. Pareto, *Cours d'économie politique* (Paris, 1897), pp. 81 ff.

10

is contrary to the gloomy expectations of Ricardo and his disciples.
It is true not only of manufacturing—as is generally admitted—but
of much of basic production.   Even mining and some types of agriculture, at one time regarded as stock examples of increasing cost
industries, exhibit this tendency.

Thus, to choose one example of what has often been regarded as
an increasing cost industry, copper mining and milling have, since
1914, been conducted on a decreasing cost in time basis, and this in
spite of rising labour costs, poorer grades of ores, exhaustion of veins,
and a falling value of money, all of which would go to emphasize
increasing money costs.

The new metallurgical techniques relevant to copper production
have been improved methods of treating slimes by gravity concentration and the introduction of the flotation process, with progressive improvements in flotation reagents and the development of
matless and rotating mat pneumatic machines.[4] The result of these
processes has been a tremendous increase in the "recovery per cent"
at copper concentrators.   Thus, whereas in 1911 a typical average
per cent recovery of copper from the concentrate was 69.53 per cent
by the Utah Copper Company, in 1930 this company was recovering
89 per cent, and another company was recovering as high as 95.7
per cent.[5]

In spite of a change in the value of money tending to exaggerate
in an upward direction all cost changes and in spite of the various
increases in variable costs we have mentioned above, the unit costs
of copper output have decreased as from 1911 to 1930. The explanation of this remarkable decrease is to be found as well as in the
improved techniques of smelting which we have noticed, in the increased proportion of fixed cost investment.   Thus in 1911 for four
typical copper companies the milling costs in dollars per ton of ore
were $.417, $.627, $.595, and $.330. The costs in 1930 for the same
companies were $.461, $.297, $.382, and $.495. Other companies
not competing in 1911 reported 1930 or 1931 costs as $.231, $.303.[6]

In some cases long-established companies show increasing costs
over the period, though these increases are scarcely in proportion to

[4]S. Chapman, *Concentration of Copper Ores in America* (United States Department of the Interior, Bureau of Mines Bulletin no. 392, Washington, 1936),
pp. 4-7.

[5]*Ibid.*, p. 11.

[6]*Ibid.*, p. 16.

changes in the value of money, and for the industry as a whole the trend is definitely towards decreasing costs.[7]

This tendency of unit costs to decrease in time can be graphically presented by means of a three-dimensional diagram, of which the third dimension is time. In Fig. 28 we plot output along the OX-

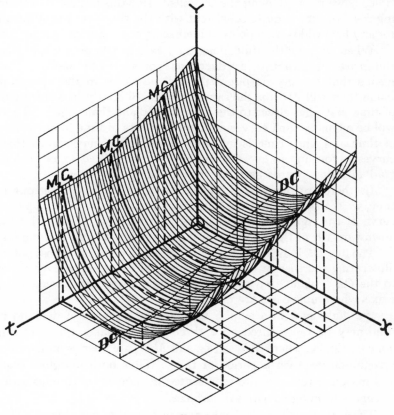

FIG. 28

axis, unit cost along the Y-axis, and time along the t-axis, which is to be regarded as originating in O at right angles to OX and OY and in the same horizontal plane as OX and the same vertical plane as OY.

Thus in the first moment of time the curve MC represents the

[7]Dr. Chapman states in private conversation that what is true of costs in copper processing holds true for the extraction of the ore, and that, with a few exceptions, copper is fairly typical of other metallurgical industries.

dependent variation of costs to output, each point on MC being the cost that would be incurred in the production of its corresponding potential output.

It will be noticed here that we retain the notion of costs increasing relative to output. The *decreasing* unit costs are decreasing in time, as we proceed along the OT-axis. But this notion of decreasing costs in time is quite consistent with the thesis that equilibrium for any firm will be at a point of increasing costs statically regarded.

When we vary the time along the t-axis to a second unit of time the entire cost structure is reduced, as represented by M_1C_1. That means that for any output M_1C_1 will lie closer to the horizontal plane than will MC for the same output. Similarly in a third unit of time M_2C_2 lies closer to the horizontal plane than M_1C_1. There will be as many such curves as there are units of time in our period of time and since time is infinitely divisible we may regard these curves as forming *in toto* a curvilinear surface tilted so as to slope gradually downwards as it moves out along the t-axis.

If, therefore, we regard the industry as increasing output in time, we see that its unit costs may continually fall, for the upward curve of the right side of our curved surface will be offset by the downward tilt of the whole surface as we proceed from O along OT.

The line DC indicates a particular series of decreasing cost points illustrating increase of output in time. The line drops ever closer to the OXT plane, and consequently falls lower and lower on the y-axis where unit costs are measured.

We may show in a similar fashion that changes of demand in time may be represented on a three dimensional graph. This is done in Fig. 29, where MR, M_1R_1, and M_2R_2 are a series of marginal revenue curves over a period of time. Thus both marginal costs and marginal revenues are represented in time as continuous series of curves forming curvilinear surfaces.

These two surfaces will intersect in a continuous curve. This curve must contain all the points of intersection of the various static marginal curves that could be drawn for each single unit of time in the series. Since each pair of static curves has a point of intersection, that intersection must be a point on the intersection of the two surfaces formed by the totality of the marginal revenue and marginal cost curves. We have two intersecting surfaces. The line of their intersection must contain every point of intersection of the intersecting curves that make up the two surfaces. Thus the static equilibrium price points form an equilibrium price curve in time, towards which, at every unit of time, price tends to approach and at which it tends to be stable.

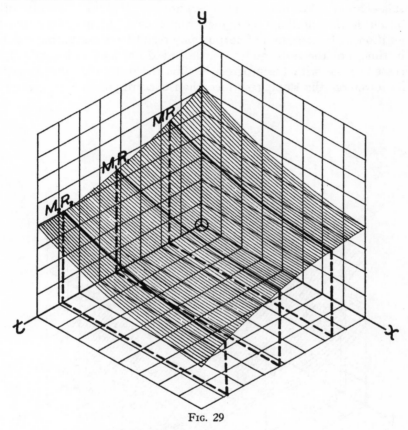

Fig. 29

This is illustrated in Fig. 30, where MR, M_1R_1, and M_2R_2 are the marginal revenue curves, AR, A_1R_1 and A_2R_2 are the average revenue or price curves, and MC, M_1C_1 and M_2C_2 are the marginal cost curves. The line of intersection of the marginal cost and marginal revenue surfaces determines the equilibrium output in time. Perpendiculars from points on this line to the OTX plane are extended to cut the average revenue or price surface along the curve PP_1P_2. This curve is the curve of equilibrium price in time.

The relative prices can be compared by measuring the lengths of OP, O_1P_1 and O_2P_2, the projections on the plane of the y-axis. The output is measured by OM, O_1M_1, and O_2M_2.

The results of decreasing costs in time are to set up a strong

tendency towards monopoly and monopolistic competition.[8] Some
of the implications of this will be examined in the next section of
this chapter.   We may notice now, however, that a restriction of
output in time need not mean higher unit costs.   Monopolistic competition with restriction of output may result from decreasing costs
in time, but the restriction of output need not lead to higher unit
costs because with the progress in time the restricted output may
lie lower on the sloping surface than a corresponding or greater

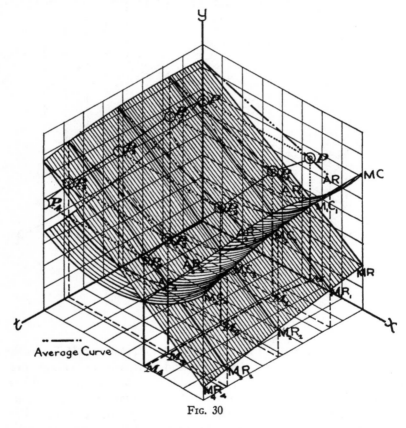

FIG. 30

output did at a previous point in time.   Under conditions of multiple equilibrium, for example, a competitive expansion of output
might result in monopoly that might then restrict output to the
most limited equilibrium point, without raising, or appreciably
raising marginal costs of production.

[8] The reasons for this are explained in chap. XII, section 5, p. 127.

SECTION 2: COMPARISON OF MONOPOLY AND COMPETITIVE OUTPUT

It is interesting to ask whether, other things being unchanged, monopoly or a competitive industry will produce the greater output.

Superficially it would appear that, since monopoly thrives by curtailing output, it is less productive than competition.[9] But this will not always be so. There are several reasons why monopoly output may equal, or in some circumstances exceed, competitive output, other conditions remaining unchanged.

In the first place it is possible that the external economies of large-scale production will so lower costs that output will be greater, even when restricted by monopolistic control of the market. It is true that there is a limit to the economies of large-scale organization. It is also true that many monopolies consist of a number of small factory units who act monopolistically through a single control but do not achieve any internal economies of organization as compared with an equal number of independent competing firms. Likewise it must be admitted that monopoly advertising as in cases of commodity differentiation may be so costly as to wipe out any economies of large-scale organization. The evidence here is confused. Studies of monopoly industries such as Wallace, *Market Control in the Aluminum Industry*,[10] Burns, *The Decline of Competition*,[11] and *The Porphyry Coppers*[12] offer conflicting evidence as to the possible economies of monopoly. The weight of evidence indicates an economy in monopoly organization of base products such as metals, and the opposite in such finished goods as cigarettes.

Undoubtedly the big monopolistic plant can effect economies of production. That is not in question. But whether those economies are such as to offset the monopolist's restriction of output so as to give the community as large a choice of commodities at the same price as would have obtained under competition is a more doubtful question.

Some light may be thrown on this question by a consideration of the shape of the cost curves. It is clear from a consideration of the curves that for monopoly output to exceed competitive would

[9]We exclude here government regulation. We wish to compare monopoly and competition as they would be if left to themselves without government "interference."

[10]D. H. Wallace, *Market Control in the Aluminum Industry* (Cambridge, Mass., 1937).

[11]A. R. Burns, *The Decline of Competition* (New York, 1936).

[12]A. B. Parsons, *The Porphyry Coppers* (Institute of Mining and Metallurgical Engineers, 1933).

be a very rare thing. We make, for the purpose of these comparisons the rather unreal assumption that the average cost curve under
monopoly will exactly coincide with the supply curve for the industry under conditions of competition.

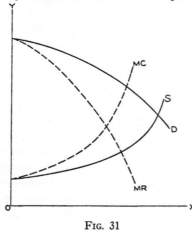

FIG. 31

Clearly, if the demand curve
is falling and the supply curve is
rising, the marginal curves must
lie inside the average curves. This
is because the marginal revenue
curve will fall more sharply than
the average revenue curve, and
the marginal cost curve will rise
more steeply than the average
cost curve. They must, therefore,
intersect to the left of the intersection of the average curves. This
is illustrated in Fig. 31, where the
curves are chosen to bring the
intersection of the marginal curves
as far to the right as possible.

Since monopolistic firms restrict output to the point of marginal
curve intersection, it follows that monopoly output must always be
less than average output if the average cost curve continuously rises.

If the demand curve is a straight line, it follows that whether or
not the cost curve is rising or falling monopoly output will be less
than competitive.

If, however, both curves are
falling, what will be the point
of intersection of the marginal
curves?[13]

If both the falling curves are
convex the marginal intersection
must lie to the left of the average
intersection. This is illustrated in
Fig. 32. Because of the convexity
of each of the average curves, the
marginal curves must fall more
steeply, dropping to negative
values as the average curves assume elasticities of less than unity.

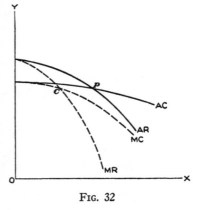

FIG. 32

If the falling average curves are concave, the intersection of the

[13]We omit consideration of the case where both curves are rising because of
the unreality of the concept of a rising demand curve.

marginal curves will lie to the left of the average curve intersection as long as there are no economies of large-scale production. If there are economies, so that the marginal cost curve drops more sharply at first than later, the intersection of the marginal cost curve, including the economies of large-scale production, may intersect the marginal revenue curve to the right of the intersection of the average curves. This is illustrated in Fig. 33, where M_1C_1 is the marginal cost curve reduced by the economies of large-scale production.[14] The MC and MR curves, however, must cut each other to the left of the average curves to which they correspond because of the increased steepness of falling marginal curves as compared with the average curves to which they are correspondent. This conclusion supports that to which we came in the first part of this argument.

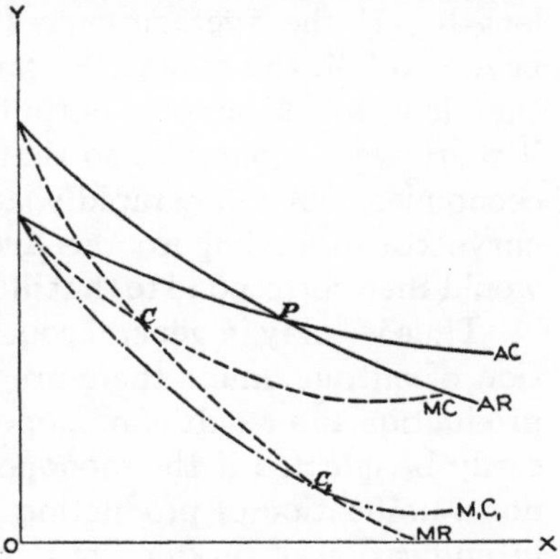

If the cost curve changes its

Fig. 33

direction, first falling and then rising, is it possible for monopoly output to exceed competitive?

It can be seen here that, if the shape of the average curves is such that the marginal curves intersect before the marginal cost curve has begun to rise, a monopoly output in excess of competitive is only possible if there are economies of large-scale production as in M_1C_1 in Fig. 33 above. If the intersection of the average curves is to the right of the swing upwards of the AC and MC curves, the marginal intersection must lie to the left of the average intersection.

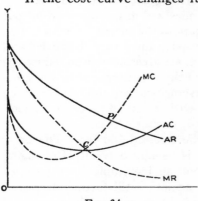

Fig. 34

[14]The construction of Fig. 33 illustrates an interesting point. The M_1C_1 curve will only intersect the MR curve if the former is drawn so as gradually to assume a more gentle slope. Thus M_1C_1 falls at first more sharply than MC, and then tends to approach MC.

This means, in effect, that the economies of large scale organization must at first be marked, but, with greater outputs, the advantages from this source will gradually diminish.

Fig. 34 illustrates the rising curves intersecting. A glance at the graph indicates the fact that the case is the same as for a pair of cost curves rising throughout their length.

If the cost curves first rise and then fall and if the intersection of the average curves takes place while the cost curves are rising, the case is the same as with curves rising throughout their entire length. If the average curves intersect after the cost curve has begun to fall, the case is the same as for curves falling throughout their length. Monopoly output here could only exceed competitive if there were economies so that the marginal curve, including the economies, fell more rapidly at first than the ordinary marginal curve corresponding to the average curve would fall. The case would then correspond to that illustrated in Fig. 33 by the M_1C_1 curve.

Thus we may in general conclude that monopoly means a restriction of output unless there are economies (external or internal) in production as a result of monopoly. These economies will not necessarily be effected if the monopoly is only monopoly of control and not a unification of production units. Again monopoly may result in unification of production units, decreasing costs, and great economies, but the economies may not mean that the monopoly can profitably put an output on the market greater than under competition. Whether or not the economies will mean increased output on the market will depend on the shape of the curves. With a falling average cost curve of sufficient concavity and a very elastic demand curve, if the economies in production are great enough to reduce the monopolist's marginal cost curve so that it intersects the marginal revenue curve to the right of the average curves' intersection, then monopoly output will exceed competitive. In all other cases, competitive output will exceed monopoly output.

These comparisons must not be stressed too far. The basic assumption is unreal. Monopoly is usually a result of changing conditions, decreasing costs in time, an inevitable consequent of unstable competition. It usually achieves still further decreased costs in time, which is to say that it fulfils the condition outlined above, so that there is a very good chance in real life of monopoly expanding output during a sufficient period of time.

We can only say that, under monopoly, output is always restricted as compared with the potential output if all the conditions of technique and organization could be maintained and competition substituted for monopoly. Another and more significant way of saying this is to say that under monopoly, output is always restricted as compared with the potential output which would cover all costs and normal profits but not surplus profits.

CHAPTER XV

CONCLUSION TO BOOK III

THAT the Industrial Revolution should result in the large-scale plant and the large-scale firm was inevitable. The new power machinery required large accumulations of capital and this meant that the joint stock company became the characteristic unit of enterprise. Once the principle of investing large sums of jointly owned capital in industry had been accepted as profitable, the world economy was committed to an historic process whereby in many lines of industry the plant units and the firm units increased in size. The internal economies of large-scale production gave the larger plant advantages over the smaller plant so that in every depression period a number of the smaller plants would disappear. But the process is not to be explained simply in terms of depression. Large plant units could enjoy the advantages of decreasing costs in time and they were thus able to expand production at lower costs and, under conditions of unstable competition, drive from the market their smaller and weaker competitors. The large-scale plant could only be owned and directed by the large-scale firm so that these internal economies led to the development of monopolistic or, at least, imperfectly competitive, market conditions. Even in industries such as brewing where the small-scale plant could still afford offsetting advantages, the external economies of the large-scale firm frequently led to amalgamations and pools, and, even when such unification of control did not occur, to price agreements and other forms of "co-operation." Under such conditions, even without unification of ownership, the advantages of a monopolistic market could be enjoyed by some, if not all, the parties to the agreement.

The first implication of the theoretic agreement is, then, that we should expect to find in all heavy industry, in all industries with a standardized product and in many industries which partake in part of one or both these characteristics, a tendency towards the large-scale plant and towards either unification of ownership or price agreements. We should expect to find, also, that the typical market for industrial products was not one characterized by price competition, but rather one where conditions of monopoly or monopolistic competition prevailed. When we examine the economic history of any of the more important industrial states, we find what we expect, the development of the large-scale plant, the big firm, decreasing

costs, unstable competition, and the growth of monopolistic practices.   In some ways the case of England, most frequently used for
examples to illuminate economic argument, is not the most reveal-
ing.   Because the Industrial Revolution began there, English firms
of moderate size long enjoyed advantages which derived from custom, prestige, personal connections, and political influence and were
able to continue to compete in markets in which their larger-scale
German and American competitors could underbid them.   The
tendency towards the large-scale unit was thus, for a time, obscured
in England, and it was not until after the War of 1914-18 when
English firms who had yielded their entrenched positions during the
war tried to regain them that the need for "rationalization," i.e. the
large-scale reorganization of industries with a restriction of price
competition, was seen to be necessary.   From that time on no one
could complain of the reluctance of English industrialists to learn
the lesson of "co-operation."

In Canada and the United States the process has been more
dramatic, the historical development speeded up by the telescoping
of stages, and it has been richer in sensational public developments.
The early efforts in the United States to break the trusts, culmin-
ating in the Sherman anti-trust legislation, are well known, and
equally well known is the relative failure of such laws.   That they
are bound to fail is apparent, for they attempt to reverse a process
which, within the framework of a purely capitalist society, is irre-
versible.   New Deal legislation, which has also attempted in some
of its aspects to prevent monopolistic practices, has, nevertheless,
been more realistic.   It has, in notable instances such as cotton,
frankly accepted the principle of "co-operation" and restriction and
brought the monopolistic marketing of the product under government regulation.   In Canada the natural environment and the
tradition of the country all favoured the rapid growth of large-scale
units.   The French had regarded the fur trade as the most important economic asset of the northern colony and they and later the
British established it on monopolistic lines.   The struggle for the
cod fisheries was a struggle for exclusive rights.   Monopolistic exploitation of natural resources was the economic tradition of the
early colonies, and tradition has been reinforced by natural forces.
In a country vast as Canada the development of railways and com-
munications was only possible on a non-competitive basis.   The
enormous fixed investment meant unstable competition, amalgamation, and regulated rates, and these services required that some
toll be levied on the country as a whole.   The development of min-

eral resources likewise required large fixed assets and the domination of the Canadian metallurgical industries by one or two large firms is a characteristic to be expected. Even in agriculture the new West was characterized by large-scale farms and very early there was co-operation in the marketing of the staple product, a co-operation now extended to government marketing and storage at public expense. In manufacturing the same process unfolded. We have already seen in Chapter XII how the number of firms in manufacturing industries in Canada steadily decreased, while the average size of firm and the value of the product were increasing rapidly. This process was accelerated by the development of hydro-electric power, a second power revolution which had in Canada more profound effects than the original steam power revolution. The development of hydro-electric power widened the power limits of the profitable size of plants in many industries and enabled firms in those areas where cheap power was available greatly to increase in size and reduce their costs with increased output. They were then able to destroy or absorb their competitors who were, for lack of available hydro, forced to rely on steam power. This development had the effect of altering the balance between industry in the Maritimes, where sources of hydro-electric power are limited and are always subject to the disadvantage that the streams are greatly reduced in the dry season, and Ontario and Quebec where great hydro-electrical development was possible. Thus Nova Scotian industry, dependent on cheap Cape Breton coal and characterized by small-scale or moderate-sized firms, lost ground steadily to the industry of the Central Provinces. We should expect to find the disappearance of the small firm most marked in the Maritime Provinces and this expectation is borne out by the statistics.[1] It is not stating it too strongly to maintain that many of the political problems of the Canadian federation have their origin in the development of hydro-electric power and the consequent decreasing costs of large-scale enterprises.[2]

The Canadian economy has been unique in the prevalence of the large-scale unit and monopolistic pricing. We have seen that there were conditions that explain why this should be. There have been interesting consequences. Canada was one of the first countries to

[1]See chap. XII, p. 127.

[2]Since writing the above the author has had opportunity to submit the hypothesis advanced to some statistical tests with disappointing results, which, though inconclusive, at least demand the admission that the importance of the hydro-electric power revolution is probably exaggerated in the text.

recognize that the price system was not always a reliable guide to investment. If the country was to exist as a nation state the building of railways, the development of the western land, and the exploitation of mineral and hydro-electric resources were essential. Yet none of these could have been accomplished had they been left to competitive private enterprise. The Canadian Pacific required assistance in the way of land grants and capital subventions and the Canadian National is maintained by levying the taxpayers annually to cover the deficit. In essence the Canadian public supports "unprofitable" enterprises because they are socially necessary. There is the tacit recognition of an alternative principle to that of profits. In spite of this, perhaps because of it, the general tradition towards monopolies has been not to attempt to protect the public but rather to encourage the monopolist by tariff or other legal protection. There is anti-trust legislation, the Combines Investigation Act and Sections 496-498 of the Criminal Code, but it is, as interpreted, not very efficient. Under the Criminal Code criminal intent and conspiracy must be shown and under the Combines Act the defence may plead that the price is a "fair and reasonable" one. Canadian manufacturers themselves say that the legislation does not prevent "co-operation" or price-fixing agreements[3] and they are clearly right. What the theoretic argument seems to indicate, however, is not that a legislative attempt should be made to prevent monopolistic practices, but rather that the state should intervene to pass on to the mass of the people the advantages of modern techniques and large-scale industrialization.

The large-scale unit effects economies in production; it makes

[3]"I happen to belong to an American association of manufacturers, and one of the most satisfying things is to step out of that association and come up here and see how we can carry on things. We have done things in our association that we would have been arrested for in the United States. There might have been some misgivings on the part of some of the Dominion officials if they had known all the details of what went on. But we went to them initially and asked them what we could do together, and they gave us a general endorsement that we could do anything in the world that was moral. They said that if you co-operate (co-operation is the business man's euphemism for price rigging) in such a way that on examining your books we satisfy ourselves that you are servicing the Canadian consumer with a fair price based on efficient production, you have nothing to fear from the Dominion government. That is just as far away as the poles from the atmosphere in the United States. When I have told them down there of some of the things we have done together they instantly look at the transom to make sure it is closed" (Proceedings of 69th Annual General Meeting of the Canadian Manufacturers' Association, quoted in *Industrial Canada*, July, 1940, p. 84).

possible the increase of output at lower cost. But these advantages, as we saw in Chapter XIV, are not fully passed on to the consumer who would frequently be better off under conditions of competition between smaller and less efficient firms. The restriction of output of the monopolist leads to high profits and unused capacity. The report of the Canadian Royal Commission on Price Spreads shows that even during the depression certain firms in monopolistic positions continued to earn high rates of profit. Professor Reynolds in his book already cited declares that Canadian monopolies in the ten years from 1927 to 1937 earned profits averaging 12 per cent per annum on common and preferred stock, surplus and reserves, while all manufacturing firms in Canada (including the monopolies) had average earnings over the same period of only 4 per cent.[4] In 1937 monopoly earnings were 20 per cent of capital invested, including reserve. Normal competitive profits are put, during good times, at a maximum of 5 and 6 per cent. Thus, we see that a second consequence of decreasing costs and the growth of the large-scale firm is a redistribution of the social income in favour of the owner of capital and at the expense of other elements of society. This general conclusion must be modified by the consideration that the trades union has enabled the organized workers to get some share of the gains. Indeed today there are some indications that the organized skilled workers may form a sort of "unholy alliance" with capital to retain the present social and economic system and to protect their joint vested interest at the expense of the mass of consumers and unorganized workers.

A further consequence which now emerges from our argument is the existence of unused capacity. If we define optimum capacity as the output at lowest unit costs, unused capacity is the amount by which optimum capacity exceeds actual output. It is *not* unused physical capacity in the sense of differential between actual output and the physical maximum that can be achieved regardless of cost or plant wastage. Under monopoly or monopolistic competition there is always restriction to less than optimum capacity as long as the maximization of profit is the determining principle. How great this unused capacity is we have no way of measuring. Some rough estimate might be attempted, however. In the year 1940 under the stimulus of war, manufacturing industries in Canada increased their output by approximately an average of 30 per cent over 1938. Prices

[4]L. G. Reynolds, *The Control of Competition in Canada* (Cambridge, Mass., 1940), p. 60.

of manufactured goods had risen, perhaps, 18 per cent or 20 per cent,[5] so that the demand curves had shifted to the right, increasing the attractiveness of expanding output. Costs had increased very little so that the optimum cost point was relatively speaking unchanged. This would suggest an actual increase in output of about 8 per cent. It is not too much to say that this represents roughly the utilization of unused manufacturing capacity, for the new plant built for war purposes scarcely affects these figures for 1940. The average figure is, however, scarcely informative for there were many industries but little affected, and many others where with a comparatively high degree of competition there was little unused plant capacity. The degree of unused capacity in the monopolistic industries must have been therefore very considerable, probably running in some instances to as much as 25 per cent or even $33\frac{1}{3}$ per cent.

Our argument consequently indicates that, though there are advantages to large-scale organization, these advantages are not socially distributed. Nevertheless, if this argument has been correct, it is futile to attempt to prevent the natural process by anti-trust legislation. The task for *political* economy is not to frame fool-proof anti-combine laws but rather to devise some method by means of which the advantages of large-scale production could be passed on to the society as a whole. The experience of the war economy seems to suggest that this is by no means impossible and that it may be done by the dual method of devising a new concept of cost accounting, and by imposing either through direct controls or by excess profits taxation, capacity production on all firms.

Finally, we may observe that our argument has suggested a notion of a dynamic rather than a static equilibrium. The equilibrium price position which we examined in Book Two was a purely static one, and, in that sense, it was unreal. But we have now progressed to a concept of a dynamic equilibrium, that is a series of equilibrium price positions changing over time under the impact of technical improvements. It is not inconceivable that under a changed social system stability would be possible. With the profit motive removed or qualified by public control under different motivation, there is no reason why the dynamic price "line" should be unstable with decreasing costs in time. There are, of course, once one admits temporal and dynamic factors, other sources of instability than technical improvements and decreasing costs. There are the frictions that prevent perfect adjustments and there are the rigidities

[5]These are not accurate calculations.

of economic institutions and conventions. There are also the vagaries—less dangerous now every day under managed money economies—of the monetary system. But all of these questions are beyond our present scope. We must be satisfied here if our theory serves to elucidate certain of the basic trends of our economic life and if it serves to indicate certain ways of formulating our problems of practical economy and methods of approaching their solution. The full discussion of these problems and the assay of solutions run far beyond the limits of the present work.

BOOK FOUR

DISTRIBUTION—THE PRICING OF THE AGENTS OF PRODUCTION

CHAPTER XVI

INTRODUCTION TO BOOK FOUR

IN primitive society producer, worker, consumer are all united in one person. Production is directly for consumption. The rude savage lives on his own production, and his one economic problem is to increase his output to the point where it will sustain him. The division of economic functions, specialization and exchange, are phenomena of a complex society in which the worker is divorced from the instruments of production. He performs a specialized task in production. The product of his work may be a small part of a machine to be used in further production, infrequently will it be a finished good for consumption, and if it is, then it is only one of the many finished goods he requires for the support of himself and his family. He becomes dependent on a money wage with which he buys the various end products of social industry which he requires for his sustenance and comfort. An increase in his output may or may not mean an increase in his standard of living; that will depend on the rate of exchange obtaining between what he produces and other goods. His living may be affected altogether apart from his capacity to produce by changes in the terms on which he receives employment or on changes in the efficiency of other non-human factors of production.

Thus the interest of men shifts from the problem of increasing physical production to the problem of the distribution of the end value of joint enterprise as among the various factors that have co-operated in production. The economic problem is not how to increase output, but how to allocate the various factors among different employments, and how to distribute the value products among the factors.

This problem is solved in practice in our society through the price system. Factors are employed in the different employments in such proportions, roughly, as to produce equal value products per factor unit. Thus if the price of bread goes up, the prices of the factors making bread will be increased. More units of the factors will be attracted to milling and baking until the value product per factor unit is equalized as between bread and the other products of industry. Similarly employers will substitute labour for capital or capital for labour if it is more "economic" to do so, that is, capital

165

will be substituted for labour as long as the ratio of value product to cost is greater in the case of capital than in the case of labour.

The theoretic problem which emerges is to explain how the result we have described takes place. If we examine what we have said, we see that this problem can be broken down into component questions. To compare the end value products per factor unit we have to devise some technique of measuring the increment of value product which can be attributed to the increase in the employment of any specific factor; to determine the ratio of value product to cost we have to know what determines the cost of using a factor, and this in turn involves an inquiry of the supply prices of the factors. The problem of substitution of one factor for another requires a technique of determining the limits of substitutability.

We may gain additional light on the nature of our present problem if we look at it another way. So far in our study of price we have taken as given the costs of the agents of production. Accepting these as given we have shown how the price of a finished good will be determined when the firm is in equilibrium. But this is only a partial equilibrium. For the system as a whole to be in equilibrium not only must all firms be in equilibrium, but they must be in equilibrium with respect to one another. This they cannot be if the rewards to one or more of the agents are higher in one firm or in one industry than in others. Equilibrium of the system must involve the concept of equal rewards. If rewards are not equalized, factors will flow from the inferior to the superior employments, and this will alter the cost structures of all the firms and force adjustments of output and price. Thus full equilibrium, the necessary assumption of a determinate price situation, involves the simultaneous pricing of the agents throughout all industries in the system.

Moreover the completion of our price theory requires that we drop the assumption that the prices of the agents are given. They are not given constants, and until we have examined how they are determined we have no complete theory of price.

There are, too, other than purely theoretic problems concerned. From the social point of view the prices of the agents (costs to the entrepreneur) form the social income. The determination of these prices is the determination of the shares of social income to be enjoyed by the various economic classes in the society. It is consequently in the field of distribution theory that we closely approach the questions of welfare economics and lay the foundations for the effort to solve questions of policy which it is the ultimate function of economics to solve, or attempt to solve.

CHAPTER XVII

WAGES AND ENTERPRISE

SECTION 1: LABOUR

OF the agents of production labour and enterprise are the two human factors, capital and land the material factors. Labour we define as the expenditure of human energy in time for the production of economic goods. Enterprise we distinguish as the undertaking and direction of production. It involves primarily the acceptance of the responsibility for the direction of the enterprise so as to minimize the risk of losses and maximize the probability of gains.

Labour, as quantity, has two dimensions, intensity and duration. But labour differs in quality. We speak of unskilled, semi-skilled, skilled workers. We have managerial and professional workers. We have specialized groups, farmers, navvies, longshoremen, fishermen, machinists, aircraftsmen, nurses, teachers, doctors, clerks, structural steel workers, and countless others.

Before we can begin to talk about the price paid to labour for a unit of labour, we must face the problem of what we mean by a unit of labour. Can we entertain such a notion at all? We mean to attempt to say how the price of labour is determined, but the concept "the price of labour" implies the idea of labour as a homogeneous whole, consisting of easily divisible units of like size and quality. Such a notion is palpably a false one. We must therefore attempt to say precisely what we mean by a "unit of labour."

Let us begin by examining the specialized groups to which we have referred. It is at once clear that these groups are not necessarily exclusive. The various skilled groups can usually move to the less skilled employments. It is only when one starts moving up the scale from the less skilled to the more skilled that one meets difficulty. An unskilled workman cannot become a skilled specialized worker over night, and, in some cases, he cannot advance to some of the specialized skills at all. It is not just training that makes a doctor. Some of the unskilled, given every opportunity for training, would never be able to become doctors. The reverse may occasionally be true. There are some doctors, no doubt, who by reason of lack of strength or other qualities could not perform the tasks of a navvy. There is, one admits nevertheless, a certain fluidity of labour from one task or type of work to another. Farmers become lumbermen in the winter season. Fishermen go into packing factories. When there is a big industrial demand for labour, men of all occupations will be found flocking from farms, mines, the sea, and retail trade into the factories. There is a certain quality, an ability to do work after a little training, sometimes very little, which is found in almost all men. At the same time there are definitely specialized tasks which require special abilities and long training. The labour to perform these tasks is scarce and cannot rapidly be increased. Ordinarily these groups of workers do not compete on the labour market with the less-skilled nor can the less skilled penetrate these special occupations. They form a distinct sort of labour, they are, with respect to one another and to all other types of labour, non-competing groups. Their rate of remuneration will not necessarily be affected by changes in the supply of or demand for other labour (though there may be certain indirect effects), and when we treat of labour, in general, we must be presumed to exclude these groups. Perhaps we might say that their remuneration is determined in a similar fashion to the determination of wages in general, admitting, however, the important influence of custom and convention, and distinguishing their remuneration from the rate of wages in general.

We have, therefore, to confess at the outset that we should think in terms of a wage rate structure rather than a single rate of wages. But, with the exception of these special non-competing groups, the great mass of industrial labour can be treated as homogeneous. It is true that there are specialized trades and specialized tasks throughout industry, but the tendency is for labour to gravitate from trade to trade and from task to task in response to wage changes. A skilled gardener requires years of training, but a farm labourer may well have been an unemployed industrial worker or a clerk a week before. A skilled mechanic may require a long period of special training, but ordinary factory operatives learn their tasks in a day or so, and they are recruited when needed from men of all sorts and types of occupation. Consequently we shall not be stretching reality too far if we speak of a base rate of wages for labour, and admit differentials from the base rate, generally additions, for special labour groups.

We still have, however, the related problem of defining what we shall mean by a unit of labour. This problem is of some difficulty and real importance. It is difficult because we are looking for a quantitative unit of homogeneous labour, an objective unit, in terms of which we can measure, for example, the different quantities of labour performed by different individuals. It is important because the decision as to the proper unit has, for some writers, determined the course of their subsequent argument. If we define, for example, a unit of labour as a single man, it follows that, at any time, the supply of labour is fixed in amount and incapable of variations with variations in remuneration. Only as population changes over a long period of time will there be any variation in the supply of labour. If, on the other hand, we take as a unit of labour, a man's services over a period of time, say an hour, it follows that greater or lesser quantities of labour can be supplied in response to fluctuations of wages. Whether or not the supply of labour can be increased in the short-run period is an important consideration in wage theory. Rigid adherents of the "marginal productivity theory" argue that marginal productivity determines the level of wages for any given supply of labour and that any effort to raise wages above the determined level by collective action can only do harm, because it will end either in penalizing other wage-earners, or in bankruptcy and general unemployment. The whole theoretical case against trades unions is based on this argument, and it is still commonly presented in public discussions. Discretion and care in establishing a proper definition of a unit of labour is essential if we are not to prejudge important issues of theory and practice.

It seems obvious that to define a unit of labour as a man, or as an integrated group of men is false to the facts. When labour is sold a man does not sell himself, he sells his services for a period of time. In a slave state labour may be sold and paid for in terms of individuals, but in a free state there is no legally admitted alienation of individual rights. A man is his own master and holds title to his productive services.[1] It is these which he sells when he contracts to work and he sells them at so much per unit of time. The labour supply consists not of men, but of men's services which constitute a flow in time and are actualized over a period.

But if we are to measure the labour supply in units of time effort, we must solve certain difficulties. Different men supply services of differing intensities in any given unit of time and the same man supplies services of differing intensities in different hours of the day's work. To some extent we avoid this problem by the division of labour into different grades or classes, but even within one class, say

---

[1]The worker does, of course, have to be on the spot to deliver his services, and this fact constitutes a restriction on his freedom of movement and has important sociological consequences.

the semi-skilled, we find different men work with different intensities
and efficiencies. As we have previously said, labour has two dimensions, time and intensity. If we choose to measure labour in units
of time, that is one of its dimensions, what are we to say about
differences in the other dimension? Might we choose as a standard
some representative man's labour effort for one hour? But if we
do, are we to choose the best man's, or the worst man's? Are we to
choose the first hour of the day or the last hour?[2] If we try to avoid
this problem of choosing hours by selecting the day as the time unit,
we create still worse difficulties for ourselves, because a common
method of increasing the quantity of labour used in industry is to
work "overtime," that is to increase the length of the working day.
Thus our day unit would not be a stable one.

Efforts to solve this dilemma have commonly been made by
asserting that labour effort is a universal attribute that various
particular men can supply, and that they supply it in various quantities. This universal labour effort, "socially necessary labour," or
whatever it may be called, can be measured in terms of output. If
we say the labour necessary to produce one pair of shoes is the unit
of socially necessary labour in the shoe industry, we then have a
standard unit of measurement for the various quantities of labour
effort supplied by shoe-makers. This definition is a perfectly possible one in the sense that it satisfies the immediate requirements
of a good definition. It does give a standard, reasonably stable, unit
of measurement. But if we accepted it we should soon, as have
others who have used it, get into difficulties. When we attempted,
on this basis, to explain the determination of the entire price system,
we should have circular argument. We should be saying that the
prices of commodities are determined by their marginal costs of
production. But one of the cost factors is labour. What is the
price of labour? It is the marginal cost of a unit of labour. But a
unit of labour is the amount necessary for the production of a unit
of the commodity. The cost of the commodity is determined by the
cost of a unit of labour—leaving aside the other factors for clarity
in this moment—and a unit of labour is measured by units of the
commodity. Perhaps the circular argument emerges most clearly
when we drop the pecuniary concept. In that case the value of
a commodity is determined by the amount of labour necessary to
make it, and the amount of labour necessary to produce a unit
of the commodity is the unit of measurement in terms of which

[2]Industrial studies have shown labour to be less efficient in the closing
hours of the day's work.

the value-determining labour quantity is measured. Thus any commodity is worth itself, a fair enough truism, but not very helpful.

We are forced back to our original difficulty. We want a standard unit of measurement for quantities of labour, and we want it, for the sake of realism, in terms of time and intensity, but we have no way of measuring different intensities as between different men in the same unit of time, or as between the same man in different units of time. To measure intensity in terms of output would only land us in difficulties later on in our argument, so that avenue is closed to us.

Adam Smith and Ricardo have been laughed at for relying on the "higgling of the market" to get them out of this difficulty, but perhaps their device, with some modifications, though not logically satisfactory, is the one which creates the fewest difficulties. It will give us a working unit, approximate only, but adequate for practical purposes. Indeed we might say that what is a difficult theoretic problem for the economist is no problem at all in industry, and the practical solution may be carried over as a possible, if not entirely satisfactory, one in theory.

Today modern industry has established what is known as the "standard quota." This is the quantity of work in each task which the average man must do in each hour of the day. The work is organized on the belt system. A conveyor belt carries the raw materials to the first station in the plant. The men at this station perform the first task in the productive process and the partly finished goods then move along the belt. Thus they go from station to station. At each a unit task is performed until the finished product emerges or until the various finished pieces are transferred to the assembly rooms where they are assembled, again on the conveyor belt. The speed of the belt determines the speed and "standard quota" of each man. That is to say the intensity of labour is fixed at a standard rate.

Under such a system it does not matter much whether time or piece wages are paid. In one case a man is paid 75 cents an hour and the belt is set so that he handles 100 pieces in an hour's time. In the second case he is paid 75 cents a piece and handles 100 pieces in an hour so that his wage works out to 75 cents an hour.

Now it will at once be argued that the belt system, though characteristic of mass production industry is by no means universal throughout industry and is not to be found at all in agriculture, construction, fishing, lumbering, and many other productive operations. This is true. But the notion of a standard or average intensity of labour is universal. Foremen have in their minds a notion of the intensity with which they may expect their men to work. They may not have very clear ideas as to how this notion has been formed. Actually it rests on experience and amounts to a rough average.[3] They know about how hard and how fast an average man can work on a certain task and maintain his rate over the day. Foremen on road construction have a pretty standardized concept of an average or normal intensity of labour. Men who cannot work to this intensity will be discharged or paid a lower wage. Men who work at more than the standard intensity may receive promotion or superior remuneration. If neither is forthcoming, it is surprising how rapidly the men learn to adjust the intensity of their work to the standard expected of them.

We shall consequently define a unit of labour to consist of an hour's work by a single man at the standard intensity of employment.

Section 2: Marginal Productivity

Of the various theories that have been advanced to explain how the social income is divided among the various productive agents, that known as the "marginal productivity theory" has won for itself the foremost place. Previously economists had developed the "subsistence theory" which explained wages as being fixed at the minimum level necessary to maintain the life and health of the workers. But this theory could not define that subsistence level in terms sufficiently precise to give any real measure of wages, nor could it properly account for the fact that wage levels persistently exceeded a bare subsistence level. When the theory defined the subsistence level in precise terms as the minimum of foodstuffs, heat, and shelter necessary to maintain the supply of labour, it defined a wage level which departed from the actual wage level, and when it tried to account for the actual wage level by defining subsistence in terms of "standards of living" its definition lost the precision and definite-

[3] It is doubtful, indeed, how far the notion of average intensity in a task is derived purely from industrial custom. It will depend in part on certain extra-economic conditions, such as light, ventilation, and hygienic protection in the factory and on the general health, energy, interest, ambition, and standards of behaviour in the community. These sociological determinants will depend in turn on the social structure of the community, its political enlightenment and the soundness of its government and on its general economic well-being. Thus the industrialist may well benefit in terms of increased labour intensity from an improvement in the tone of the community as set by his fellows and himself.

ness necessary in an explanation of the determination of the rate of wages.

Residual theories which explained wages as the share left after capital costs had been paid on the no-rent lands left wages as non-determinant in the theory of production. Capital and labour are substituted for one another. The rate of return to capital will vary with the amount of capital employed, and the amount of capital employed will in part be determined by the amount which must be paid for a unit of labour. Thus if wages are regarded as residual, no logical theory of distribution is possible.

Bargain theories, which regard wages as the result of a bargain between labour and entrepreneur, are more realistic. Indeed wages are determined as the result of a bargain. But it is the function of economic science to state if it can the conditions determining the bargain. The so-called "bargain theory of wages" generally finds that the price of labour is indeterminate between certain limits, the minimum limit being the lowest rate at which workers will supply their labour and the upper limit being the highest rate that entrepreneurs can afford to pay and continue in business. Between those limits there are no determined points, and wages may fluctuate from the lower to the upper limit and back again. This form of indeterminate bargain theory obscures or neglects those forces which actually do determine wages and denies the possibility of any general equilibrium theory of price and distribution.

The marginal productivity theory, most immediately associated on this continent with the name of Professor J. B. Clark, was an attempt at a precise theory of the determination of the distributive shares of the agents of production.[4]

Professor Clark's theory assumes a given or fixed supply of labour in the short run. It further assumes that this total supply will all be employed, and that it will be employed, on the equilibrium assumption, in such quantities in each employment as to yield an equal marginal product in all employments. If labour is more productive, i.e. yields a higher marginal product in employment A than in other employments, employment A will be able to offer a higher rate of wages and this will attract more labour to employment A. This process will continue until the marginal product of the increased labour supply in employment A is no greater than the marginal pro-

[4]We have already given the mathematical formulation of this theory in Book Two. The marginal productivity of labour can be written $\frac{dP}{dL}$, that is the change in product with respect to a change in the quantity of labour.

duct of labour in other employments in the economy. Professor
Clark thus assumes complete mobility of labour from one employment to another.

The argument is based on three further fundamental assumptions. These are: the law of diminishing returns, the doctrine of the
flexibility of capital, and the conviction that the specific product of
a factor is discernible.

The law of diminishing returns is used in this theory in its static
and correct form. It asserts that if all factors but one are kept constant and if the employment of that variable factor be increased,
there will be a less than proportionate increase in product. We have
already observed that in this form the law of diminishing returns is
a valid generalization from observed fact. Thus when the quantity
of labour working with the same total amount of capital on the same
amount of land is increased, the increments in product will be smaller
and smaller as the increase in the employment of labour is continued.
This increment in product which results from this increase in labour
marks the maximum which the entrepreneur can afford to pay to
labour. Rather than pay more he will forgo employing the final
unit of labour. Since all units of labour are regarded as similar and
interchangeable the rate of reward offered to bring the final unit of
labour into production will likewise mark the maximum the employer will be willing to offer to retain any other unit in employment.
It is also argued that the competition among employers for labour
will be such that they will bid up to the amount of the marginal productivity in order to obtain labour. Thus the argument is that the
marginal productivity of labour determines the rate of wages.

A similar argument is advanced to explain the rate of return on
capital. Thus on no-rent land the product is divided between capital and labour. If labour is regarded as the variable factor, wages
will be determined by the marginal productivity of labour and the
residue will be interest. If capital is regarded as the variable factor,
interest will be determined by marginal productivity and the residue
will be wages. This is illustrated in Figs. 35 and 36. In Fig. 35
labour is regarded as the variable factor and wages are shown as the
rectangular area $MOAB$ and the residual interest is represented by
the triangular area ABC. In Fig. 36, where capital is treated as the
variable factor, interest is represented by the rectangular area $NODE$
and wages by the area DEF. It is supposed that $MOAB$ in Fig. 35
is equal in area to DEF in Fig. 36 when the figures are drawn to the
same scale, and that ABC is equal to $NODE$.

But if labour is to be increased, working with the same amount of capital, obviously this presumes that the actual forms of capital equipment will change. Capital must be sufficiently flexible to alter its forms to meet the needs of an increased body of workers. The total amount of capital will remain the same, but the actual capital equipment of which that total consists will have to be different. More workers will require more raw materials, probably more machines, even if these machines have to be cheaper and of poorer quality. That capital has not this flexibility is one of the criticisms of this theory. Indeed it is hard to see how, in actuality, if the

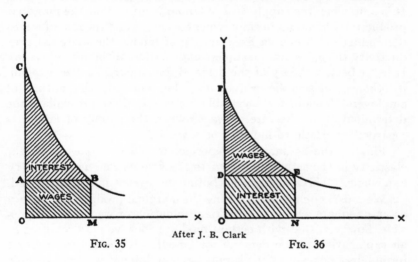

After J. B. Clark

FIG. 35   FIG. 36

quality and kind of capital equipment is varied it is possible to conceive of its quantity being unchanged, or, even, if the total quantity is unchanged, how even changes in quality and type can be treated as having no effect upon output. That is, if there are changes in the quantity of labour and changes in the kind and organization, if not the quantity, of capital equipment, can the variations in product be attributed specifically and entirely to the quantitative change in labour? Is there a specific marginal product of labour discernible? In actual industry—and we are attempting to explain how in actuality the employer decides what he can offer labour as a wage— are increments in the employment of labour possible without accompanying changes in the employment of capital? And is there a discernible marginal product of labour?

If we turn to the other assumptions on which the theory rests, are we better satisfied? There is a fixed supply of labour in the short-run period only if we accept as our unit of labour the individual worker. But if we select, as we have done, a time unit, then it is clear that even in the short run there is a considerable elasticity in the supply of labour. Once you grant that there are changes in the supply of labour the marginal productivity theory ceases to be, of itself, a complete and determinate theory. The marginal product of labour in the economy can only be determined when all of a fixed supply of labour is employed. If the reader will turn to Fig. 35 (p. 175) he will see that the marginal productivity is a varying quantity and that until the point M is given the rate of wages is not determined. It is only when the supply OM of labour is given that the marginal productivity of labour in employment is known and the rate of wages determined. Without a fixed supply of labour the marginal productivity theory is not a complete explanation of the rate of wages. It is, at best, a theory of the demand for labour. It does explain, if other criticisms be waived for the moment, the nature of employers' demand for a variable factor. It does not explain the determination of the rate of wages when the supply of labour is regarded as elastic to industry as a whole.

Finally, the assumption of perfect mobility implies a perfect elasticity in the supply of labour to the firm as well as to industry as a whole. This assumption is both unnecessary and unwarranted.

We must conclude by rejecting the marginal productivity theory as an adequate account of the determination of wages. It is possible, however, that with certain modifications we may retain it as an explanation of the demand for labour. If we can in addition formulate a concept of the supply price of labour, we shall be able to proceed to an equilibrium wage theory, which will form a part of a full equilibrium price system as adumbrated in Book Two.

Section 3: The Demand for Labour

A unit of labour is worth to a firm what it adds to the firm's revenues. What it adds to the firm's revenues is its marginal physical productivity multiplied by marginal revenue. This product we shall know as marginal value productivity. When a firm is in perfect competition so that marginal and average revenue coincide, then marginal value productivity is always marginal physical productivity times price, and the marginal value productivity and marginal physical productivity curves will fall with exactly the same slope and elasticity. But when the firm is in imperfect competition or is monopolistic the marginal and average revenues will not coincide. Marginal revenue will fall with a steeper slope so that marginal value productivity will always decline more sharply than marginal physical productivity.

The problem of distinguishing the marginal product of labour, a problem we observed in connection with the marginal productivity theory in its classic form, remains to be faced. For any equilibrium employment of labour it is clear that the labour must be employed conjointly with capital and other factors and in such quantities as leave the entrepreneur no motive to change the combination, substituting more labour for capital or *vice versa*. Capital and labour are combined in integrated economic units to the margin of substitution, i.e. to the point where no further substitution of labour for capital or capital for labour would pay. It is only by small variations at this margin of substitution that we get small variations in output which we can attribute specifically to labour and impute as the specific marginal product of labour.

If, within these limits, we decrease the combination of the productive factors by one unit of labour and we get a diminution in output as the dependent variation, we define the diminution in output as the marginal physical product of labour. More exactly, marginal physical productivity is a rate, the rate of change in total product with respect to a change in the employment of one of the factors of production.[5]

The difficulty of distinguishing the specific marginal physical product of labour may be overcome by the method of distinguishing "marginal net productivity."[6] We assume as given the marginal costs of all other agents in the productive combination and subtract this cost from the marginal value productivity of the integrated labour-land-capital combination. The remainder can then be directly imputed to labour and can be called "marginal net value productivity." This device has the merit of being more realistic than that used above, which is logically correct only when we suppose the units to be the infinitely divisible ones of the differential calculus. But this method seems to be open to the objection that when one attacks the problem of the pricing of the other agents of production one has to assume the rate of wages to be given. It seems to be circular argument to assume the rate of wages as given when determining the rates of remuneration for the other agents and to assume them as given when determining the rate of wages.

Perhaps we ought not to exaggerate this logical difficulty. In actual practice the firm never determines exactly the marginal phy-

[5]See Book Two, pp. 56-7.
[6]Joan Robinson, *Economics of Imperfect Competition* (London, 1933), chap. **xx**.

sical productivity of any factor, but it does obtain an approximation of this marginal physical productivity. We shall use the phrase "marginal net productivity" to refer to the marginal physical productivity that can be imputed to any one factor, and the phrase "marginal net value productivity" to refer to the marginal value productivity that can be imputed to any one factor.

A consideration of these definitions will show that we can no longer assume with certainty the existence of diminishing returns. If the increase in the employment of labour is accompanied by alterations in the efficiency of capital, it is conceivable that the firm will enjoy internal economies as it increases its employment of labour through time so that the marginal net productivity curve will be rising rather than falling. In a perfectly competitive industry, of course, the equilibrium assumption requires that all firms will be operating under diminishing returns; otherwise the industry would cease to be perfectly competitive.[7] But if the firm is a monopolistic one the recognition that there may be a reorganization of capital and internal economies accompanying the increase in the employment of labour alters the conditions and premises of diminishing returns. On the whole we are justified in basing our main argument on the assumption of diminishing returns, but we must admit the theoretic possibility of an upward sloping marginal productivity curve.

Under imperfect competition, however, the marginal revenue curve slopes downward to the right. Thus the marginal value productivity curve, the product of marginal physical productivity and marginal revenue, will, when marginal physical productivity is increasing, slope upwards or downwards according to the relative slopes of the marginal physical productivity and marginal revenue curves.

The marginal factor cost curve represents the increase in cost to the firm incurred by unit increments in the employment of the factor. In the case of labour the marginal cost of labour is derived from the average cost in the usual way, and the average cost will be given once we know the shape of the supply function of labour to industry generally. For the purposes of our present argument we shall have to assume, what we shall later establish, that in the short run the supply function of labour is positively inclined. This means that the marginal labour cost curve (of the firm) slopes upwards to the right. When the firm is in equilibrium it is apparent that the sum of all the marginal factor costs will, by

[7]See Book Three, p. 127.

definition, be equal to the marginal cost of production, and since
the sum of the marginal costs in equilibrium will be shown to be
equal to the sum of marginal productivities, and since marginal
cost of production is equal to
marginal revenue, then the sum
of marginal productivities of the
factors must be equal to marginal
revenue.   Total   revenue   less
total factor income (equals total
factor cost) must equal profit.
How this differential of profit
arises we shall be able to show
in the development of the argument.

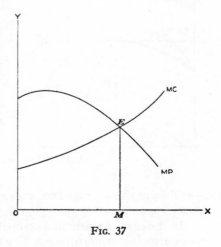

FIG. 37

A monopolistic firm will employ labour to the point where
the marginal cost of labour to
the firm will equal the marginal
value productivity. This case is
represented in Fig. 37, where
MP is the marginal value productivity curve, MC the marginal
labour cost curve, and OM the amount of labour employed.

A firm in a competitive industry will have a straight-line factor
cost curve, parallel to the x-axis. It also will employ to the point

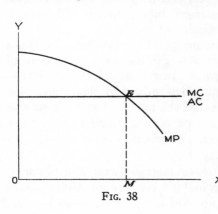

FIG. 38

where marginal factor cost
and marginal net productivity
are equal. This is illustrated
in Fig. 38. This rule is based
on the principle of maximiz-
ing profits.

As long as marginal pro-
ductivity exceeds marginal
factor cost, increases in employment bring increases in
net profits. But when marginal factor cost exceeds marginal net productivity, in-
creases in employment lead to a diminution in net profits. Thus
profits are at a maximum when marginal factor cost and marginal
productivity are equal.

The marginal firm employs to the point where marginal factor cost and marginal productivity are equal, and, because by definition it is a no-profit firm, this point must coincide with the highest point of the average productivity curve. This is illustrated in Fig. 39.[8]

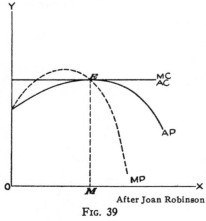

After Joan Robinson

FIG. 39

But marginal labour cost is not the rate of wages. It is the rate at which total labour cost increases with an increase in employment. The supply price of labour—the rate of wages at which additional labour units will be available for employment —will form the average cost curve to which the marginal cost curve is correspondent.

In the case of a firm in a competitive industry the average labour cost curve (and the corresponding marginal curve) will be a straight line parallel to the x-axis. See Figs. 38 and 39. This is because changes in the employment of a factor by any one firm will have no appreciable effect on the terms at which labour is available in the total industrial market. The supply curve of labour to a monopolistic firm, however, will have less elasticity and will be inclined upwards because if the firm increases employment it will have to pay more to attract additional supplies of the factor.

It will be seen, therefore, that marginal net productivity is not necessarily identical with the rate of wages, as was the argument of the marginal productivity theorists. In a competitive industry— see Figs. 38 and 39—employment is determined by the intersection of the marginal curves, and, because the marginal factor cost and average cost curves coincide, the rate of wages and marginal net productivity are equal. In that case marginal net productivity can be said to measure the rate of wages.

But in a monopolistic firm, where average factor cost is rising, the marginal factor cost and marginal net value productivity curves must intersect to the left of the intersection of the average productivity and average factor cost curves. In this case, marginal net value productivity in conjunction with marginal factor cost determines the amount of employment. The rate of wages, however, is

[8]See also pp. 104-6.

measured by the average cost curve and must be less than marginal net value productivity. The monopolist thus earns a surplus on the employment of each unit of labour, including the marginal unit.[9] This is illustrated in Fig. 40, where AP and MP are the average and marginal value productivity curves, and AC and MC the average and marginal factor cost curves. The amount of employment is determined by the intersection of MP and MC, and is measured by the amount OM. The rate of wages is MW and the entrepreneur's surplus is represented by the shaded rectangle WPW_1P_1.

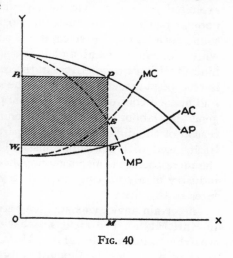

Fig. 40

It must not be thought that this surplus is entirely made up of profit which the entrepreneur enjoys from the "exploitation" of labour. Exploitation is one of those dangerous words that has been used by propagandists until it has lost precise meaning and has become a sound signifying moral indignation. Nevertheless there is a process for which exploitation may be the best word we have. But we must try to give it definite meaning. We shall say a productive factor is exploited when it receives as a reward less than the marginal increment it adds to the product. The surpluses earned by the entrepreneur from the employment of labour have to cover the other costs. Thus in Fig. 40 a certain portion of the rectangle WPW_1P_1 goes to pay capital and other costs. But a certain section represents a profit enjoyed by the entrepreneur by reason of his ability to pay labour less than the specific marginal value productivity of labour in the firm. Thus in Fig. 40 the amount EW measured off on the line PM represents the degree of the exploitation of labour per unit in the firm pictured in this figure. It must be remembered that labour is not the only factor so exploited. Any firm which is the only buyer of a factor which is not sufficiently mobile to seek other employment, what we shall call a monopsonistic firm,

[9]This surplus is not all monopoly profit. Out of it the other costs and rent must be paid. A certain portion of it, however, represents the monopolist's profit. The proportion of profit we do not for the moment attempt to state.

is able to exploit the factor in this way. Capital may find itself so exploited, or land or even managerial enterprise. Nevertheless the popular belief that labour is the most exploited factor is based on a sound social sense. Free capital is sufficiently mobile to move any-where for employment and it is seldom that a single buyer finds himself without competitors in the capital market. The same thing is true of managerial ability. The owner of land may sometimes find himself confronted with a monopsonistic buyer. But it is most generally labour which, by reason of specialized training, or by reason of the difficulty of moving from one place to another, finds itself faced with a monopsonist. This is particularly likely when the monopsonist is also a monopolist. If a single firm controls the industry of toy-making, then all toy-makers have to sell their ser-vices to this firm.

A certain analogy exists here between our conclusions and those of Karl Marx. The great socialist economist believed that labour was the source of all value. However, when it was employed it received as a wage, he thought, only the value of those commodities necessary to keep it alive, viz. to maintain the supply of labour. This might correspond roughly with our average cost, though the reader will be aware of fundamental differences between the two concepts, and, more important, between the premises on which they rest. But, Marx believed, the use of labour in conjunction with capital gave rise to "surplus value," a value over and above the supply price of labour. This we have shown to be true: our average product per worker exceeds the average cost or wage. Marx did not believe that capital should be rewarded beyond the value of the "stored-up labour" represented in the capital instruments, and he regarded this surplus value as the source of profits. He drew the conclusion that this surplus value which was extorted from the workers represented "exploitation." As we have seen, much of what Marx called "surplus value" must go to cover the costs of industry. Nevertheless there are conditions, not infrequent, under which labour, and possibly other factors, may be exploited in the sense that less will be paid them as a reward than the net marginal value product they create.

We have yet to consider the industrial demand curve for labour when there is perfect competition within the industry. When this is the case the supply curve of labor to the firm is perfectly elastic within the relevant range. This, we repeat, is because changes in employment in any one firm will not be sufficiently large to alter the prevailing industrial remuneration. If the supply is perfectly elastic the average and marginal cost curves will coincide as a straight-line parallel to the x-axis (see Fig. 39). Now since all firms employ to the point where marginal factor cost and marginal net value productivity are equal, and since marginal factor cost will be the same for all firms in the industry, it follows that when each firm in the industry is in equilibrium marginal net value productivity throughout the industry will be equal. Thus it is possible to speak of the marginal net value productivity of labour in the industry as a whole, and the industrial demand curve for labour must consist of the totals of the units of labour which will be employed by all the firms for a series of marginal net value productivities.

We have so far imagined diminishing returns to exist in all industries. In a progressive economy average and marginal productivity curves may be rising throughout, with no turning point from the rising to the falling position.[10]

If the marginal productivity curve for labour is rising throughout there may be no stable equilibrium wage. There is no guarantee that the marginal cost curve will rise so as to intersect the marginal productivity curve. In this case there would be no determinate rate of employment and wages in the industry. If, however, the curves do intersect, as in Fig. 41, the fact that marginal productivity continues to rise would not cause the firm to increase employment because marginal labour cost would be increasing at a more rapid rate than marginal productivity, and total profits would be reduced.

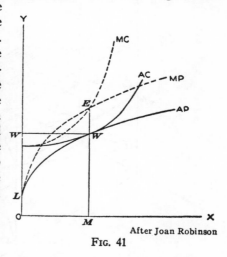

After Joan Robinson

Fig. 41

Actually these internal economies take place through time. We

[10]This is included as being theoretically necessary for complete argument, but it is highly improbable. In a progressive economy most of the internal economies come from improved capital techniques and they will make the demand curve for labour more elastic by increasing the degree of substitution of capital for labour. Economies that actually result in a rising labour marginal productivity curve are consequently unlikely.

should get a more accurate and correct picture of what really happens if we once again make use of the three-dimensional treatment we adapted for the treatment of decreasing costs in time. Because of diminishing returns the marginal productivity curve of labour must always decline at any moment of time. A series of such curves over a period of time may, however, shift gradually upwards towards the right. If we make use of a time axis we may represent this increase in marginal productivity over a period of time as a curvilinear surface which rises higher and higher on the Y-axis as we move outward from O along the T-axis. This is represented in Fig. 42. In this figure the marginal and average factor cost curves

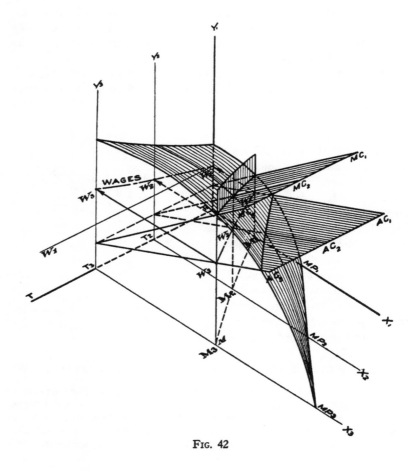

Fig. 42

(the MC and AC curves) are pictured as representing exactly the same factor cost situation over the total period of time, from time 1 to time 3. But the MP, marginal net value productivity curves, though each falls at any moment of time, are set each time higher on the Y-axis, indicating the increased factor productivity attendant on internal economies through time. Thus the amount of employment, indicated by M_1, M_2, and M_3, increases over the period, and at the same time the rate of wages, W_1, W_2, and W_3 rises continuously. The rising rate of wages is clearly shown by the rising line $W_1W_2W_3$ drawn against the background of the Y-axes.

It is difficult, if not impossible, to obtain statistical verification of theoretic argument based on marginal productivity analysis, because of the nature of the marginal productivity concept, which practically defies statistical analysis, except on the, unwarrantable, assumption that changes of marginal productivity in time correspond to the functional rate of change of marginal product to volume of employment. These difficulties are partly overcome, however, by the three-dimensional temporal analysis rather than the static or two-dimensional definition of marginal productivity. The theoretic argument would lead us to expect certain relationships between productivity, employment, and wages which would obtain over a period of time. If internal economies lead to a rising average productivity we should expect wages to increase, but less than in proportion. We should expect, under such conditions, an increase in employment in those industries experiencing an expansion of demand but in industries where there are only slight increases in demand, if any, we should expect the internal economies to result rather in higher wages than in increased employment. These conclusions are not repugnant to the more traditional static theory based on the notion of falling marginal productivity, for they presume a falling marginal productivity curve with increases in employment and follow from the increases in productivity over a period of time.

These expectations, formulated in concepts which now permit of reference to historical and statistical information receive striking corroboration from a recent study of the Brookings Institute.[11] This study shows the changes in productivity, wages and employment for the two-year average 1936-7 over 1923-4. The following composite table summarizes some of the findings:

[11]Spurgeon Bell, *Productivity, Wages and National Income* (Washington, 1940).

TABLE XIV

PERCENTAGE CHANGES IN SELECTED INDUSTRIES
1923-4 TO 1936-7

	Automobiles and Parts	*Iron and Steel*	*Paper and Pulp*	*Cotton Textiles*	*Tobacco*	*All Manufacturing*	*Mining*	*Railroads*	*Light and Power*
Productivity......	+47	+56	+52	+39	+140	+50	+89	+43	+111
Physical volume of output	+46	+16	+50	+ 7	+17	+25	+12	−17	+141
Man-hours of employment.......	− 0.7	−25	− 1.5	−24	−51	−16	−41	−42	+ 14
Number of wage-earners.........	+25	− 1	+12	− 7	−35	+ 3.5	−14	−39	+ 36
Hourly earnings...	+19	+24	+ 9	+ 4.5	+17	+13	+ 1.7	+13	+ 30
Weekly earnings ..	− 4.8	− 7	− 4.5	−14	−13	− 9	−30	+ 7	+ 9
Weekly earnings—real............	+11	+ 8	+11	+ 0.3	+ 1.6	+ 6	−19	+24	+ 27

An analysis of these figures shows that money wage rates increased with increases in productivity, but more markedly in expanding industries like the automobile industry and electric light and power than in comparatively stable industries like mining, textile manufacturing, and railroads. Real earnings, however, which differ from wage rates because they reflect the steadiness of employment throughout the year as well as the purchasing power of the wage dollar, are higher in industries of steady employment, like railroads, while in industries which are highly seasonal or seriously interrupted by strikes, like mining, real earnings show less improvement than money wage rates. Indeed in mining, real wage earnings showed a slight decline for the period. Nevertheless the long-run wage trend is upwards with increases in productivity, and this is particularly marked in the rapidly expanding electrical group. Employment, measured in man-hours, real quantity of labour, is on the other hand, reduced. The reduction, one observes, is rather in hours worked than in men employed, a phenomenon the theoretic argument had already suggested, but it is nevertheless a reduction in the quantity of labour employed. Interestingly enough the reduction is most marked where productivity was most increased, which might seem to suggest that productivity was increased by reducing employment, that is a statistical verification of static marginal productivity analysis. But this conclusion is not warranted by the facts; the increased productivity here occurred over time and was presumably due to internal economies and technical improvements. The reason employment was so sharply curtailed is indicated by the relatively small increase in the volume of output. There was little improvement in demand and consequently the technical improvements by means of which each worker in 1936 produced about one and a half times as much as in 1924 necessitated a reduction in employment. Only in the expanding electrical group was there an increase in employment, necessitated by the fact that the volume of output had increased more than in proportion to the productivity of the worker.

While we must not push these conclusions too far, we can see that they correspond in a most gratifying manner with the theoretic argument pictured in Fig. 42, where the increasing productivity of labour over a period of time is reflected by higher wages, which rise, however, less than in proportion to the increase in productivity. We chose, however, to illustrate an expanding industry, like the electrical goods industry, where the expansion of demand results in increased employment. The actual diminution of employment found in most of the other industries is, however, perfectly consistent with the theoretic argument.

Section 4: The Supply of Labour

We have so far assumed the cost of labour to be given. The marginal cost of labour to the firm is the pecuniary cost of employing an additional unit of labour. It depends on the price labour is willing to accept to supply an additional unit of labour effort. We have now to ask what forces affect the rate at which labour's services will be supplied to industry, and how changes in the supply of labour will affect wages.

The marginal productivity theorists regarded the total supply of labour as being fixed and therefore completely inelastic. They also regarded labour as completely mobile in moving from one employment to another, and thus implied that the supply of labour to the firm or to the industry was completely elastic. We have already shown that, on our definitions, there will be a certain elasticity in the supply of labour to industry as a whole, and we have admitted that labour is imperfectly mobile as between employments, so that the supply of labour will not be perfectly elastic to the firm (except when perfect competition is assumed) and that there will be certain differentials in wage rates as between employments.

We shall consider variations in the supply of labour under the following heads: short-run variations in the total supply of labour; short-run variations in the supply of labour to the firm; long-run variations in the supply of labour.

A. *Short-run variations in supply*

Alterations in the short-run supply of labour are sometimes forgotten. But the tremendous increase in the supply of labour which occurs, for example, in time of war is an indication that such short-run variations are possibly independent of changes in population. There are three ways in which the supply of labour is increased in the short run. The working hours in the day may be increased. This is a direct increase in the number of labour units employed. The fact that "overtime" wages are at higher rates than the usual pay is an indication that the increased supply of labour is obtainable only at a higher remuneration. That is to say that the supply curve of labour to industry as a whole is inclined upwards.

Women may be brought into industry. In time of war, to choose again a clear example, women flock into industry and trade in great numbers to replace the men who are employed in the armed services of the state. A superficial examination here might suggest that the women were employed at reduced wages. But such is not, in fact, the case. It is true, of course, that the women are frequently employed at wages less than those of the men they replace. But the women's intensity of work is less than—or is regarded as less than—that of men. If the ordinary differential between the unit of labour supplied in an hour by a man and that supplied by a woman is measured by the differential in pay, then the women brought into industry during periods of expansion in the supply of labour are brought in at increased remuneration. This is because wage rates for women are increased. Thus if women's wages are increased and if the old differential between men's and women's wages represented the employers' estimate of the difference in worth between male and female labour, then the increase in the supply of labour accomplished by the introduction of increased numbers of women into industry is at an increased wage per unit of labour. Thus once again the supply curve of labour to industry as a whole is seen to be inclined upwards.

Finally, young persons will be introduced into industry in response to a social demand for increased labour. School-leaving ages may be lowered and children or young persons above the legal school-leaving age who would normally have remained voluntarily in schools or technical colleges or universities will be attracted into industry or trade. Once again the attraction exercised to draw these young persons into employment will be higher wages.[12]

We cannot in a work of this sort make any attempt to estimate the elasticity of the short-run supply curve of labour to industry as a whole. Any such effort as Professor Robbins says, can only "proceed by inductive investigations of elasticities."[13]

The supply of labour to the firm we have treated in our preceding argument as positively inclined, except under perfect competition. We showed both average and marginal sector cost curves to slope upwards to the right. It is clear that, whatever the slope of the supply curve of labour to industry as a whole, any particular firm must offer higher rewards to increase its own available supply of labour and to attract workers from other occupations. Only under very special conditions might the supply curve of labour to the firm be negatively inclined.

We have now to ask what affects the shape and elasticity of this curve and what effect alterations in the elasticity of the supply of labour to the firm will have on the quantity and terms of employment. We assume monopsonistic conditions throughout. Ordinarily the supply curve of labour to the firm will slope upwards to the right. The firm must offer higher rewards to attract larger quantities of labour. If no specialized skills are required we may expect

[12]The matter covered in the previous paragraphs is somewhat controversial. Professor F. H. Knight has argued in his *Risk, Uncertainty and Profit* (Boston, 1921), p. 117ff., that the supply curve of labour is negatively inclined. This contention has frequently been made by various schools of economists. Professor Knight's argument is based on the thesis that there must be an equality between the worker's disutility of labour and the utility of his money wage at the margin of indifference. If wages are raised the marginal utility of the money wage will be reduced. Thus the added disutility of the last unit of labour time would now exceed the added utility of the last unit of money wage. Consequently the worker would want to shorten the working day. A critical examination of this interesting theory from the point of view adopted here can be found in Lionel Robbins, "On the Elasticity of Demand for Income in Terms of Effort" (*Economica*, vol. X, 1930). Professor Robbins shows that if the elasticity of the demand for money income is less than unity the supply curve of labour may be negatively inclined, but if the elasticity of the demand for income is greater than unity the supply curve of labour will be positively inclined. It is a matter of opinion but it is probable that the demand for money income is elastic for low income groups. The units of effort expended to gain an increased unit of income will remain high for all workers with low incomes for whom increased income means more of the necessities and barest comforts of life. Thus for the mass of labour, which is in this condition, the supply curve would be, if Professor Robbins's argument is correct, positively inclined.

[13]Robbins, "On the Elasticity of Demand for Income in Terms of Effort."

the curve to be reasonably elastic, though nothing more precise can be said by way of generalization. As the supply is taken up the curve may well become more inelastic as greatly increased wages are required to obtain small increases in labour time. The more specialized the labour the less elastic the supply curve will be. The supply curve of highly specialized labour may eventually reach an almost perpendicular position, the limiting position of zero elasticity.

When there are improvements in industry or when there is an increase in demand, the factors in less elastic supply are able to take a larger share of the benefits than those in more elastic supply. The classical economists of the Ricardian tradition regarded land as being completely inelastic in supply and they believed that gains from all improvements, either in technique or from an increase in demand, were entirely passed on to land. They were wrong in singling out land as the only factor in inelastic supply, but they were right in believing the inelastic factors received the lion's share of such improvements. If we imagine two factors, A and B, A being perfectly inelastic in supply and B being perfectly elastic, and if the marginal value productivity curve of each is raised by proportionate amounts, A will have the total benefit passed on to the same number of units in employment in the form of higher remuneration, and B will have more units employed at the same rate of remuneration.

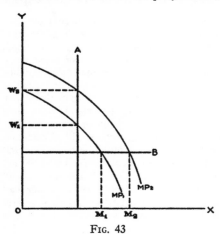

FIG. 43

This is illustrated in Fig. 43.

In this Figure the improvement in marginal value productivity of the two factors is shown by the shift to the right of the MP curve. The new MP curve cuts the supply curve of the inelastic factor A at a higher point. The full benefit is passed on as higher remuneration. In the case of the elastic factor B there is no improvement in the rate of remuneration. The whole benefit is passed on as increased employment.

This, of course, is an extreme case. But where one factor is less elastic than another the less elastic factor obtains a greater share of the benefits. Thus if factor A is inelastic, while factor B is elastic in supply and if there is an improvement in marginal value productivity the less elastic factor will be employed in but slightly increased numbers. Because there is no large increase in employment, the marginal productivity per unit will remain high, and remuneration will be at a higher level than before. Where the factor is elastic, however, there will be a big increase in employment and the new marginal productivity per unit will be but slightly higher than the previous. There will be more units employed but the improvement in remuneration will be slight. This is illustrated in Fig. 44.

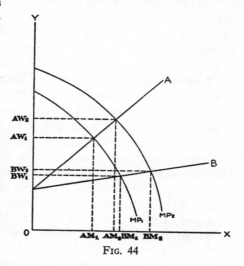

FIG. 44

Thus the war boom in Canada has meant higher wages for the skilled workers and more employment for the unskilled and semi-skilled. If, for example, we compare the increase of wages in the metal industries, we find that the average wage increase among the skilled craftsmen from June, 1939, to June, 1940, was 4.4 per cent. The increase, within the same industry (there is thus no difference in the degree of war stimulus), in the wages of unskilled workers averaged over the same period 2.8 per cent.[14] In the building trades in fifteen cities in Canada skilled workers' wages rose by 3 per cent in eight trades and unskilled workers' wages had risen during the same period by only 2 per cent.[15] In all probability the disparity will become more apparent by 1941. Moreover, one should bear in mind the increased hours worked at overtime rates which would give an even greater differential between the skilled and unskilled workers. Employment figures are less satisfactory, since employment figures by trades within industries are not separately obtainable. We are justified, however, in making the broad assumption that the employment figures reported by the trades unions will be heavily

[14]*Wages and Hours of Labour in Canada, 1940* (Ottawa, Dominion Bureau of Statistics). These figures are taken from proof as the publication is, at the time of writing, not available. The author wishes to thank the officials of the Bureau for access to this information in advance of publication.
[15]*Ibid.*

biased by the skilled crafts and that the general employment index
will include the unskilled as well as the skilled workers. In June,
1939, the Canadian trade unions reported 11.7 per cent unemployed, in June, 1940, 7.9 per cent; that is employment had increased
as from 88.3 to 92.1 or 4.3 per cent.[16] The general employment
index in June, 1939, was 113.1 (1926 = 100) and in June, 1940, it was
120.9, an increase of 7.1 per cent.[17] When we consider that this latter
figure includes both skilled and unskilled, that it is, roughly speaking, an average between the 4.3 per cent increase in the employment
of skilled workers and some unknown increase in the employment
of the unskilled, we must conclude that the improvement in employment of the unskilled must greatly have exceeded that of the skilled.
The increased demand of war-time has benefited the workers in
inelastic supply through higher wages with some increase in employment. Workers in elastic supply have benefited through increased
employment with some improvement in wages.

For similar reasons the less elastic the supply of a factor the less
the factor suffers from reduction of remuneration or reduction in
employment when there is a decrease in demand for the product or
when for other reasons the firm's position is worsened. Thus in the
vicissitudes of the business world the factors in inelastic supply benefit most in good times and suffer least in bad. It is perhaps for this
reason, among others, that trade unionism is frequently more successful with skilled craftsmen than with unskilled labourers. An
improvement in bargaining position, due to unionization, will bring
greater improvements in wages to workers if they are in inelastic
supply than if they are in elastic supply. But unionization has a
definitely beneficial effect on wages. The fallacious notion that
wages were fixed by marginal productivity alone (the supply of
labour being fixed in total amount) and that unions could only raise
wages for one group by reducing employment or lowering wages of
another group was only tenable on the assumption that labour was
in completely elastic supply to the firm. Then it would be true that
an increase in wages would result in a reduction of employment.
But if labour is supplied along a positively inclined curve with an
elasticity of less than infinity, unionization will mean a definite
improvement in the position of labour. It is impossible to say *a
priori* whether the increase in wages will be more or less than
proportionate to the reduction in employment. This will depend
on the elasticities of the factor supply curve and the marginal pro-

[16]*Canada Labour Gazette*, July, 1939; July, 1940.
[17]*Ibid.*

ductivity curve. If, for example, both are inelastic so that one is rising sharply while the other is falling steeply, the probable effect of unionization will be that the total share of the end product going to labour will be increased. This is pictured in Fig. 45.

In this figure the curve $BB_1B_2B_3$ represents the probable effect of unionization upon the shape of the original supply curve of labour A. The group from B to B_1 are those workers who are not union members but who are able to demand higher wages as a result of the shift in the centre of the curve resulting from unionization. The flat part of the curve from B_1 to B_2 represents the wage set by the collective agreement

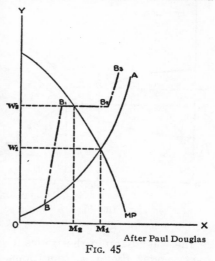

After Paul Douglas

FIG. 45

of the union for which all members of the union will work. The balance of the curve B_2 to B_3 represents overtime at increased rates. The result of unionization in this case is that the rate of wages is increased by more than the reduction in employment so that the total wage bill, or the total share of labour in the end product of the industry, is increased.

It is for this reason, as we have previously intimated, that unionization has been most successful among skilled workers. This also explains why, in times of war or other periods of boom when the labour supply is being largely utilized and the factor supply curves are becoming pretty inelastic, there is intense organizing activity among workers of almost every grade. Such conditions permit of rapid and evident improvements in the lot of labour after organization and thus are most favourable to union activity. It is small wonder that the workingman finds it a strong temptation to take every possible advantage of his strong position; it is not often he has the opportunity.

If, however, the supply curve of labour and the marginal productivity curve are both very elastic as in Fig. 46, it is possible that the increase in wages resulting from the organization of the workers will result in a decrease in employment more than in proportion to the increase in wages. In this case it is true that the total wage bill

would be reduced and labour's share of the end product of the industry would be less than before the organization of the union.   But

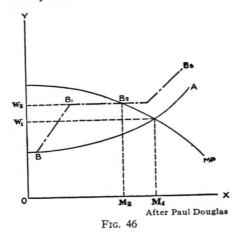

FIG. 46

even here one must be very
careful what conclusions one
draws. For the truth is that
we are treating here ab-
stract, purely static conditions.   Unionization has
been shown empirically time
and again to have achieved
solid benefits for labour
quite apart from wage
changes. All sorts of social
reforms which might not
otherwise have been
achieved have been won by
the pressure of organized
labour. Outside the realm
of the wage bargain the trades union has shown its worth. Moreover, under dynamic conditions the unions have succeeded in
making the rate of wages "sticky" and have thus improved the
position of labour in comparison with other factors during periods
of economic depression. The trades union has also an important
function in the social economy as a "stabilizer." When confronted
with a monopsonist buyer, labour, if unorganized, is in a helpless
position. It is only when organized as a monopolist seller of labour
services that labour can hope to achieve an equal bargaining
position.   It is probably not true, we might add here, that a
monopsonist buyer will actually reduce employment to the "equilibrium point" of maximum profit when confronted with unionization
of his workers. Public opinion, which strongly resents a reduction
of employment by an important industry, may have an important
modifying effect on the monopsonist's behaviour. In such a case the
higher wages are achieved by the union without any reduction in
employment and the monopsonist is content with a reduced surplus. Empirical studies have shown that frequently organization of
labour has led, not to a reduction in employment, but to technical
improvements that have raised the marginal productivity curve so
that the full staff continues to be employed at a higher wage.

     When there is perfect competition among the buyers of labour,
the factor cost curves to the firms are then perfectly elastic.   But,
in such cases, what has been said above with reference to the supply

of labour to the monopsonist firm will apply to the supply of labour
to the industry. An important qualification is that positive shifts
in the bargaining position of labour may then have the effect of
driving the marginal or least efficient firm out of business. This
infrequent case is the one most generally considered by those who
have a strong bias against trades unionism. The case is a limiting
one in theory and deserves mention. In actual practice it would be
hard to show many, if any, cases where union organization had in
itself resulted in the closing down of a firm.

Union organization results in a positive shift of the supply curve
of labour. In theory there are certain conditions of elasticity under
which the consequent increase in wages would be less than proportionate to the reduction in employment and the resultant share of
labour in the end product would be less. In actual fact the reduction
of employment may not take place, or, if it does take place, may be
very much less than purely theoretic considerations would lead one
to expect. Trades unionism, then, with infrequent exceptions, is
beneficial to labour; but it is more beneficial to those specialized
groups which are in comparatively inelastic supply.

B. *Long-run variations in supply*

The long-run supply of labour will depend on population changes.
The long-run rate of change of labour supply will be roughly measured for any country by the formula $\dfrac{B-D\pm M}{P}$, where B is the
number of births, D the number of deaths, and M the net immigra-
tion or emigration. P is the total population.

It is only since the American and French Revolutions that any
public attempt has been made to take a regular census of population.
Prior to that estimates were sometimes made, but they were not
accurate and they were not made at regular intervals. The first
American census was taken in 1790 and the first British census in
1801. Population theorists are thus faced with the difficulty that
accurate statistics of population change are available for little more
than a hundred years, a comparatively short time in the population
history of the communities of the western world.

For a long time it was believed that population was nearly static
and that there were forces at work which would prevent any sub-
stantial increase in population. The economic and political writers
of the eighteenth century believed that the population of England
was either static or decreasing. Writers in France were aware of

increases, but they believed that the population of France had reached its maximum.   These beliefs were given a more scientific appearance by Malthus[18] who tried to show that population if unchecked increased by a geometric ratio, 1, 2, 4, 8, 16, 32, 64 . . . , while food resources or subsistence increased, at best, according to an arithmetic ratio, 1, 2, 3, 4, 5, 6, 7, 8, 9. . . . Thus, he concluded, population must rapidly outrun the means of subsistence.   Famine and the diseases bred by famine and overcrowding would soon impose a check on the natural increase of population.   An upper limit to population was thus imposed by the available resources of food. Though these resources might be increased with an increase of workers, the increase in resources was proportionately small and the rate of increase of population would, by the forces of nature, be restricted to the slow rate of increase of food production.

Malthus ought not, perhaps, to be blamed for the uses to which his theory was put by those who were relieved to find in it a justification for their continued comfort in the face of misery and starvation.   These disciples interpreted the Malthusian argument to mean that if the workers were given better pay and better living conditions, they would marry earlier, have larger families and live longer.   Their rapid multiplication would lead to pressure on the means of subsistence, eventual famine, and the sorry reduction of the entire population to an even worse state of misery than that from which the original reforms had lifted them.   This comforting theory included the corollary that it would be a pity for the rich to give up any of their comforts when the long-run results would be so disastrous for the poor.   Malthus had, of course, an Anglican clergyman's sympathy for the poor, "who in the great lottery of life have drawn a blank,"[19] and he believed that they might find comfort in Christian resignation and a dignified acceptance of their lot; the accident of birth was final and could not be repaired. Less biased thinkers, however, were unable to find comfort in the evident fact that population and the standard of living were increasing together throughout the earlier years of the nineteenth century.   Ricardo and Mill were alike gloomy and believed that diminishing returns on land were bound to impose a check on population.   Population might increase because of certain technical improvements but eventually the failure of subsistence to increase with population would result in overcrowding and a check to

[18]T. R. Malthus, *An Essay on the Principle of Population* (6th ed., London, 1826).

[19]*Ibid.*, p. 350.

population. Ricardo believed that if real wages rose appreciably above subsistence for any considerable period of time population would rapidly increase until wages were once again lowered to a bare subsistence level.

The failure of these gloomy prophecies led some later writers to believe that the long-run supply curve of labour was negatively inclined. That is they thought that as real wages were raised the birth-rate would decline; though the death-rate also would decline it was believed that the larger proportionate decline would be in birth-rate. Thus, it was believed, a rise in real wages would be accompanied, were it sustained over a sufficient period, by an actual decline in population. This theory receives some support from the observed fact that fertility and reproduction rates are lower among the upper, or higher paid, strata of the population. There has also been a very pronounced decline in the birth-rates in western countries since approximately the middle of the last century[20] and in net reproduction rates since the beginning of the present century. We may see that this view is in flat contradiction to the former one. Whereas Malthus held that a rise in real wages would lead to an increase in population, an increase that would be rapid until checked by failure of the means of subsistence, this new view holds that a rise in wages will be accompanied by a fall in population. Whereas Malthus held that the long-run supply curve of labour was positively inclined, the other view holds that it is negatively inclined. Whereas Malthus held that the gains to labour from any advance would be short-lived, the alternative view holds that labour will consolidate its gains and, by lower-

[20]It is not possible to say in general just when this decline set in. Thus in Sweden a definite decline in the birth-rate was pronounced after 1870, the net fertility rate increased with occasional lapses until about 1860, was fairly constant till 1890, and thereafter slowly declined until 1920. Since 1920 the decline has been sharp. The Norwegian figures are similar, except that the decline in the birth-rate is not pronounced until after 1880. The Danish figures are similar to the Norwegian. In Great Britain the birth-rate reached its peak in 1875, and thereafter declined. The net fertility rate declined with the exception of the immediate post-war years from about 1905. In France the birth-rate has been declining since 1820, and the decline in the net fertility rate set in about the time of the War of 1870. In Germany the decline in the birth-rate begins in 1876, or thereabouts, and the decline in the net fertility rate about 1902. In Italy the birth-rate has declined since 1885, and the net fertility rate since the Great War. In the United States the two declines set in, of course, at a later date. There is no marked decline in the birth-rate until after the first decade of the present century and the net fertility rate does not decline until after the Great War.

ing its net reproduction rate, actually accentuate them by reason of increased marginal productivity.[21]

The truth would seem, however, to lie somewhere between these two views, or, perhaps one should say in a modification of Brentano's position. Clearly labour tends to hang on to its gains by reducing its birth-rate when real wages increase. The evidence in favour of this view may be regarded as conclusive, or nearly so. Certainly the improvement in standards of living that began in Malthus's day has been accompanied by a cessation not an augmentation, as he expected, of famines and famine-bred epidemics. There are few people today, outside Dr. Goebbels's Propaganda Bureau, who would attempt seriously to argue that our wars and our depressions were the result of over-population.

On the other hand, it is hard to believe that the long-run supply curve of labour is negatively sloped. As Professor Douglas points out in his comments on Brentano's theory,[22] Brentano seems to have considered birth-rates and to have neglected death-rates. After all, the rising real wages of the nineteenth century were accompanied by an unprecedented increase in population. The workers did secure their improved standards of living by reducing their rate of reproduction, but the improved living conditions and the improved techniques of medicine combined to effect even greater reductions in the death-rate. Professor Douglas sums up the evidence in favour of the view that the long-run supply curve of labour is positively inclined in the following words:

(1) Real wages increase both because the quantity of capital grows more rapidly than the supply of labor and hence raises the marginal productivity of the latter and because of improvements in technique. (2) As real wages rise the standard of living of the workers also rises. Since the standard of living fundamentally consists of the commodities and services which people prefer to having children, the result is that the birth rate through the practice of birth control adjusts itself at a lower point from that which it would be were the previous and cheaper standard of living to persist in the presence of the higher wage. (3) As wages continue to increase, the same process tends to be repeated. So far as the European and American experience of the past decades is concerned this process tends to continue until the true rate of natural increase either falls to nothing or actually becomes a minus quantity.[23]

We have, of course, to face the fact that in recent years there

[21]For a presentation of this view, see L. Brentano, "The Doctrine of Malthus and the Increase of Population during the Last Decades" (*Economic Journal*, vol. XX, 1910).

[22]Paul Douglas, *Theory of Wages* (New York, 1934), p. 351.

[23]*Ibid.*, p. 379.

has been a marked lowering of net fertility rates and that population experts, projecting their population curves into the future foresee a definite decline in population in the western countries. But this decline is probably due to causes extraneous to the rate of real wages. It is, in part at least, the result of the practice of birth control. To some extent, at any rate, population trends continue independent of economic causation; given the present-age distribution of population in western Europe and the United States and the continued practice of birth control, and the population curves of the immediate future are practically determined irrespective of the trend of real wages. Indeed we may anticipate a reciprocal action. The continued accumulation of capital and improvement in techniques, with a reduced population, may well result in marked increases in real wages for all working sections of the population. This view, so bright in contrast with the gloomy prognostications of Malthus, is marred only by the prospect of continued devastating wars.

Section 5: Enterprise

The function of enterprise is to accept the responsibility, and attendant risk, of the direction of the firm. This risk and responsibility are of a peculiar nature. The man who lends capital to an enterprise accepts a certain risk. If the enterprise fails he may not receive either his interest or his full capital back. The worker, too, runs certain risks. His tenure of his job is not certain: if the firm fails he may find himself out of employment. In many occupations he put his health, his limbs, and even his life in hazard. But the pecuniary risks of enterprise are peculiar to the entrepreneur. Without the guarantees of the bondholder or the bank he puts up capital, is the owner—or an owner on shares—of the enterprise and as such accepts the full pecuniary risks of the enterprise and the responsibility for decisions affecting its market behaviour.

Actually in modern practice the position of the enterpriser is undergoing certain modification. Infrequently do we find the owner-manager type of business where a single person puts up the bulk of the capital and runs the business. More often the firm is corporatively owned. A group of people put up the capital and have little more to say in the direction of the business than the bondholders, who have merely lent money on a guaranteed interest basis. These stockholders receive in return for their capital a return which amounts in fact to normal interest plus a small reward for the additional risk which they accept over and above the risk accepted by the bondholder.

The actual management and direction of the company are delegated to a managing director and a board of the chief stockholders. These men take the real responsibility of ownership and direct the market behaviour of the enterprise. The professional manager is paid a salary, he is an employee of the corporation, and the stimuli which operate on him are not those which operate on a man who runs his own privately owned business. This point deserves consideration. It is frequently said that the great advantage of private capitalism is that the managers of enterprises have the incentive to "efficiency" which arises from their concern for their own capital. This is not strictly true. Many times the manager is handed a block of stock to give him a personal interest in the concern he is managing, but his incentives to efficient management do not primarily derive from this fact. On the contrary, they come from his dependent position, the fact that his job and his advancement depend on his success; the fact that his ambition and professional pride are involved; the fact that, presumably, his interest is in his work. These are all incentives which would equally well be operative under alternative methods of ownership of capital.

It is difficult to say that there is any precise determination of the wages of management. The manager must be paid at least as much as he could obtain in alternative employments of similar size and responsibility. If he shows himself superior over his rivals, he may well expect an extra return which might be called a quasi-rent of management, a differential earned because of his superior skill. If he owns some of the stock, he will receive in addition a share in the profits of the enterprise.

In order to retain capital in an enterprise the owners must receive the normal remuneration prevailing over industry as a whole. That is there must be a return equal to the interest they could receive if they invested their money elsewhere plus some additional reward for the extra risk of ownership. But the measurement of risk, of necessity cannot be precise. Frequently, instead of an actual reward for risk, there is substituted the possibility of exceptionally large rewards, and the investor is invited to speculate, setting up the extra risks against the possibilities of exceptional profits.

Finally, the owners of the enterprise receive whatever profits are earned additional to the normal return. These extra profits may come from three sources; they may come from monetary fluctuations, from technical advantages, or from a monopolistic position in the market.

If there is a monetary inflation so that there is a general advance in prices, firms holding large stocks of raw materials, bought at the old prices, will be able to sell at higher prices than they anticipated and to realize unexpected or "windfall" profits.

If there is an advance of demand so that old machinery which had previously been written off as amortized and which was no longer profitable may once again come within the margin of employment. On such no-cost machinery all earnings are of the nature of rents or surpluses; they may be called after Marshall "quasi-rents"[24] and these rents accrue as profits to the entrepreneur. Or a firm may enjoy certain technical advantages over its rivals. If these advantages are directly attributable to land, they will be paid out in the form of rent and will not go to the firm unless it is the owner of its own land. But there may be certain technical superiorities enjoyed by reason of machinery or organization for which no rent is paid an agent. Surpluses earned as a result of such superiorities may likewise be regarded as "quasi-rents" and may be received by the firm.

Finally, as we have seen, a firm which enjoys a special position on the market, a monopolistic position, is able to maximize its net returns. These returns will be determined by the shape of its marginal cost and marginal revenue curves and will bear no necessary relation to the normal returns being earned on capital in competitive industries. These profits may be known as monopoly profits. They are made up of the surpluses, enjoyed by monopolies as a result of restriction of output, over and above the "normal return" to ownership. These surpluses may not all be distributed in the form of cash dividends. Frequently, indeed, firms wish to conceal the magnitude of their rate of profit. Large surpluses are set aside as "reserve" and stock dividends are issued. A stock dividend is a further issue of stock entitling the recipient to an increased equity in the business. Thus a firm may issue over a period of five years stock dividends amounting to $20 each year on every $100 par value of original stock. The cash dividends may be kept at 5 per cent. Yet in five years' time the owner of $100 worth of stock has received profits to an amount which gives him a capital holding of $200 and an annual cash yield of $10 on his original investment. Thus, though the rate of dividend as published in the newspapers remains at 5 per cent, the actual profits far exceed this modest figure.

In view of the tendency towards monopolistic industries the phrase "normal profits" or "normal return" has ceased to have, if it ever had, any very precise meaning. It cannot mean an average return, nor the return in an "average" industry. It can only mean

[24]Alfred Marshall, *Principles of Economics* (2nd ed., London, 1891), p. 418.

the return to capital under "normal" competitive conditions, but since such competitive conditions are no longer normal in any sense of the word the phrase is apt to be misleading.   It might perhaps be read to mean normal rate of interest, but here, again, there are difficulties, as we shall see when we come to the study of interest rate.   In any case the concept, if imprecise, is not important, for the whole picture of modern industry is dominated by the firms in imperfect or monopolistic competition whose profits are maximized by restriction of output.[25]

[25]The use of the word "normal" in economic literature might well be the subject for a much longer discussion than we have seen fit to give here. Clearly it cannot mean "usual." We should be nearer a true interpretation if we regarded "normal" as synonymous with "equilibrium" used as an adjective.   Thus "normal" price is not usually to be found in the actual market, it is the "equilibrium price" of abstract theory: normal returns to capital are not the returns usually found; there is no warrant for the belief that there is any greater probability that any particular firm will be earning normal than abnormal profits. Normal returns to capital consist of the equilibrium rate of interest which brings into the investment market an amount of free capital whose marginal net value productivity in employment is anticipated as just equalling the interest rate, plus a small allowance for risk.

CHAPTER XVIII

RENT AND DIFFERENTIAL SURPLUSES

SECTION 1: DEFINITIONS

IN this chapter we shall use "rent" to refer to a special sort of return from enterprise. We shall use it to mean any differential return on an agent of production. How this differential arises we shall describe in detail in the following sections. In common language rent usually means the charge made for the use of land or a house or factory or similar fixed asset. In economics rent was first used to refer to the charge made for the use of land. This was distinguished as "economic rent."

The earlier rent theories, notably that of Ricardo, explained rent as arising as a result of the increased returns on the better lands as compared with the marginal lands which produced only enough to pay the "real costs" of production. Rent, then, was the differential surplus of the return from better lands over that of the marginal land. Ricardo also pointed out that the more intensive cultivation of land under diminishing returns meant that there would be surpluses earned by all intramarginal units of the variable factors. These surpluses would also give rise to rent.[1]

Later economists pointed out that rents or "quasi-rents," as Marshall called them, might arise from the intensive use of any fixed or relatively fixed agent of production. Other economists also showed that land had a "scarcity" cost comparable to the costs of other agents. Consequently the distinction between land and other capital has become blurred. We no longer speak of rent as being the return on the use of land, but speak of it as being a differential return over and above other costs of production. Part of the payment for the use of land will be a capital expense of production and will be reckoned as such. All differential surpluses arising from the use of an agent we shall call rent.

We must distinguish rent from other surpluses. We know that certain "profits" are surpluses, and, as we have seen, the distinction between "normal" profits and "surplus" profits is becoming difficult by reason of the disappearance of the "normal" condition of perfect competition. However, it is traditional to define normal profits as consisting of the average return on capital invested plus the average

[1]For further explanation see section 2 of this chapter.

wages of management. Every firm in competitive equilibrium must make normal profits. Otherwise it is not covering its average costs. Thus "normal profits" are not a surplus of any sort. "Surplus profits" are returns to the entrepreneur over and above costs of production. They may, as we have seen, arise as a result of three sets of circumstances.

A monetary inflation may raise prices and if a firm has a good stock of raw materials bought at old prices and is able to delay raising wages, it will sell at more than the anticipated price while keeping its costs for the time being at the old rate. The consequent profit is "money surplus profit," or more briefly, "money profits." The reverse movement, monetary deflation, creates "negative money profits," i.e. losses due to monetary changes. Such profits may occur in a competitive or monopolistic industry.

An industry may not have reached equilibrium or it may be in transition from one equilibrium position to a new one necessitated by a spontaneous change in demand or by a change in technical processes. This transition may create profits, by increasing marginal revenues or lowering marginal costs or both. These profits will continue until further competition has reduced them to zero. These profits we shall call "transitionary profits." They may appear in either competitive or monopolistic industries.

Finally, there are monopoly profits which arise because of the ability of a firm to withhold and restrict supply and thus to sell at a point where price exceeds average unit cost. These profits arise in monopolistic industries only.

In a competitive industry under equilibrium—so that neither money nor transitionary profits exist—no surplus profits may arise. The surpluses of the intra-marginal firms are rents. That is they arise because of superior advantages enjoyed by reason of better land, better situation, better equipment, or better management— in a word, they are surpluses which arise as a result of some agent or group of agents. As such the supplier of the agent can demand them from the entrepreneur and will receive these surpluses as an additional reward. Thus to the entrepreneur rent appears as a cost of production which he must pay. It is because of this that we said[2] that when rents are included in costs of production each firm of a competitive industry is in equilibrium when its total average unit costs, including rent, are just equal to average revenue or price. Thus the marginal firm pays no rents, and the intra-marginal firms pay as rents the differential surpluses they enjoy as compared with

[2]See Book Three, pp. 105-7.

the marginal firm. For all firms in competitive industry in equilibrium, profits are normal, and no surplus profits are earned.

We can thus distinguish between *rents* and *surplus profits*. Rents are surpluses that are earned by specific agents of production. They can be claimed by the agents and will be paid as additional rewards.

Surplus profits arise from the market situation and are not attributable to any particular agent. Thus money and transitionary profits are obviously the result of non-equilibrium forces on the market and are not present in perfect equilibrium. Monopoly profits are present in equilibrium and are normal to it in monopolistic industries. They are not attributable to any particular agent, but arise as a result of the firm's dominant position on the market, and are retained by the owners of the enterprise and not paid to the owners of any agent.

Even when the owners of the corporation also own the agent (as when a corporation owns its own land), corporation accountants distinguish between the returns paid to the agent and "profits earned." Thus surplus profits are surpluses earned by and payable to the enterprise as a whole, whereas rents are surpluses earned by and payable to a specific agent or agents.

SECTION 2: THE THEORY OF THE RENT ON LAND

The Ricardian theory of land rent was based on the supposed fact of diminishing returns. For Ricardo and his contemporaries "the law of diminishing returns" had a partial and specialized meaning. It meant for them that the increased use of land, either by more intensive or extensive cultivation, would yield less than proportionate increases in product. The best land would, Ricardo assumed, be first put under cultivation. As population increased and more food was demanded poorer and poorer lands would be cultivated. The poorer lands would yield less than the better lands. The poorest land of all, which it would just pay to cultivate, would be on the extensive margin of cultivation and could be called "marginal land."

Similarly the more intensive cultivation of the better land would result in diminishing returns. "Doses" of labour and capital would be applied to the land until the last or marginal dose just increased the total yield by enough to cover the marginal cost of that dose. This determined the intensive margin for the cultivation of land.

Now land differed from the other productive agents, according to Ricardo, in being fixed in supply and freely provided by nature.

It had therefore no supply cost. Improvements to land naturally had a supply cost, but they were reckoned as capital. The "natural and indestructible" qualities of the land were given by nature. Thus there was no "real cost," comparable to labour and saving connected with the supply of land. It had no supply price.

The prices of commodities would be determined by the equilibrium of demand price and supply cost of the variable factors at the margin of cultivation. The marginal value product would cover the marginal costs of the variable factors and each unit of these factors would receive no more than this by way of income. At the margin, then, there would be nothing left over for land. Ricardo argued that the existence of free land (as on the frontiers of settlement in America) was evidence to support his view that marginal land was no-rent land.

But on all intra-marginal land and on all intra-marginal applications of labour and capital a surplus return was earned. This differential surplus the landlord could claim as rent. The enterpriser would reluctantly pay the full differential as rent because he was making a normal return after he had paid it and rather than cease production he would pay. If rent was increased beyond the differential he would go to marginal, no-rent land. Thus the amount of the differential surplus determined the level of rent, and the value amount of the surplus would be determined by the determination of price and output. Thus rent was "price-determined," not a "price-determining cost."

A brief illustration may clarify and clinch the argument. Let us suppose there to be five different grades of agricultural land, according to fertility. Let us also suppose that we have a labour-capital unit consisting of one man working ten hours a day with $100 worth of capital (including raw materials and machinery). Let us further suppose that 10 labour-capital units on 1,000 acres of Grade A land produce 10,000 bushels of produce, worth $1.00 a bushel; on the B land, 10 units produce 8,000 bushels, on the C land, 6,000 bushels, and on the D land, 4,000 bushels, on the E land, 2,000 bushels.

This may be represented graphically as in Fig. 47.

The E land is on the extensive margin. Its value product of $2,000, by definition, just covers the cost of employing 10 men and $1,000 worth of capital. But wages and interest will be uniform. Hence on Grades A, B, C, and D, the return to capital and labour will be $2,000 in each case. Thus an additional value product over and above capital and labour costs will accrue on the 4 intra-marginal grades, amounting to $8,000 on Grade A, $6,000 on Grade B, $4,000 on Grade C, and $2,000 on Grade D.

But if it pays to apply agents on E land it will pay the cultivators of the intra-marginal lands to cultivate more intensively. They will apply more agents to working the 1,000 acres each of Grades A, B, C, and D, and will apply them to the point where, due to diminishing returns, the marginal value product just covers the marginal factor cost. We know the marginal factor cost to be $2,000 for 10 capital-labour units.

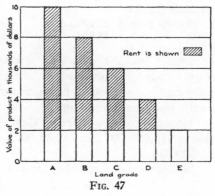

FIG. 47

Let us suppose that diminishing returns set in as follows:

		Marginal Differential Product
On Grade A Land		
10 units produce $10,000		
20 " " $18,000		$8,000
30 " " $24,000		$6,000
40 " " $28,000		$4,000
50 " " $30,000		$2,000

		Marginal Differential Product
On Grade B Land		
10 units produce $ 8,000		
20 " " $14,000		$6,000
30 " " $18,000		$4,000
40 " " $20,000		$2,000

		Marginal Differential Product
On Grade C Land		
10 units produce $ 6,000		
20 " " $10 000		$4,000
30 " " $12,000		$2,000

		Marginal Differential Product
On Grade D Land		
10 units produce $4,000		
20 " " $6,000		$2,000

Marginal
Differential
On Grade E Land   *Product*

    10 units produce \$2,000.................(On extensive margin   \$2,000)
    20   "   "   \$3,000....................................   \$1,000

It is clear that 50 units will be used on Grade A, 40 on Grade B, 30 on Grade C, 20 on Grade D, and only 10 on Grade E land. Twenty units on Grade E would produce a marginal product less than equal to the marginal factor cost.

Now the total product on Grade A land is \$30,000 and the total cost is \$10,000 (50 units at \$2,000 per 10 units). Thus the rent will be \$20,000.

Similarly rents on other lands will be:

               On Grade B...................... \$12,000
               On Grade C...................... \$ 6,000
               On Grade D...................... \$ 2,000
               On Grade E...................... zero

Intensive cultivation has increased the rents on all lands but Grades D and E. On E no intensive cultivation is possible; it is no-rent land. On D the intensive cultivation reaches the margin in one "dose" so that the differential is not increased and the total surplus is exactly as before intensive cultivation took place. In all other cases rents accrue as differentials on both intensive and extensive margins.

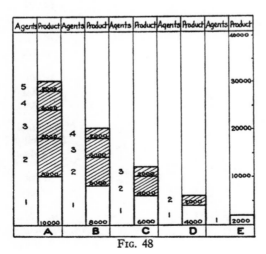

FIG. 48

Graphically the two cases combine as in Fig. 48. In this figure the rectangles represent the total value product and each subdivision of the rectangles represents the marginal product due to the use of a "dose" of 10 units. The number of such "doses" applied is indicated by the figures to the left of each rectangle. The total amount of rent is shaded. The fact that in each case the unshaded, or cost, area corresponds with the value yield of the first dose is of no significance and is merely the result of the correspondence of our selected figures for returns from the intensive and extensive margins.

The classical economists, in support of this theory, frequently draw attention to the free land of the American and Canadian West. This land, excellent as most of it was, had to be cleared or at least put under the plough, and it was far from the centres of world population and, in the early days of settlement, but indifferently served by railways. Both the American and Canadian governments offered free land to settlers or "homesteaders" who would take up a certain quantity of land, develop it, and live on it for a certain time. It was, in this sense, "free" or "no-rent" land and was regarded as being on the extensive margin of cultivation. This illustration serves as a striking exemplification of the classical rent theories, but only so long as it is not too closely examined. Actually the Ricardian Theory of rent requires an extensive margin in economic quality and the land of the new West was by no means on the extensive margin of cultivation in that sense, but was rather "frontier" than "marginal" land. Moreover it is doubtful how far it was "free." The history of western railway development and of the land speculators, which we can scarcely take up here, might suggest considerable modification of the classical view.

Section 3: Development of, and Controversy over, the Differential Surplus Theory of Rent

The theory we have just elucidated has been the subject of much economic controversy. It was almost immediately challenged, and has been subjected to criticism from Ricardo's times to our own. Unquestionably it is unsatisfactory in the form stated.

The criticisms may be classified as falling into two divisions: (a) those which sought to show that land had a supply cost like other agents and (b) those which sought to show that agents other than land could remain relatively fixed and suffer intensive exploitation thus yielding differential returns.

Our definition of rent has already shown that we are prepared to admit both these criticisms. The one thing we do not admit is that there are no differential returns or "rents" (as we defined the term) whatever and that all so-called rents are costs of one sort or another. In order to establish our own position we wish to trace briefly the history of one of the rent controversies of English economic thought during the past century.

J. S. Mill followed Ricardo in his rent theory. But he admitted

14

as an exceptional case that the rent which land could earn in one employment formed a cost which must be paid when it was used in some other employment.[3] This admission was seized upon by W. S. Jevons, who in the preface to the second edition of his *Theory of Political Economy*,[4] asks:

> But wherefore this distinction between agriculture and other branches of industry? Why does not the same principle apply between two different modes of agricultural employment? If land which has been yielding two pounds per acre rent as pasture be ploughed up and used for raising wheat, must not the two pounds per acre be debited against the expenses of the production of wheat? .... The principle which emerges is that *each portion of land should be applied to that culture or use which yields the largest total of utility as measured by the value of the produce?*[5] ... But when the matter is fully thought out it will be seen that exactly the same principle applies to wages. ... Precisely the same thing may be applied, *mutatis mutandis*, to the rent yielded by fixed capital, and to the interest of free capital.

In the course of this section, Jevons says: "There is no such thing as absolute cost of labour; it is all a matter of comparison ... thus wages are clearly the effect not the cause of the value of the produce. But when labour is turned from one employment to another, the wages it would otherwise have yielded must be debited to the expenses of the new product."

These passages may be observed to imply a theory of value quite different from that implied in these pages. For Jevons value (price) is determined by marginal utility and the rewards of the productive agents are determined by their marginal value products. He does not admit costs to be price determining. With this view we have shown reason to disagree. But we see from these passages in Jevons a doctrine of "opportunity costs" that bears a resemblance to the doctrine of "transfer costs" we are shortly to formulate.[6] Jevons's doctrine seems to be that the expenses of any enterprise must in-

---

[3]"But when land capable of yielding rent in agriculture is applied to some other purpose, the rent which it would have yielded is an element in the cost of production of the commodity which it employed to produce" (J. S. Mill, *Principles of Political Economy*, People's ed., London, 1885, Book 3, chap. VI, section 1, article 9).

[4]Fourth ed., London, 1911, p. 49.

[5]Jevons's italics.

[6]Compare also in this connection Professor Gustav Cassel's theory of "scarcity cost" (*Theory of Social Economy*, McCabe translation, New York, 1924, p. 277). "In general the explanation of ground rent as a surplus over the amount of produce of waste land is not very satisfactory. The ground rent of land of a certain quality is in its innermost nature a *scarcity price* [my italics] referring primarily to this land and determined by the supply of and demand for it."

clude charges to cover what could be earned by each agent in its most remunerative alternative employment.

Marshall does not deny the law of apportionment of the agents implied in this view, but he does show it to be consistent with the Ricardian theory of rent. The relevant passage in Marshall runs as follows:

Jevons in the Preface to the Second Edition of his Theory of Political Economy argues in the direction of treating agricultural rent on the same footing as ground-rent. But he goes on:—"If land which has been yielding two pounds per acre rent, as pasture, be ploughed up and used for raising wheat, must not the two pounds per acre be debited against the expenses of production of wheat? It is true that Mill was inconsistent in answering this question in the negative, while he maintained that when land capable of yielding rent in agriculture is applied to some other purpose, the rent which it would have yielded is an element in the cost of production of the commodity which it is employed to produce. But still the proper answer to Jevons' question is in the negative. For there is no connection between this particular sum of two pounds and the expenses of production of that wheat which only just pays its way. The amount of capital applied in cultivation is elastic; and is stretched until the return to it only just repays the outlay: this limit is determined by the general circumstances of supply and demand; and is independent of the particular sum of two pounds which the land will afford as rent. Mill ought to have said: "When land capable of being used for producing one commodity (whether agricultural produce or not) is used for producing another, the price of the first is raised by the consequent limitation of its field of production. The price of the second will be the expenses of production (wages and profits) of that part of it which only just pays its way; that which is produced on the margin of cultivation or building. And if for the purposes of any particular argument we take together the whole expenses of the production on that site, and divide these among the whole of the commodity produced, then, the rent which we ought to count in is not that which the site would pay if used for producing the first commodity, but that which it does pay when used for producing the second!" [7]

Thus we see that, with a proper apportionment of the agents as between alternative uses, a differential surplus will arise from the intensive use of the agents or from the extensive use of inferior grades of the agents, and it must be equal to or exceed the differential which could be gained in any alternative employment. This differential is most commonly and clearly observed in the case of land but it may arise from the employment of labour[8] and capital. It is this differential surplus which forms rent.

[7] Alfred Marshall, *Principles of Economics* (2nd ed., London, 1891), p. 462.

[8] It is, for example, arguable that superior talents are rewarded by a rent as a result of the extensive employment of inferior grade labour of the same classification.

SECTION 4: TRANSFER COSTS AND RENT

Now we must inquire if there is no truth in Jevons's contention that the reward offered to an agent in any employment must cover what it could earn in any alternative use. We have quoted Marshall to refute Jevons's main position here that these costs form the only possible "cost" of an agent and that "rent" and "cost" are one and the same thing.

But in one point Jevons is clearly right. No employment can offer to an agent less than the reward it could earn in the most remunerative alternative employment.[9] Thus the cost of an agent to any industry cannot be less than the agent could earn in any other employment. This minimum cost which "is necessary to retain a given unit of a factor in a certain industry may be called its *transfer earnings* or *transfer price*, since a reduction of the payment made for it below this price would cause it to be transferred elsewhere; and any particular unit of a factor may be said to be at the *margin of transference*, or to be a *marginal unit*, if the earnings which it receives in the industry where it is employed are only just sufficient to prevent it from transferring itself to some other use."[10]

These transfer earnings must, by definition, correspond to the marginal cost of the agent to the industry at what we have called the margin of substitution.[11] The earnings of any agent over and above these transfer earnings are rent, and are not a cost of production from the social point of view, or from the point of view of the industry as a whole. We must remember, however, that, from the point of view of any firm, rent forms a cost of production which must be paid and which must be covered, like any other cost, by the price.

A mathematical statement of the position of rent in the price system as a whole is given in Book Two.

[9]Non-competing groups are expressly ruled out here. If the rigidities or frictions are such that the agent cannot be transferred, the superior employment is not an "alternative."

[10]Joan Robinson, *Economics of Imperfect Competition* (London, 1933), p. 104. Compare also H. D. Henderson, *Supply and Demand* (London, 1922), p. 94 (cited by Mrs. Robinson).

[11]See Book Four, chap. XVI, p. 177.

CHAPTER XIX

INTEREST

Section 1: Definitions

WE turn now to the theory of the price paid for the use of capital, which we have already defined as consisting of goods for further production. Capital may be of three sorts: fixed capital, liquid stocks, and working capital. Fixed capital consists of capital goods of long life, such as factories, machinery, trucks, railways, etc. Industry must pay the cost of maintaining its efficiency plus the cost of replacing it when it is worn out. In addition industry must pay a reward to the owner who *advances or lends the funds* for the purchase of this capital. These costs are a part of fixed costs, already defined.

Liquid stocks consist of raw materials in process of manufacture and distribution. Examples of liquid stocks would be raw rubber in the hands of the rubber companies, treated rubber in the plant of tire manufacturers, partly finished tires in the same plants, and finished tires in the warehouses of jobbers and distributing agencies. The cost of carrying raw materials *consists of the cost of borrowing funds to buy and store them* and, since they are only in process a limited time, is a short-term cost. It naturally varies directly with the quantity of output and thus forms a part of "variable costs" as previously defined.

Working capital consists of goods necessary to supply the energy of production. It consists of coal, electric power, advances of consumption goods to labour, etc. Its cost *is the cost of borrowing the short-term funds necessary*. It is also obviously a part of "variable costs."

Capital is never borrowed as such. What is borrowed is the money or purchasing power to purchase the capital instrument or instruments. This process of using funds for the purchase of capital is commonly known as investment. We shall, however, define investment more precisely as the process of adding to the total of capital goods. The funds we shall call capital disposal. Capital goods are quite often known as investment goods. Titles to wealth in acknowledgement of investment are known as securities. Securities are of various sorts, depending on the duration of the loan and its legal status. Thus short-term investment is represented by short-term paper, such as notes, drafts, bills of exchange, etc., and long-term investment by long-term paper, such as stocks, bonds, mortgages, etc. A bond is the title held by a long-term creditor of a corporation. It represents a loan of funds from one legal person to another. The interest on it is a first charge on the earnings of the borrower and if it cannot be paid, the borrower is bankrupt. A stock, however, is the title of ownership. By investing in the corporation the stockholder has become a member of it. He is a part owner of the corporation. Legally he has not lent money to someone else, but has invested directly, assuming the responsibilities of ownership. He is not guaranteed any interest, but receives dividends, viz., a share of net profits proportionate to his share of the direct investment. These dividends include a "risk" rate which is a rough effort to provide a differential to measure the varying degrees of risk involved in different employments, and they also include a share in the net profits. When a firm is in perfect competition there will be no profits over and above the various elements of interest, risk, and rent, but when a firm enjoys a special position on the market under imperfect competition, it may, as we have seen, earn profits over and above these other rewards. In such a case it would appear that there is theoretically a marked difference between interest and dividend yields. Actually the stock market adjusts this difference. The price of a share of stock in such a company rises to the point where new investors find the dividend rate expressed as a ratio of the price of the stock equal to the prevailing rate of interest, so that new investors in the company are much in the position of supplying capital disposal for interest. The original owners, of course, receive the surplus profits through the appreciation in the value of their stock, from inflated directors' fees, stock bonuses or "stock dividends" and by other devices.

From the point of view of economic theory the distinction is not as important as it is in law. The realities of modern corporation finance are that in either case a group of enterprisers are obtaining funds from the public. In the one case (of bonds) they borrow the money, guaranteeing a fixed and reasonably certain return. In the other case (of stocks) they do not guarantee any interest but attract the investor by the prospect of dividends at a better rate than bond interest. In either case the economist sees that funds are supplied to enterprisers at a price, in the one case guaranteed in advance, in the other not guaranteed, but in either case a price for the use of capital disposal. Stocks must pay dividends that over a period of time are at least equal to the current long-term rate of interest.

They pay more than this, perhaps, as a result of surplus profits, but they must pay at least this much.[1]

SECTION 2: THE DEMAND PRICE FOR CAPITAL DISPOSAL

We must distinguish between the price paid for capital goods as such—a price determined in the ordinary way of commodity pricing—and the price paid for the use of borrowed capital disposal, the price paid, that is, for the right to dispose of accumulated savings or unused purchasing power. It will be seen that at any given time capital instruments engaged in production will be earning rewards that will be similar to rents. Like land these instruments will be fixed in supply and their more intensive use will give a series of yields to the point where it would be uneconomic further to intensify their use. These yields will be similar in every way to the returns from land so that the differentials earned by superior instruments, or from the more intensive use of instruments, or from instruments that have already repaid their full cost, will be of the nature of rent. But when the entrepreneur comes to consider whether or not he will increase his use of capital, he has to weigh the expected or *anticipated* increase in product the new capital will make possible against the cost of employing the new capital. There are two elements in this cost; there is the cost of the capital instrument itself, which can be charged at so much a year over the life of the instrument, the amortization charge, it is called, and there is the cost of borrowing the use of capital disposal, a cost that is usually set out as so much for every $100 borrowed, as a percentage rate. This rate is the rate of interest.

Difficult accounting problems and some problems of business cycle economics[2] are involved in the notion of amortization charges but the main principles relevant to price theory are sufficiently clear. The price of the capital instrument will be determined by the demand for it, a demand derived from the demand for its product, and its cost of production. The total price may then be simply divided by the number of years the instrument may be

[1] That is dividends, like all profits to owners, consist of "interest" plus "surplus profits."

[2] An interesting peculiarity of depreciation charges is that they alone among costs are not a source of income. Compare J. M. Keynes, *The General Theory of Employment, Interest and Money* (London, 1936), p. 69, also p. 371; and R. G. Hawtrey, *Capital and Employment* (London, 1937), p. 96. Both make acknowledgement to Major Douglas for his emphasis on this point. Mr. Keynes makes considerable use of this peculiarity in his cycle theory, arguing that if a part of costs does not generate consumer's income there will be a deficiency of demand.

expected to serve.   Thus if a capital instrument costs $10,000, and if its life is reckoned conservatively at ten years, $1,000 a year must be charged for its amortization.[3]   But if the new instrument is worth employing it will yield a marginal product of more than $1,000 a year.   The surplus, which we may call the net marginal product of the capital instrument, will constitute what the entrepreneur is able or willing to offer for the use of the funds necessary to purchase the capital instrument.   It is thus the determinant of the demand price and the source of the ability to pay interest. But it is probably not the "cause" of interest, which, presumably, lies in the conditions which govern the willingness of people to make capital disposal available.

In the cases of liquid stocks and working capital there is no problem of long-term amortization.   The replacement cost is immediately known from the price of the raw materials necessary to replenish stocks.   In a stationary state this price will not vary.   The price of the finished goods must cover the price of the raw materials plus an increment in value to cover the costs of working them.   If labour and other non-capital costs be subtracted, the remainder must be the net marginal value productivity of capital.   This determines the quantity of short-term capital to be used and the average net value productivity corresponding to it determines the demand price of the firm for short-term capital disposal.

Some economists have attempted to explain interest rate in terms of marginal productivity only, without reference to the supply price of capital.   An effort has been made to say that a capital good or machine is worth its cost of production or its cost of replacement. It will add an annual increased net product over and above the annual retiring or sinking fund charges put aside to meet its cost of replacement.   It is said that the percentage ratio of its marginal yield to its total cost determines the rate of interest.

If we say the capital instrument costs $100,000 and adds an increased product of $7,500 a year, and, if it will wear out in about twenty years, so that approximately $2,500 a year, accumulated at compound interest for twenty years, will replace the machine when its productive life is over, we have left a net annual increment of product worth $5,000.   Then it would be said that, if this machine was the marginal unit of capital, the rate of interest would be 5 per cent per annum.

[3]Actually, because the amounts put aside earn interest, it is not necessary to put aside as much as $1,000 a year.

The trouble with this is that actually the capital worth of all old capital instruments is calculated by taking the rate of interest as given, and capitalizing the yield. This process means that, if a house for rent, or any other capital instrument, is earning a net rental or dividend of $300 a year and if the long-term rate of interest is 5 per cent, we say the house, or capital instrument, is worth, not what it cost to build, but $6,000, which is the sum which, if invested on the long-term market at the present rate, viz. 5 per cent, would yield $300 per year. This means that we cannot calculate the rate of interest as the percentage yield on the capital worth of old instruments, because, to calculate their capital worth, we have to know the rate of interest. There are too many unknowns in that equation.

It is only on new capital that we can do this and then the yield must be anticipated, so the marginal productivity of new capital is guessed at, not known by experience. Moreover the quantity of new capital is not a fixed amount. It will vary with the rate of interest. Thus the marginal productivity theory of interest in the form that the rate of interest is determined by the net marginal productivity of a fixed or given quantity of capital must, by itself, be an inadequate explanation. Only in the stationary state[4] would the amount of new capital be given and the marginal productivity known. In the stationary economy the demand price of capital is determined by the marginal productivity of capital in use.

A $100,000 loan will buy a machine priced at $100,000. If this machine will pay all replacement costs and, as well, a net income of $5,000 per annum, it is worth offering up to $5,000 or 5 per cent for this loan. Thus in the stationary state the net marginal productivity schedule of capital is known as is the rate at which new capital disposal will be available. Under such conditions we have a typical demand-supply equilibrium in the capital market.

In a progressive economy, in which technical advances are being made, the demand for new capital must depend on the entrepreneurs' expectations of its yield. It is fair to assume that these estimates will be, if not accurate, at least sufficiently reliable to approach the yields which will be realized when the capital is employed. Any firm will have, then, an estimated marginal productivity schedule for borrowed capital (i.e., net productivity after amortization charges) which can be graphically represented in a manner similar to the marginal productivity curve for labour

[4]The stationary state for our purposes may be defined as one in which no technical changes are occurring and in which the aggregate supply of the factors of production remains unchanged.

(see Fig. 37). The factor cost curve to the firm will be determined by the prevailing market rate of interest, and since almost all firms are in perfect competition for the use of capital disposal, the factor cost curve will be a straight line parallel to the x-axis. Thus the determination of employment of capital by a firm will be exactly similar to the case illustrated in Fig. 38. The position of the firm in equilibrium presents, therefore, no unusual features. But our argument, as it stands, tells us only how capital is allocated among different employments—to the point where its marginal value productivity is equal in all employments—and how the quantity of capital to be employed is determined by each firm. It does not tell us how the rate of interest is determined throughout the economy as a whole, for we have not yet discovered what governs the rate at which funds are made available to industry.

SECTION 3: SHORT RUN ADJUSTMENT OF SUPPLY OF CAPITAL
DISPOSAL AND INTEREST

Interest, we have seen, is the reward paid by the borrower, not for a capital instrument, but for the use or disposal of funds. The borrower, it is clear, will be willing to pay for the borrowed funds up to the net amount by which the control over these funds will enable him to increase his value product or revenue. We have to ask on what terms people are willing to lend funds to industry and what determines the aggregate supply of these funds. In Book Two we indicated an answer to this question, which satisfied the conditions of that highly simplified model economy with which we were then working. We indicated that new real capital would be provided from savings if a sufficient reward were offered to attract people to save. Thus both the demand for capital in employment and the supply of capital were functions of the rate of interest and equilibrium would be reached at the point where the rate of interest effected an equality between the demand and supply of new capital. But we have to ask if this hypothesis satisfies the conditions of a complex economy in which speculative and other motives affect the willingness of people to hold their savings in the form of loans, in which the alternative of holding stores of money is open to them, and in which the business enterpriser is in a far stronger position to determine the total aggregate of savings than he was in our model economy. These complexities force us to reconsider not only our own hypothesis of Book Two but the basic tenets of much interest theory, the main outlines of which, were, indeed, what we presented in that Book.

Past interest rate theory has explained the supply price of capital disposal to be determined by the marginal cost of saving. This supposes that the act of saving is abstinence or lacking, which people are reluctant to undergo. In order to encourage them to do this, some incentive or reward must be offered. If they will abstain for a time, postpone their enjoyments, they will be given increased enjoyment at a future date. Some economists have even supposed that future satisfactions, as compared with present, are discounted and that the rate of this discounting determines the supply price of capital. Others have said that, however this may be, the quantity of capital disposal varies with the interest rate offered, that is, with the price offered as an incentive to get people to save. On this argument, it can be seen that the demand price for capital, determined by its marginal productivity in employment, is a function of the available capital supply and that the supply price of capital disposal is also a function of the amount supplied. There must, therefore, be a point where the demand and supply prices for some quantity of new capital will exactly coincide. If more capital is offered, the demand price would be less than the supply price and savers, disappointed in their yield, would save less. If the quantity fell short of this amount, the high yields of investment would attract more savers. The price for the use of capital, or interest, would tend to become fixed at this point of equilibrium and this was called the "normal interest rate." The interest rate as charged by the banks, which is called the "market rate," tended, it was thought, to approach this point.

Most new investment comes not out of the savings of the people, but out of the amounts put aside for this purpose by the big corporations. This is not true of government investment, which does come out of individual savings, but of new industrial investment[5] which comes almost entirely from the big corporations. Corporations reinvest their profit and the owners of great fortunes invest their large surpluses according to what they have to invest. Now, what they have to invest depends on their profits; that is, on the yields of past investment and not on the anticipated yield of new investment—not, that is, on the rate of interest. We say not on the rate of interest because the marginal demand price for the use of new capital is based not on the yield of old capital, but on the anticipated yield of the new capital instruments, which will be put into production as the result of this new investment. Thus, the supply

[5]Mr. Carl Snyder proves this conclusively in his article "Capital Supply and National Well Being" (*American Economic Review*, vol. XXVI, June, 1936).

of capital disposal is independent of the rate of interest; and the amount demanded is a function of the anticipated yield. They are functions of different things; they share no point of equilibrium; they are determined by different forces.

But not only do entrepreneurs make many of the major decisions as to the amount of savings themselves, they are able to impose their will in part on other peoples' decisions to save. Over any given income period the amount of new investment, the amount, that is, added to the stock of producers' goods must be equal in sum to the amount of savings. The total money income of the period is, from one point of view, the total amount of income, including profits, paid out to individuals; from another point of view it is the total value of all the goods, investment and consumption goods, produced. Now the total amount of income which is spent on consumption goods must equal the money value of those goods. Therefore the amount of income which is not spent, that which from the point of view of individuals is saved, must be equal to the value of investment goods. Thus, over any period, savings must equal investment. The decisions to invest, it is true, are made by one set of people, the business enterprisers, and the decisions to save are made by another set of people which includes the enterprisers, though not necessarily in their capacity as enterprisers, the public as a whole. Now the fact that savings always equal investment, while the decisions to save and to invest are made independently of one another suggests either the most extraordinary manifestation of coincidence or some causal relationship. Since one could scarcely expect the coincidence to reappear in every income period one must seek for the more credible causal connection. If enterprisers decide to invest more than the public decides to save the effect will be that fewer consumption goods will appear on the market than consumers wish to buy at prevailing price levels. Prices will change to limit the demand for consumers' goods and there will be an increase in money incomes to the poi t where a sufficient amount is being saved to sustain the level of investment. Thus a sort of forced saving is imposed on the public as a result of the decisions of entrepreneurs to invest. This is most clearly apparent in time of war, when the major entrepreneur in the economy is government. The military authorities decide on the level of investment necessary to sustain their strategic programme, and the public is asked to save what is necessary to pay for the new investment. If the public does not respond voluntarily the government must impose the necessary level of saving. It may do this by fiscal means, by taxation, and this is probably the fairest way to do it. But if fiscal methods are not sufficiently stringent the government may permit the adjustment to take place as it does when ordinary business and not government decides to invest more than the public is voluntarily saving, that is by inflation of prices. Whatever the method the equality of savings and investment is always maintained, and it is done by methods which very definitely restrict the freedom of the public as a whole to decide what shall be saved. Hence we are obliged to give up the notion that the supply of capital disposal comes from the supply of savings voluntarily undertaken by the people as a whole in response to the stimulus of interest.

Now people always have a choice between holding their savings in the form of money or in the form of securities. By money we mean both legal tender (gold, token coinage, and notes of the government or government bank) and bank money (bank deposits and bank notes), and by securities we mean stocks, bonds, insurance policies, and similar promises to pay. Clearly what is held in the form of securities is available directly or, through the insurance or trust company, indirectly, to industry. But what is held in the form of money is not available for industry. When you hold a bank deposit you do not "put money in the bank" which the bank can lend to business; on the contrary the bank has to hold a portion of its cash as a reserve against your deposit and since the bank has only so much cash and since it must hold a certain ratio of cash against its total deposits, the existence of your deposit constitutes a claim against the bank's cash reserve and limits its ability to lend to industry and commerce. Consequently the amount of money the public as a whole is willing to lend to industry—the amount of capital disposal available to support investment—will depend not only on the total amount of savings, but also on the willingness of people to *lend* the money, to hold their savings, that is, in the form of securities rather than in the form of money. At first it might seem odd that there should be any difficulty in getting people to hold securities rather than money, because to hold money is to forgo the opportunity to receive an income from one's savings. Stocks of money held idle either receive no interest or, at the best, if held in a savings or time account at the bank, a very low rate. The answer is two-fold: (*a*) money is more liquid and (*b*) money is always stable in value in terms of itself. Thus several distinguishable motives emerge for the holding of money. If for several reasons one desires to hold one's savings in liquid form, money is preferable to securities. Perhaps one is saving for some definite purpose to be attained in the not-too-distant future, so as to buy a car or take a trip to Europe, or something of that sort. In such a case one is more apt to hold a savings deposit at the bank than to buy securities or an insurance policy. Again large classes of the society are paid monthly or quarterly by cheque, and they deposit their cheques in current accounts which they use to meet their current expenditures over the income period. Thus at any time these classes will be holding in money form average deposits which will be equal to the total income so received and so deposited divided by two.[6] The amounts held for these reasons will be reasonably stable in total amount in the short run and will only change slowly over the long period with changes in the habits and customs of the society. Fluctuations in the desire for liquidity itself will not, therefore, be great and will not have any important effect on the short-run supply of capital disposal. On the other hand the *speculative* motive for the holding of money may exhibit sudden, rapid and considerable changes. People who buy securities are interested not only in the income which they obtain from these securities, they are also interested in the probable increase or decrease, what is called the appreciation or depreciation, in the value of their securities. If people believe that security prices are going to decline they will refrain from buying securities, and those who hold securities will want to sell them and hold money instead. They will prefer to hold money to securities until they believe that the price of securities is going to rise. Then they will prefer to buy securities and give up their holdings of money.

There is a definite connection between the rate of interest and the price of securities. Any security offers a certain return, say $5.00 a year, and, because there is perfect competition in the capital market, the *rate* of return on all old issues and on new borrowing must be equalized. Thus when the rate of interest is 5 per cent the security which paid $5.00 a year is worth $100. But if the rate of interest declines to 4 per cent a security paying $5.00 a year becomes worth $125, and if the rate of interest rises to 6 per cent, the security comes to be worth $83.33. Thus when the rate of interest falls security prices will rise and when the rate of

[6] If R is the total income so received and so deposited and if we assume that at the end of the income period the deposits are entirely paid out, the *average* amount held will be $\frac{R}{2}$. The longer the income period, the greater this average will be.

interest rises security prices will fall. Hence at any given time in the securities market there will be a prevalent expectation of the future of securities' prices and a consequent willingness or unwillingness to hold securities rather than money. The desire to hold money has been given the name "liquidity preference,"[7] and, at any time, there will be a liquidity preference schedule. Given this schedule at any one time the rate of interest has to adjust the demand for, and supply of, capital disposal. Thus the instantaneous rate of interest effects the short-run adjustment of the demand for funds and the willingness of people to forgo liquidity in holding their savings. This adjustment is ordinarily made through the money market. At any one time all the money then in existence has to be owned by someone. The rate of interest must be such that at any moment the amount of money that people taken together are willing to hold is just equal to the total amount of money in the economy. If the rate is below this point there will be a demand for more money than there is; if the rate is above this point, people will be demanding securities rather than money.[8] Thus at any moment the rate of interest is "determined"—in the sense that its proper level is indicated—by the amount of money. But this would seem to mean that the instantaneous rate of interest must satisfy two conditions of equilibrium: it must equate the demand for loans with the supply, and it must equate the total demand for money with the existing stock of money. The total stock of money is made up of the *inactive* deposits of those who are holding money because of a preference for liquidity and the *active* deposits of the commercial and industrial circulation. Thus any rate of interest that leaves no one at the current liquidity preference schedule and the current marginal productivity schedule anxious to increase his holdings either of active or inactive deposits, that is any rate of interest which equates the total demand for money with its supply, automatically and at the same time must effect the equilibrium between the demand and supply of loans. Consequently the two apparent conditions are really one.

We have been speaking above of the "rate of interest" and we have assumed an identity between the rate on the short-term money market and the long-term rates on various categories of

[7]Cf. J. M. Keynes, *The General Theory of Employment, Interest and Money* (London, 1936), a book to which we owe the main argument which is developed in this and the succeeding section.

[8]See Joan Robinson, *Introduction to the Theory of Employment* (London, 1937), p. 71.

securities. In Section 1 we showed that the rates on different securities might differ to allow for differing elements of risk, and when we speak of *the* rate of interest we refer, of course, to the common rate which must be paid to obtain loans irrespective of the differentials which must be paid to cover varying elements of risk. What has been said of different types of long-term securities may apply to the difference between long- and short-term loans. Because of various purposes for which short-term loans may be used there will be a difference in rates, so that a short-term Treasury note will bear a lower rate than short-term commercial notes. There will also be a difference according to the length of time for which the loan is made. Notes for ninety days, or short-term demand notes are, in a sense more liquid, more nearly like cash, than notes for longer periods. On the other hand short-term commercial notes have a higher administration cost, that is a certain charge has to be made to cover the cost of maintaining the financial institution to negotiate the loans. In the case of small short-term borrowings these administration charges form a relatively high proportion of the total charge. All these differences of risk, length of time, and administration charges have to be allowed for and they cause differentials to appear in the actual market rates of interest. But common to all rates is the single charge for lending funds, a rate which, when it changes, affects all the rates together, so that the interest rate structure tends to move always together and in the same direction, and it is this common element to which we refer when we speak of "*the* rate of interest."

SECTION 4: LONG RUN SUPPLY OF CAPITAL DISPOSAL

Given the existing schedule of liquidity preference, the existing state of entrepreneur's anticipations of the future productivity of new capital and the existing level of national income, the rate of interest adjusts the demand for money with the total stock of money and at the same time adjusts the demand for loans with the supply of loanable funds. But over a period of time the schedule of liquidity preferences, the anticipations of entrepreneurs, and the national income will change, and the nature and direction of these changes will govern the long-run adjustments of the supply of capital disposal and the rate of interest.

The liquidity preference schedule will depend on the prevailing attitude towards the probable movement of securities' prices and on the level of income. If the tendency of the stock market is downwards—if there is a "bear" or selling market—more people will want to increase their holdings of money and if the tendency is the opposite way—if there is a "bull" market—liquidity preference will decline. The prevailing attitude towards the market is in part a whimsical, unpredictable and inexplicable thing, seeming to follow a sort of manic-depressive psychological cycle,[9] but there are certain forces that have clearly discernible effects on this attitude, forces and effects that can be observed, though the full study of them lies beyond the scope of this volume. The fiscal and monetary policies of the government and central bank will have a definite effect on the stock market. Heavy or "regressive" taxation, a "tight" money policy, a policy, that is, that tends to raise the rate of bank interest on commercial loans, particularly when coupled with open market selling of securities by the central bank, will tend to lower security prices, and the reverse policies will have the opposite effect. A big spending programme by the government will tend to make the market optimistic, though if this is coupled with an administration unpopular with the business community, as in the case of the New Deal in the United States, this effect may be negligible.

Changes in the level of the national income will have a definite effect on the willingness and ability of people to save and to lend. Individuals who experience an increase in their individual incomes generally tend to save a larger proportion of the increase than of the original income. A man with an income, say, of $2,000 a year is apt to establish a living standard that requires a great part of that income to sustain. He may put aside in the form of insurance as much as $100 a year. But if his income is increased to $2,500 a year he is likely to save a much larger proportion of the additional $500, he is apt, in our example, to spend an additional $300 or $400 and to save the balance. Again people with large incomes save a higher proportion of their incomes than people with low incomes. Thus when the national income is increased, the increase in savings will be more than in proportion to the increase in income, for an increase in the national income means both a higher fraction of the society in the large income brackets, and higher personal incomes for the majority of income-earners. A fall in the national income will have the opposite effect on savings.

Before we can pull these various considerations together to see if they tell us anything about the long-run trend of capital supply and interest rate, we must ask what the long-run trend of

[9]Cf. Sam Lewisohn, "Psychology in Economics" (*Political Science Quarterly*, vol. LIII, no. 2, June, 1938).

the demand for capital is likely to be. It is clear that during a period of technological advance the increased use of capital, with consequent increases in the proportion of fixed to variable capital in employment, results in lowered unit costs and increased profits. During such a period the demand curve for capital disposal will be shifting upwards and to the right, entrepreneurs will be willing to increase their use of capital over time at a given interest rate, or they will be willing to increase what they pay for loans to obtain the same amount of capital. But if there is a slowing up of the technical improvements, or even if the process of increasing fixed investment continues unchecked long enough, there will eventually come a point beyond which lowered costs from the employment of increased quantities of fixed capital will be offset and more than offset by diminishing marginal productivity. If the reader will think in terms of the three-dimensional diagrams, he will see that the increased use of capital along the x-axis will lead to diminishing marginal productivity as measured on the y-axis. This diminishing return will be offset as one comes out along the t-axis by the increased technical efficiency of capital, but if there is a slowing up of the technical improvements in the increased use of capital in time, the extension of the employment of capital along the x-axis will eventually lead to a decline in productivity greater than the improvement effected by technical advances. Consequently the long-term trend in the demand for capital is apt to be cyclical in nature, the demand is apt to increase and entrepreneurs are willing to pay higher rates for loans, then comes a period in which they are apt to be unwilling to borrow as much at high rates, a period when, to sustain the level of investment, lower interest rates must be charged for loans.

In the period of technical advance, when entrepreneurs are increasing investment, the very fact that they are investing more means that employment is increasing and the national income is growing. There is apt to be confidence on the stock market and a low liquidity preference schedule. Thus, on the supply side, loans are offered at low interest rates, and with the demand in a state of eager anticipation, this means that equilibrium is shifting towards an ever-expanding use of capital at falling rates. But the falling rate has the effect of encouraging entrepreneurs to invest to the point of diminishing productivity and, of course, the keen competitive bidding for loans will also lead eventually to an increase in the rate of interest. At this point a reverse movement will be initiated. Entrepreneurs are now less willing to pay higher rates for loans, and will curtail their investment. The only thing which could sustain the rate of investment and employment would be a continually falling interest rate to the limit of zero. But the check to investment is likely to create some pessimism on the market, a shift in the liquidity preference schedule to increased preference for liquidity, to a higher equilibrium rate of interest. If entrepreneurs now reduce investment, as each one acting individually must do in his own protection, there will be a reduction in employment and in the national income and this will further reduce the supply of loanable funds and the willingness of people with savings to forego liquidity. This process must continue until savings and investment are reduced to the point where entrepreneurs can once again see gains in increasing their investment and the cycle enters again on its positive or upward swing. Thus the supply of capital, in the long run, seems to oscillate, to be first positively and then negatively inclined, so that there is generated a cycle of equilibria points at different levels of investment and employment.

SECTION 5: CONCLUSION. THE RATE OF INTEREST, THE RATE OF INVESTMENT AND THE RATE OF EMPLOYMENT

In the past economists have argued that under conditions of competing private capitalism equilibrium will be attained at full employment of the factors of production. This argument was based on the assumption that if any factors of production were left idle they would bid down the price for their employment. If more capital was being saved than entrepreneurs wanted to use, the rate of interest would fall until the capital was borrowed for investment, and until the lowered rate of interest discouraged people from saving. Entrepreneurs used their plants to full capacity under the pressure of competition. A firm with unused capacity had high fixed unit costs which soon forced it to the margin of production and beyond. Labour could not afford to withhold its services; if wages were too low population would fail to increase and "in the long run" the labour supply would adapt itself to the demand for its services.

On arguments such as these economists based their doctrine of full employment. They admitted that during "transitional" periods there would be unemployment of agents of production. But they maintained that the introduction of new machinery or other dynamic changes would soon lead to new equilibria at full employment. Men displaced by machinery in one industry would soon be reabsorbed into another industry as the demand for other goods increased by reason of the lowered prices of the machine-produced goods.

So thoroughly has this idea permeated economic literature that, in spite of indisputable evidence to the contrary, argument that there can be equilibrium at less than full employment was first received rather coldly.   Nevertheless such seems the inescapable conclusion of contemporary economic investigation.   The rate of interest is a determinant of the rate of investment and the rate of investment for technical reasons sets the rate of employment.   Given fluctuations in the attitude of the public towards liquid assets, fluctuations in the quantity of money, or fluctuations in the expectations as to the future by entrepreneurs, it follows that there will be fluctuations in the rate of interest and the rate of employment. The forces that determine the rate of interest are quite distinct from the forces that make for full employment of the social capital.   An unfavourable balance of trade, an increase in preference for liquidity by the public, will raise the rate of interest and reduce investment and employment without respect to whether or not there is full employment of the factors of production.   Moreover, there is no reason to believe that such restriction carries compensating forces that correct it and restore full employment.   On the contrary, the reduction of employment may reduce income and lead indirectly to a still further reduction in investment and employment.

Thus the study of pricing and distribution leads us naturally to the study of economic dynamics so that it is misleading to make the sharp distinctions that are sometimes made between "pure theory" and "economic dynamics."   In "pure theory" it is true we are dealing with the determination of the prices and output of goods and the prices and employment of the factors of production under static conditions.   But as we pursue this theory one of the determinants of output emerges as the rate of employment of factors, and the rate of employment of the factors is dependent on the rate of investment.   Thus the theory of the determination of price and output is incomplete without the theory of the determination of the rate of investment.   This theory, to which the theory of interest introduces us, involves, as well, dynamic, temporal, and social forces that we have not discussed and cannot discuss within the compass of this book.   In a free capitalist system the rate of investment is the creature of a wide variety of forces which cause it to fluctuate widely and fitfully and are therefore the source of many of the social ills of our age.   The war is indicating some of the possibilities of control and it may be that, after the war, we shall know better how to obtain economic stability and security of employment for the mass of the people.   But if this is so it may well mean modification of some of our basic economic concepts along lines which as yet remain vague and indistinct.

CHAPTER XX

CONCLUSION

SECTION 1: THE PRICE SYSTEM AND SOCIAL COSTS

THE theory of interest which was outlined in the last chapter is
not one to which all economists will give assent. It is a definite
departure from the orthodox notion of interest as an equilibrium
rate between the anticipated marginal productivity of new capital
and the marginal disutility of saving, a departure which it seems
one has to make under pressure both of the logic of the method of
analysis and of recorded fact. By its own nature interest cannot
be treated on the static assumption; it is a rate in time, and for the
static assumption one has to substitute the assumption of a stationary state, one that exists in time but is subject over a period of
time to no changes either in the quantity of capital supplied, in
labour supply, or in industrial techniques. There is a sense in which
the static assumption is far more real, and perhaps more valid, than
this stationary assumption. The static assumption is a method of
abstracting from the time dimension for purposes of equilibrium
analysis, and it is both logically valid and justified by its results.
The stationary assumption is a more violent distortion of reality in
the sense that it is not a step in abstraction, but a working hypothesis
which says not "let us work out of time," but "let us work in time
but as though all the changes that actually do take place through
time are absent." Such a working hypothesis can only be justified
if it yields valuable results. When in this case we set the results
against the facts they are seen to be inconsistent, for new capital
formation does not vary with the rate of interest. In the Dominion
of Canada, today, it is apparent that the monetary and fiscal authorities are acting as though new capital formation was independent
of the rate of interest and they have been justified in their faith.
War borrowing has been carried out at a stable or even slightly
declining interest rate and, in 1941, the Minister of Finance is asking
the people of Canada to save for war purposes, in addition, that is,
to any new saving for ordinary civilian purposes, about $1,250 mil-
lion. This sum by itself is more than the Canadian people have
ever before saved. When added to the probable saving for non-
military purposes, which can scarcely be less than $400 million or
$500 million, the sum will amount to about one-third of the national
income, and this in a year when taxation is heavier than at any time

in history.   It is true that there is present in war-time the powerful patriotic motive, which is not ordinarily operative in the economy, but this consideration does not seriously qualify the argument, because not more than half the total will be raised by an appeal for popular loan subscriptions.   The balance will be raised by appropriate monetary action imposing savings on the people; that, at least, was what was done in 1940, and is presumably what will be done in 1941.   It was for these reasons, reinforced by many and similar cases, that we were forced to a modified position on the theory of interest.

To some minds these and other considerations have suggested that the whole position of price theory and, in particular, the doctrine of real costs must be abandoned.   A "realistic" view of the price system, it is sometimes urged, must see it as the product of a particular epoch and as the characteristic institution of the system of private capitalism during a certain stage of its development. There is nothing fixed or immutable in its laws.   Already the price of capital has ceased to appear as a typical supply-demand relationship and soon, it is urged, under pressure of revolutionary changes in our social institutions, the other prices will likewise appear to be fixed by other than the forces of free demand and freely responding agents of supply.   The great war which is at present raging has resulted, in all the belligerent countries, in prices fixed by the intervention of the state, by the rationing, instead of the free sale, of consumers' goods and in state regulation of the supply and employment of the agents of production.   After the war, whatever the outcome, much of this control will remain.   What then is there left of the free price system and the forces which are supposed "to determine" prices?

Rather more, perhaps, than some imagine.   During war-time there is, in a belligerent country, complete or nearly complete unanimity on the subject of what goods to make, what employment to give to every available agent of production.   But let us imagine a nation at peace, with, nevertheless, the full complement of war-time regulating agencies empowered to ration goods, establish raw material priorities, fix prices, impose saving and new capital formation, mobilize and direct labour into selected employments, and distribute among the various productive enterprises the human and material instruments necessary to their successful conduct; let us now ask ourselves how, in such a society, the agencies of government are to decide, once war-time stringencies and the urgency of military needs have disappeared, what quantities of which goods are to be produced and put on the market, how far to restrict consumption in favour of new capital or how far to encourage spending in the present at the expense of a larger capital equipment for the future, how many men to employ in different industries and how long to employ them, whether to sacrifice leisure for greater production or to sacrifice material output for the intangible benefits of rest, health, and greater cultivation of the sensible and intellectual faculties, when output is to be increased along one particular line, when a diminution would be desirable, and, most vital, what proportionate share of, or claim on, the social income must be awarded each factor in production.   As we pose these questions it becomes apparent that a price system, or some mutation of it, is essential in a free society. A completely rationed society, in which all individual and social needs are determined by bureaucratic authority, is a condition which the mind refuses to accept.   No man or set of men could successfully undertake in a complex society to make the multitude of decisions involved in determining consumption, output, and distribution without some form of guidance from the consuming and producing public, and, if they did undertake such a truly Herculean task, no public would ever submit to it.   But once one admits the social necessity of a price system, one need not assume that it will carry with it all the implications of that to which we have been accustomed during the past one hundred and fifty years.

It is not too presumptuous to suggest that the near future may discover two concepts which will be accepted as of genuine and definite economic significance, social need and social cost.   Already the concept of social need plays a most important but not too clearly recognized part in our economic system.   Under our "free" price system we have permitted consumers to indicate their preferences by bidding on commodities and we have permitted the productive agents to enter, freely, such employments as, from the existing price situation, seemed most profitable.   But we have limited this freedom by taking, in the form of taxation, a considerable proportion of consumers' purchasing power from them and we have directed new employment by using the proceeds of taxation to invest and employ in the production of certain "social goods" for the fulfilment of "social" or "collective" wants.   With these collective wants we are all familiar.   They comprise such commodities or services as can only be enjoyed or used collectively, education, public health services, roads, bridges and public works, and so forth.   The field is steadily growing as more and more services are undertaken by the state and as public opinion comes to accept as public responsibilities the supply of those services which can be efficiently and adequately supplied only by public agency. In war-time the service of defence absorbs as much as half the national income of the principal belligerents, the economies of these states are to the extent of 50 per cent absorbed in the satisfaction of collective wants. In these cases the method of taxation and spending through the ordinary price mechanism has proved inadequate as a method of directing the maximum productive energy from the "individual" to the "collective" economy, that is from the satisfaction of individual to the satisfaction of collective wants. But, as we have seen, the situation in war-time is simplified by the unanimity of opinion on the major social need, successful defence, and by the willingness of the mass to sacrifice personal satisfaction without complaint or rebellion. In peace-time the methods of rationing and of "priorities" would be scarcely endurable and some method of providing for social needs through the price system ought not to be impossible of attainment, either by means of taxation, or, if the state comes to own the major enterprises, out of the "profits"[1] of industry.

There is a sense in which some of these social needs might well be provided for from the costs of enterprise, for many of them are but the obverse of the real costs of production; they arise because of the wastage of human resources in the productive process. The maintenance of public health, adequate living and housing standards, of skills and industrial morale, the rehabilitation of workers are all charges on the social economy, necessary to the maintenance and growth of its efficiency, as much so as the provision of new capital. Perhaps in a state in which the nature of collective wants was given full and formal recognition there would also develop recognition of the concept of real social cost.

In formulating a concept of social cost, it is necessary to go back to the doctrine of real cost and re-examine it in the light of current social experience. It has been frequently suggested that the doctrine of real cost is unreal and of no importance to economic theory. The attack on the doctrine of real costs, for example, made by Professor Cassel in his *Theory of the Social Economy*, assumes that the basic notion of scarcity can be made into a definite principle which will appear as a constant determinant in the system of price equations. The doctrine of real costs is assailed as purely subjective, incapable of objective measurement. This position is only valid on the assumption that the agents are in fixed supply, and

---

[1]"Profits" in quotation marks because it remains to be seen just what meaning could be attached to the concept of profits under such conditions.

when Professor Cassel admits that there may be short-run variations in the supply of the agents he is driven into some strange devices to make his system of price equations a determinate one. The reluctance of workers to increase the supply of labour and of investors to increase the supply of capital disposal, which he admits, is surely nothing more nor less than what Marshall calls "real cost," yet without this admission of the real cost concept Professor Cassel's price system is only determinate when he assumes fixed supplies of the productive agents. A glance at our price equations of Chapter VII will show the necessity of the real cost doctrine in a determinate price system. Without equations 6, 7, 8, and 9 the system would not be determinate. In other words, the willingness of the owners of the productive agents to put on the market any quantity of the agent they control will vary with the reward offered, the nature of the variation depending on the reluctance which has to be overcome to increase the supply of the agent, and this fact is one of the determinants of the quantity of output which will be sold and the price which will be charged for it. Without this relationship we could not have a theory of price determination; it would be logically impossible, for we should have to say that prices would vary with what consumers were willing to pay for varying quantities put on the market, but we should lack any guide to the quantities producers would be willing to put on the market. For the two unknowns, quantity and price, we should have one equation, the demand equation, but we should lack the other, necessary, simultaneous equation, the supply equation.

To say that the doctrine of real costs is a necessary one if we are to have a determinate theory of price is not enough to justify it, because if a concept is a false one, not in accord with the facts, the logical need for it does not render it valid. It is always conceivable that prices are inexplicable in terms of a determinate theory, that they vary in so many ways under so many influences that they cannot be explained by the methods economic theory has traditionally used. That is rather a council of despair to the economist, but it would be better to admit it frankly than to impose a logical formalism which had no justification in the facts. But there is sound reason to believe that the doctrine of real cost is in accord with the facts. There are real human costs involved in production. Work is not accomplished without the pain of thought, of effort and fatigue, without the wastage of energy and resource. This regular consumption of human effort is real cost, a basic fact in man's struggle to exist. The doctrine of real cost is not accepted because it is logically necessary, it is logically necessary because in the scheme of real human forces which determine behaviour on the market real cost is one of those determining forces. The logic of abstraction is not a distortion of reality, but a clarification whereby analysis becomes possible and insight is afforded into the nature of the pricing system.

But when the doctrine of real cost was extended to cover the "pain" of saving it was misused because the nature of saving was misunderstood. Whereas the traditional notion of saving was that it was a voluntary putting aside of income by the individual at the real cost of the postponement of enjoyments, "the disutility of temporary lacking," we have come to see that savings are made irrespective of any such "pain" and that the volume of saving depends on the earnings of corporations, the decisions of their managers about the wisest use of corporation earnings, and by the monetary and fiscal policy of the central bank and the state. Savings are thus imposed and the real cost of providing new capital is a social cost rather than an individual one. True, it is felt by individuals, but the decisions governing the volume of savings are social or collective decisions, which impose a reduction in the flow of consumers' goods onto the market. At present the decisions are made by various individuals, with purely individual motives. In a society where the state owned the larger enterprises or controlled the rate of private investment, all these decisions might be made by the state through its various agencies and thus assume their proper form as social decisions. Thus the cost of maintaining and increasing the supply of the social capital is really a social cost, though none the less a real one because the decisions to save, however they may now be made, impose on the economy as a whole a reduction in the present volume of consumers' goods, and mean that individuals, who have no choice in many of the decisions, are forced to reduce, or not to expand, as the case may be, their current satisfactions from consumption.

Though the primary real cost of labour is individual, there are probably certain social costs connected with maintaining and increasing the supply of labour, none the less real for being social, yet only partly admitted as such in the pre-war economy and in economic literature. These are the cost of maintaining and developing skills, i.e. elementary and vocational education, the cost of maintaining social and industrial morale, i.e. the cost of providing through cultural education and creative recreation an antidote for the deadly monotony of modern factory work, the cost of public health, which would include in addition to the usual public health facilities the maintenance of adequate and healthy housing and nutrition standards and of child welfare agencies and probably of clinics, crêches, and similar institutions at present in their infancy and too usually available only to those of the more comfortable classes. Undoubtedly in a progressive social economy the tendency would be continuously to widen the concept of social cost to the economic limits.

SECTION 2: QUESTIONS OF POLICY

We have definitely excluded from the compass of this work the discussion of questions of what may be properly called political economy, questions which have to do with the economic policy of the state. Nevertheless such a study as this would not be very valuable if it did not enable us to formulate certain questions, which might well serve as a guide to any future discussion of policy. As Professor Collingwood points out in his *Autobiography*, the proper and exact formulation of a question is the essential first step in obtaining an answer. It is perhaps the function of abstract economic theory to formulate, on the basis of its analysis of what is, the questions as to what ought to be, and the function of political economy, the study of economic policy, to try to afford the answers to these questions suitable to the then existing state of society.

If we suppose a society which recognizes in a formal way as determinants of the economic system the concepts of social need and social cost, we shall have to ask how these concepts are given expression within the price system. We see that any political agency empowered to exercise certain regulations over the economic system would have the duty of directing the state agencies for the fulfilment of social needs, and of estimating and apportioning social costs. We may observe that such a body need not function as an irresponsible bureaucracy, for within a democratic society it would receive, as the state does now in determining its taxation and spending policies, the general guidance of a free electorate, and in the second duty it would have as criteria the advancing standards of health, education, and social welfare. But these general political considerations will not solve the technical problems of the economic method to be adopted by any such state agency for the measurement and apportionment of costs among industries and for the accurate expression of social demand through the price system.

A second question of considerable importance, which arises if we suppose an answer to have been given to the first, has to do with the equilibrium position of a socially owned production unit.[2] Presumably it would have a revenue from the sale of its produce from which a marginal revenue curve could be derived. Presumably also it would have a factor cost curve which would include wages, capital maintenance, a charge for new capital supply, determined ultimately by the social decision as to what real cost of savings was to be borne by the economy as a whole, and finally its share of other real social costs. If question one is answered so that these costs can be apportioned quantitatively among industries, the production unit will presumably have an average cost curve from which a marginal cost curve can be derived. Presumably also the state-owned or controlled enterprises will dominate those industries in which the advantages of large-scale production are most evident, and in which competition has broken down under the pressure of long-run decreasing costs. Under these circumstances ought the equilibrium position of the production unit to correspond to the equilibrium position of the private firm, viz., at the point of intersection of the marginal curves? Would the state wish to maximize profits which would be used presumably for some socio-economic purpose or would it wish to hand on to the consumer the full advantages of both external and internal economies? In the latter case what long-run determinant of equilibrium output could be substituted for maximization of profit?

The third question of considerable interest would concern the determinants of the rate of investment and the general level of productivity and employment. Is it possible given such state powers of regulation and control to eliminate the vicissitudes at present associated with the profit cycle and the attendant fluctuation in investment and employment? What are the causes of this cycle and are they such as could be eliminated in what is called a planned economy? If they could be eliminated, how would this be done and would the measures adopted to achieve stability be consistent with the acceptance of the principles of social cost and social need as determinants of the economy? In other words, is the achievement of the highest level of social economic efficiency consistent with the elimination of fluctuations in the rate of investment and the level of employment?

That these questions may be formulated is something though it is always possible that they may have to be recast in the light of events now in process. Their solution awaits the outcome of the

[2]We avoid the word "firm" because it carries the connotation of private ownership.

war, both in the sense that the economic experience of the war-time organization will be a guide in tackling them and also in the sense that they presume political institutions dedicated to the maintenance of civil and political liberty and social security. Within such a political society their solution, or partial solution, while creating other problems of political organization of great difficulty and perplexity, is nevertheless always possible to men of intelligence and goodwill.

INDEX

A

A. A. A., 120
Abscissa, defined, 31
Abstract method, 12-15
Abstraction, as isolation, 12; level of, 42-4
Advertising, and the consumer, 90; and commodity differentiation, 133; and price discrimination, 140
A. F. of L., 89
Agriculture, and large-scale organization, 83; specialization of crops, 83; disappearance of small proprietor and enclosure movement, 83-6; in New World, 85; acreage and crop restriction, 120; and reserved supply, 120; decreasing costs in, 146; development in Canadian West, 157
Amalgamations. *See* Trusts
Amortization, 215-16
Anaconda Copper Inc., 82
Anti-trust laws, 156
Apprentice, 87
Argentine, 80
Armaments industry, kartel in, 130
Assignats, 22
Assumption, nature of and place in economic method, 11; basic economic, 12; of price system in Book Two, 62-3; of Book Three, 91
Austrian school, 25
Automobile industry, 86, 186
Availability of raw materials as limit to size of firm, 85

B

Baconian method, 15 fn.
Baking industry, 86
Baldwin, Earl, 20
Banks, in eighteenth-century commerce, 79 fn.; to marshall savings, 90; money policy of and rate of interest, 221-4
Bargain theory of wages, 173
Bargaining, units, 78-90; collective, 87, 193-5
Bear market, 224

C

Bell, Spurgeon, 185 fn.
Benjamin, A. C., 13 fn.
Birth rate, 197, 198
Blum, Leon, 120
Bonds. *See* Securities
Boot and shoe industry, 86
Brentano, L., 198, 198 fn.
Brewing industry, 86
Brick and cement industry, 87
Brookings Institution, 185
Bull market, 225
Burns, A. R., 132 fn., 151 fn.
Butler, Bishop, 12

C

Canada, 80, 82, 83, 86, 120, 123, 126 fn., 132, 132 fn., 133, 137, 156-9, 191, 209, 229
Canada Labour Gazette, 192 fn.
Canadian Criminal Code Sec. 496-8, 158
Canadian Manufacturers' Association, 158 fn.
Canadian National Railway, 158
Canadian Pacific Railway, 158
Capacity. *See* Unused, Excess, Optimum
Capital, rewards to under simple conditions, 57-9, 65-73; first explained, 58; employed in eighteenth-century enterprise, 79 fn.; accumulation, 79-83; market, 90, 222-5; investments in Canada, 123; flexibility of, 175; disposal, 213; fixed, 213; liquid, 213; working, 213; rewards to, 213-28; demand for, 215-18; supply of, 218-27
Carryover, 120
Carson City, 82
Cash nexus, 83, 83 fn.
Cassel, G., 65 fn., 210 fn., 232-3
Cassirer, E., 13 fn.
Cause, nature of, 10
Census, 195
Chamberlin, E., 129 fn.
Chapman, S., 146 fn., 147 fn.
Chartism, 88

Lightning Source UK Ltd.
Milton Keynes UK
UKHW010003210722
406167UK00001B/161